Students Activities M
Workbook/Lab Manual/Video Manual

Viajes

INTRODUCCIÓN AL ESPAÑOL

Robert Hershberger
DePauw University

Susan Navey-Davis
North Carolina State University

Guiomar Borrás A.
Glendale Community College

Prepared by

Jill Pelletieri
Santa Clara University

Silvia Rolle-Rissetto
California State University, San Marcos

Verónica Añover
California State University, San Marcos

Australia • Brazil • Japan • Korea • Mexico • Singapore • Spain • United Kingdom • United States

For product information and technology assistance, contact us at
Cengage Learning Customer & Sales Support, 1-800-354-9706

For permission to use material from this text or product, submit all requests online at **www.cengage.com/permissions**
Further permissions questions can be emailed to **permissionrequest@cengage.com**

ISBN-13: 978-1-4282-8987-1
ISBN-10: 1-4282-8987-9

Heinle
20 Channel Center Street
Boston, MA 02210
USA

Cengage Learning products are represented in Canada by Nelson Education, Ltd.

For your course and learning solutions, visit **www.cengage.com**

Purchase any of our products at your local college store or at our preferred online store **www.ichapters.com**

Printed in the United States of America
1 2 3 4 5 6 7 14 13 12 11 10

Table of Contents

WORKBOOK

LAB MANUAL

Preface

Workbook

The ***Viajes*** Workbook has been written and designed to accompany the ***Viajes*** textbook. Through a tightly structured instructional sequence that closely parallels the main text, the workbook leads students first through a set of highly contextualized form-focused activities and then through more open-ended contextualized activities that foster the development of skills for creative expression in Spanish.

Each chapter of the ***Viajes*** Workbook contains activities targeted at vocabulary and grammar building, as well as at the development of critical skills and strategies necessary for the comprehension and production of written texts. Following are some suggestions for the use of each of the chapters' sections:

Vocabulary and grammar exercises parallel each vocabulary and grammar section of the main text and can be assigned as homework as these sections are covered in class. They are designed to help students memorize and comprehend the words, phrases, and structures as well as to practice their application in context. This type of work will support students' active comprehension and production in their more open-ended and creative classroom oral activities.

Viajemos por... This section is designed to help students view and comprehend the **Viajemos por...** video segments that accompany each chapter. These activities include previewing activities that lead students to recognize cognates they will hear in the video narration and post-viewing activities to check their comprehension of key cultural points made in the video. These activities can be assigned as stand-alone homework or as support to a class session in which the video will be presented.

¡A escribir! This writing section mirrors the strategies and tasks presented in the main text. The section's **pasos** guide students through the process of composing and editing in Spanish.

Autoprueba This section provides a short set of exercises that allow students to check their mastery of the target vocabulary and structures of a chapter. Students should complete these exercises prior to a review session or an exam. The answer key is located in the back of the Student Activities Manual.

Laboratory Manual

The ***Viajes*** Laboratory Manual and Audio program have been written and designed to accompany the ***Viajes*** textbook. Each chapter is designed to help students improve their listening and speaking skills through vocabulary-based and form-based activities that parallel the analogous presentations in the main text. Listening tasks have been carefully written to allow practice of the material presented in the main text. They were crafted to target the appropriate proficiency level.

Like all of the components of ***Viajes,*** the Laboratory Manual embeds culture and provides examples of authentic oral expressions. The audio recordings feature native speakers and, where possible, speakers that exhibit accents typical of the countries featured in the main text.

The following sections appear in a typical Laboratory Manual chapter:

Vocabulario corresponding to each vocabulary section checks the core of the lexicon presented in each chapter of the main text with enhanced listening comprehension and pronunciation activities.

Estructura y uso parallel each grammatical structure and function presented in the main text. The activities in this section reinforce listening comprehension, as well as the handling of structures, forms, and expressions from the aural perspective.

Pronunciación provides a complete review of sounds of the Spanish language. This section is comprised of pronunciation and listening activities targeting difficult sounds and pronunciation rules.

¡A ver! allows students to expand their comprehension of the situational video clips featured in the ***Viajes*** video program. The Real World-inspired video presents the target vocabulary and structures in the context of an engaging storyline.

All sections in the Laboratory Manual follow the same format, and are composed of three activities per section, with the exception of **¡A ver!** In each activity, students are asked to provide a set number of answers. This will allow students to more easily gauge both the length and time it will take them to complete their work.

Acknowledgments

I would like to thank my husband, Bruce Storms, for his love and support throughout the completion of this project. I would also like to thank my dear friends and coauthors, Dr. Silvia Rolle-Rissetto and Dr. Verónica Añover, for their expertise, inspiration, collaboration, love, and humor. Without them, this manual would not be the excellent pedagogical tool that it is. Finally, I would like to thank all of the Heinle team for their support and good spirit throughout the production of this project.

Dr. Jill Pellettieri

I would like to thank my family for its unfaltering love and support throughout the process of recreation, revision, and completion for *Viajes*. I would also like to extend my gratitude to my two dear Musketeers/Mousquetaires, co-authors, Dr. Jill Pellettieri and Dr. Verónica Añover. Their unparalleled expertise, diligent work, and friendship have made *Viajes* a sheer joy.

Dr. Silvia Rolle-Rissetto

I would like to thank all the members at Heinle involved in ***Viajes***. I am very grateful to my husband and son for allowing ***Viajes*** to steal away my presence and for always supporting my work. I would like to express my most sincere gratitude to my two coauthors and dear friends Dr. Silvia Rolle-Rissetto and Dr. Jill Pellettieri for forming a great team, and for working so smoothly together.

Dr. Verónica Añover

Workbook

Nombre ______________________ Fecha ______________________

P ¡Mucho gusto!

VOCABULARIO 1 Saludos y despedidas

WB P-1 | **Saludos y despedidas** For each picture, circle or select the most appropriate of the three greetings or responses.

WB P-2 | Presentaciones Your roommate wants to practice meeting and greeting people in Spanish. Help her by selecting the appropriate response from the first column to each expression in the second column. **¡OJO!** Some expressions may have more than one response.

______	**1.** ¡Encantada!	**a.**	Bien, gracias.
______	**2.** ¡Hola! ¿Qué tal?	**b.**	Muy bien, ¿y Ud.?
______	**3.** ¡Mucho gusto!	**c.**	Soy de San Diego.
______	**4.** ¿Cómo se llama?	**d.**	El gusto es mío.
______	**5.** ¡Buenas noches, Carolyn!	**e.**	Nos vemos.
______	**6.** ¿Cómo está Ud.?	**f.**	Bastante bien, ¿y tú?
______	**7.** ¿De dónde eres tú?	**g.**	Felicia. Y Ud., ¿cómo se llama?
______	**8.** ¡Hasta luego!	**h.**	¡Buenas noches, señor Guzmán!

WB P-3 | En una fiesta At a party you overhear a conversation between two new students, Tomás, from Puerto Rico, and Carlos, from the Dominican Republic. Based on the answer, write out the question that was asked. **¡OJO!** Remember that students would probably use the informal form of address.

Modelo CARLOS: *Hola.*
TOMÁS: Hola.

1. CARLOS: Me llamo Carlos, ¿______________________________?
TOMÁS: Mucho gusto, me llamo Tomás.

2. TOMÁS: ¿______________________________?
CARLOS: Bastante bien, gracias.

3. CARLOS: ¿______________________________?
TOMÁS: Muy bien.

4. TOMÁS: ¿______________________________?
CARLOS: Soy de la República Dominicana.

ESTRUCTURA Y USO I — Talking about yourself and others: Subject pronouns and the present tense of the verb *ser*

WB P-4 | ¿Qué pronombre? Which pronouns would Alberto Yáñez, a professor from Spain, use to address or talk about the following people? In the spaces provided below, write the most appropriate pronoun. **¡OJO!** Remember that Alberto is from Spain, which affects the pronouns he selects in certain situations.

1. Referring to students Alicia and Cristina ______________________________
2. Talking to Mr. Gutiérrez ______________________________
3. Referring to his brother Carlos ______________________________
4. Talking to Mr. and Mrs. Morán ______________________________
5. Talking to his two sons ______________________________
6. Referring to himself ______________________________

7. Talking to his wife ______________________
8. Referring to his wife ______________________
9. Referring to himself and three friends ______________________
10. Talking to his two daughters ______________________

WB P-5 | ¿Qué piensas? What do you think? Give your opinion by forming sentences with the words provided. Following the model, use the appropriate form of the verb **ser.**

Modelo Barack Obama / sincero
Barack Obama es sincero.
o *Barack Obama no es sincero.*

1. Will Ferrell / cómico
____
2. Michael Phelps / talentoso
____
3. yo / inteligente
____
4. Jessica Alba / atractiva
____
5. mis amigos (*friends*) y yo / interesantes
____

ESTRUCTURA Y USO 2 Identifying quantities: *Hay* and numbers 0–30

WB P-6 | El sabelotodo Juan Carlos is a **sabelotodo** *(know-it-all)* who doesn't always know it all. Mark each of Juan Carlos's sayings with **cierto** *(true)* or **falso** *(false)*. If they are false, rewrite the sentence correcting Juan Carlos's error. **¡OJO!** Use the verb form **hay** as well as numbers. Follow the model.

Modelo En el mes de septiembre hay 28 días *(days)*.
Falso. En el mes de septiembre hay treinta días.

1. En una semana *(week)* hay siete días.
____
2. Hay trece huevos *(eggs)* en una docena.
____
3. Hay nueve números en un número de teléfono en los Estados Unidos.
____
4. En un año *(year)* hay doce meses *(months)*.
____
5. Hay quince pulgadas *(inches)* en un pie *(foot)*.
____

WB P-7 | Problemas de matemáticas Test your mathematical ability by completing the following equations. **¡OJO!** Write out the numbers, not the numerals. Follow the model.

Modelo Treinta menos dos son *veintiocho*.

1. Once más tres son ______________________.
2. Ocho menos ocho son ______________________.
3. Siete más tres son ______________________.
4. Catorce más quince son ______________________.
5. Veintiséis menos dos son ______________________.
6. Dieciocho más cuatro son ______________________.

WB P-8 | Guía telefónica Laura's new "user-friendly" handheld computer won't let her input numerals! She can only store friends' and family's telephone numbers by answering the software's questions and spelling out these telephone numbers. Help Laura by writing out the numerals in words as they are displayed.

1. ¿Cuál es el número de teléfono de tu mejor amiga *(best female friend)*?

   4–0–8–26–5–15–17

   ____

2. ¿Cuál es el número de teléfono de tus padres?

   3–21–2–19–13–29

   ____

3. ¿Cuál es tu número de teléfono?

   9–19–7–10–14–28

   ____

VOCABULARIO 2 Palabras interrogativas

To learn more about **Question Words,** go to Heinle iRadio at www.cengage.com/spanish/viajes.

WB P-9 | Más preguntas Look at the following pictures and choose which questions are likely being asked.

1. **a.** ¿Qué es?

   b. ¿De dónde eres?

   c. ¿Cuál es su número de teléfono?

Nombre ______________________ Fecha ______________________

2. **a.** ¿Quién es tu profesora de español?
   b. ¿Cuándo tienes clase?
   c. ¿Cuál es tu número de teléfono?

3. **a.** ¿Cuántos libros tienes?
   b. ¿Por qué preguntas?
   c. ¿Cómo estás?

WB P-10 | ¿Cuál es correcto? Fill in the blanks with the appropriate question word.

1. ¿__________ se llama usted?

2. ¿__________ estudiantes hay en su clase?

3. ¿__________ estudias español?

4. ¿__________ es tu cumpleaños *(birthday)*?

WB P-11 | Tantas preguntas You are meeting your date at his/her house, and your date's mother has many questions for you. Complete her questions by supplying the appropriate question words below.

1. ¿__________ estás?

2. ¿De __________ eres?

3. ¿__________ años tienes?

4. ¿__________ es tu número de teléfono?

5. ¿__________ son tus padres?

6. ¿__________ personas hay en tu familia?

VIAJEMOS POR EL MUNDO HISPANO

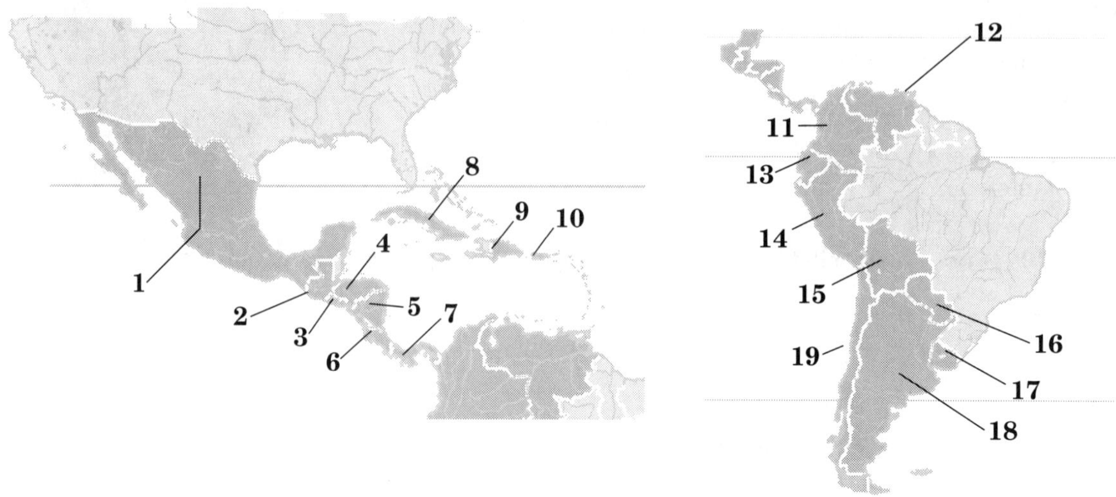

Study the maps of Latin America in your textbook and then name each of the numbered countries on the maps.

1. ______
2. ______
3. ______
4. ______
5. ______
6. ______
7. ______
8. ______
9. ______
10. ______
11. ______
12. ______
13. ______
14. ______
15. ______
16. ______
17. ______
18. ______
19. ______

Nombre ______________________ Fecha ______________________

Autoprueba

WB P-12 | Una conversación típica Below is a typical conversation likely to be heard during the first days of a new school year. Complete the conversation by supplying the appropriate vocabulary words or phrases.

MIGUEL: ______________, Tomás. ¿______________ tal?

TOMÁS: Bien, Miguel. ¡Tanto tiempo! (*It's been awhile!*) ¿Y cómo ______________ tú?

MIGUEL: Bien, ______________. Tomás, esta es mi novia (*this is my girlfriend*), Elena.

TOMÁS: Hola, Elena. Mucho ______________.

ELENA: El gusto ______________.

TOMÁS: ¿De ______________ eres, Elena?

ELENA: ______________ de Puerto Rico.

TOMÁS: Muy bien. Bueno, ya me voy (*I've got to go*). ______________.

ELENA: ______________, Tomás.

MIGUEL: ______________ vemos, Tomás.

WB P-13 | Números Write out each of the numerals indicated below, as well as the numeral that precedes it. Follow the model.

Modelo 28
veintiocho / veintisiete

1. 15 ______________________________
2. 1 ______________________________
3. 30 ______________________________
4. 17 ______________________________
5. 25 ______________________________

WB P-14 | Presentaciones Complete the following conversation with the appropriate form of the verb **ser**.

PILAR: Me llamo Pilar. ¿Quién __________ tú?

LOLA: __________ Lola Araña Téllez. Y este (*this*) __________ mi amigo, Carlos.

PILAR: Encantada. ¿De dónde __________ Uds.?

LOLA: Nosotros __________ de Cuba.

WB P-15 | **¿Sois de España?** Ramón has come from Spain to the University of California to study engineering. Complete one of his campus conversations by supplying the appropriate subject pronoun. **¡OJO!** Remember the difference between formal and informal subject pronouns, as well as the differences between Peninsular and Latin American Spanish with respect to pronoun usage.

RAMÓN: Perdón, ¿__________ sois de España?

DIANA (Y DIEGO): No, __________ somos de México. __________ soy de Guanajuato y __________ es de Morelia.

DIEGO: El profesor Carrazco es de España. ¿De qué parte de España *(From what part of Spain)* es __________, profesor?

PROFESOR CARRAZCO: __________ soy de Galicia.

RAMÓN: Mi mamá es de Galicia. __________ es de Vigo.

DIEGO: ¿De qué parte eres __________, Ramón?

RAMÓN: __________ soy de Toledo.

DIANA: Bueno, profesor y Ramón, __________ son compatriotas y van a ser *(are going to be)* buenos amigos.

Nombre ______________________ Fecha ______________________

En una clase de español
Los Estados Unidos

VOCABULARIO 1 En la clase

WB 1-1 | Colores revueltos *(scrambled)* Unscramble the letters to reveal each color.

1. ojor ____________ **3.** ramnór ____________

2. conlab ____________ **4.** lamirola ____________

WB 1-2 | Una de estas cosas no es como las otras. (*One of these things isn't like the others.*) For each series, circle the word that does not form a set with the others.

1. el lápiz, la tiza, la pluma, la pizarra

2. el libro, el diccionario, la lección

3. la silla, el escritorio, el lápiz

4. la pizarra, el borrador, el bolígrafo, la lección

WB 1-3 | Asociaciones Write in Spanish the color you usually associate with the following items.

Modelo snow *blanco*

1. a crow ____________ **6.** chocolate ____________

2. an orange ____________ **7.** a banana ____________

3. grass ____________ **8.** the sky ____________

4. cherries ____________ **9.** eggplant ____________

5. paper ____________

WB 1-4 | En mi clase Joaquín, a pen pal from Quito, Ecuador, is interested in how college classes are different in the United States from college classes in Ecuador. Choose the most appropriate response to his questions.

1. ¿Cuántos estudiantes hay en tu clase de español?

a. Hay veintitrés. **b.** Hay tres exámenes. **c.** El diccionario.

2. ¿Cómo se llama tu libro de texto de español?

a. El libro. **b.** Viajes **c.** Mucho dinero

3. ¿Cómo se llama tu profesor(a) de español?

a. Se llama Profesora Muñoz. **b.** Bien, ¿y tú? **c.** Está aquí.

4. ¿Cuántos bolígrafos tienes *(do you have)*?

a. No hay muchos estudiantes. **b.** Tres. **c.** Dos novias.

5. ¿Tienes computadora? ¿De qué marca *(what brand)*?

a. Sí, es una Mac. **b.** La Dell no tiene pantalla. **c.** Hay muchas PCs.

ESTRUCTURA Y USO I Talking about people, things, and concepts: Definite and indefinite articles and how to make nouns plural

WB 1-5 | Los artículos For each of the nouns listed below, select **F** for **femenino** or **M** for **masculino.** Then write the appropriate definite article needed to accompany the noun. **¡OJO!** Be sure that the definite articles agree with the nouns in number as well as in gender. Follow the model.

Modelo F *la* calculadora

1. F / M ______ diccionarios
2. F / M ______ lápiz
3. F / M ______ luces
4. F / M ______ escritorio
5. F / M ______ mapa
6. F / M ______ computadoras
7. F / M ______ calendario
8. F / M ______ mesas
9. F / M ______ relojes (*watches*)
10. F / M ______ pizarra

WB 1-6 | ¡Qué exagerada! *(How exaggerated!)* Mari Bocazas is one of those people who often exaggerates. Whatever you do, she says she does it better, and whatever you have, she says she has more. What would Mari say if you were to tell her that you had each of the following?

Modelo una mochila
dos mochilas

1. un amigo

____

2. una computadora Mac

____

3. una clase de español

____

4. una pluma Cartier

____

5. un reloj (*watch*) Rolex

____

Nombre ______________________ Fecha ______________________

WB 1-7 | Inventario Your roommate works at the college bookstore and is taking inventory on school supplies. How many of each item are there? Follow the model.

Modelo cuaderno (18)
dieciocho cuadernos

1. bolígrafo (15)

____

2. diccionario (1)

____

3. lápiz (12)

____

4. mochila (29)

____

5. calendario (14)

____

6. computadora (1)

____

VOCABULARIO 2 Lenguas extranjeras, materias y lugares universitarios

WB 1-8 | Internacional Below is a list of the countries available for next year's Study Abroad programs. For each country, indicate the language in which interested applicants must be minimally fluent. **¡OJO!** In Spanish, country names are capitalized, but the names of languages are not. Follow the model.

Modelo Alemania: *el alemán*

1. Japón: ______________
2. China: ______________
3. Portugal: ______________
4. Italia: ______________
5. España: ______________
6. Francia: ______________
7. Rusia: ______________
8. Inglaterra: ______________

WB 1-9 | Cursos The following is a course list for the Universidad de Buenos Aires's Semester Abroad Program. Write the name of the major to which each course would normally pertain. Follow the model.

Modelo genética y evolución: *la biología*

1. anatomía: ______________
2. análisis de mapas: ______________
3. legislación ambiental: ______________
4. teoría literaria: ______________

5. programación de computadoras: ______________________

6. cálculo: ______________________

7. filosofía del derecho: ______________________

8. literatura española: ______________________

WB 1-10 | Lugares universitarios Where on campus are you most likely to do each of the following activities? Use a different location in each sentence.

Modelo practicar deportes *en el gimnasio*

1. comprar *(to buy)* un sándwich ______________________
2. hablar con mi profesor ______________________
3. estudiar ______________________
4. comprar libros ______________________
5. dormir *(to sleep)* ______________________
6. hablar *(to talk)* con mis amigos ______________________

ESTRUCTURA Y USO 2 Describing everyday activities: Present tense of regular *-ar* verbs

WB 1-11 | Actividades Jorge and his friends talk about some of their more common activities during the school year. Complete their sentences with the appropriate present tense verb form.

1. Yo ______________ (tocar) mis instrumentos.
2. Noelia y yo ______________ (bailar) en la discoteca.
3. Tú ______________ (practicar) el español con Noelia.
4. Amanda ______________ (estudiar) mucho en la biblioteca.
5. Jaime y Teresa ______________ (mirar) la televisión toda la noche.

WB 1-12 | Conversando Manu is an exchange student from Spain studying at the University of Massachusetts. Below is one of the conversations he has with Alicia and Tomás, two Mexican-American students. Complete their conversation by supplying the appropriate form of the verb in parentheses.

ALICIA: ¡Hola, Manu! ¿Qué tal? ¿Cómo está todo?

MANU: Muy bien, pero *(but)* **1.** ______________ (tomar) muchos cursos y **2.** ______________ (estudiar) mucho.

TOMÁS: ¿Cuántos cursos **3.** ______________ (tomar) tú?

MANU: Seis. ¿Y vosotros? ¿Cuántos cursos **4.** ______________ (llevar) este semestre?

TOMÁS: Nosotros... solamente dos. Alicia y yo **5.** ______________ (tomar) los mismos *(the same)* cursos. **6.** ______________ (Estudiar) fisiología y química.

ALICIA: Manu, ¿**7.** ______________ (trabajar) en la biblioteca?

MANU: No, mi compañero de cuarto **8.** ______________ (trabajar) allí *(there)*.
Yo no **9.** ______________ (necesitar) trabajar.

ALICIA: Sí, entiendo *(I understand)*. Tú compañero se llama Juan, ¿no? ¿Cómo es él? ¿Es simpático *(nice)*?

MANU: Sí, es muy simpático. Nosotros **10.** ______________ (hablar) mucho y siempre **11.** ______________ (mirar) «Baywatch» juntos *(together)* en nuestra casa. Y después del *(after the)* programa, nosotros **12.** ______________ (practicar) inglés.

ALICIA: ¡Manu! ¿Uds. **13.** ______________ (mirar) «Baywatch»? ¡Ese programa es horrible!

MANU: ¿Horrible? ¿Cómo que horrible *(What do you mean it's horrible)*? ¿Vosotros aquí en los Estados Unidos no **14.** ______________ (mirar) «Baywatch»?

ALICIA: ¿Yo? ¡Para nada! *(Not a chance!)*

TOMÁS: Pues *(Well)*...

ESTRUCTURA Y USO 3 Telling time and talking about the days of the week

WB 1-13 | **¿Qué hora es?** Write out the time indicated.

1. 12:15 ______________________
2. 1:30 ______________________
3. 6:45 ______________________
4. 12:50 ______________________
5. 5:03 ______________________

WB 1-14 | ¿Qué cursos tomo? Roberto Torres, an exchange student, is having trouble reading the new course catalog for next semester. Help him by writing out in Spanish the time the course begins and the days of the week the course meets. Follow the model.

Modelo la clase de psicología
Es a las dos de la tarde los martes y los jueves.

Course code	Course title	Units	Time	Days	Instructor
55940	Art 120	4	0900-1000	T/Th	Paredes
24965	Biology 10A	4	1730-1945	W	Smith
84804	Computer Science 101	3	1500-1600	M/W	Richardson
48997	Chemistry 7C	5	0700-0745	MWF	Nelson
94942	English 205	4	1400-1630	T	Hershberger
40900	Geography 10	3	0900-1000	Th/F	Cox
28817	Literature (US) 1A	3	1000-1150	T/Th	Rolle
38822	Mathematics 6C	4	1300-1400	MWF	Añover
99944	Music Appreciation 20	2	1120-1350	Sa	Fernández
19902	Psychology 1C	4	1400-1645	T/Th	Velasco
53229	Zoology 167	4	0900-1045	W/F	Clark

1. la clase de biología

____

2. la clase de química

____

3. la clase de geografía

____

4. la clase de literatura

____

5. la clase de matemáticas

____

VIAJEMOS POR LOS ESTADOS UNIDOS

In this video you will learn about Latinos in the United States and three principal U.S. cities where the influence of their cultures is most visible.

Nombre ______________________________ Fecha ______________________________

WB 1-15 | Cognados You will view three video segments, and in them you will hear a number of Spanish words that are cognates of English, that is, they look and sound like English words and have similar meanings. Identifying these words and their meanings will help you understand the Spanish used in the video. Before viewing the segments, try to pronounce each of the following Spanish words, and then try to match each with their meaning in English.

1. _____ destino turístico	**a.** population
2. _____ misión	**b.** mission
3. _____ símbolo	**c.** commerce
4. _____ clubes nocturnos	**d.** symbol
5. _____ población	**e.** tourist destination
6. _____ cosmopolita	**f.** millions
7. _____ bulevares	**g.** cosmopolitan
8. _____ millones	**h.** night clubs
9. _____ comercio	**i.** boulevards
10. _____ mayoría	**j.** majority

WB 1-16 | Cognados en contexto Watch the video and listen for the following sentences, in which some of the cognates you just identified in activity **WB 1-15** will appear. Complete each sentence with the correct cognate.

from Segment 1 (San Antonio):

1. La ciudad es un ________________ muy popular, con muchas atracciones y actividades.

2. El Álamo, en el centro de la ciudad, es una ________________ española parcialmente reconstruida.

from Segment 2 (Miami):

3. Miami es una ciudad ________________ donde llegan personas de muchos países para trabajar, vivir y pasarlo bien.

4. En las playas y en los ________________ se vive un ambiente festivo, gracias a su gente.

from Segment 3 (Nueva York):

5. Casi tres ________________ de puertorriqueños viven en los Estados Unidos.

6. La ________________ vive en las ciudades de Nueva York y Nueva Jersey.

WB 1-17 | Comprensión Watch the three video segments again and determine whether the following sentences are true (T) o false (F).

1. _______ In San Antonio, Texas, it is still easy to see its Mexican roots.

2. _______ The Paseo del Río in San Antonio is where one will find the Alamo.

3. _______ About 65% of Miami's population is of Cuban origin.

4. _______ The famous Calle Ocho is a part of Miami's La pequeña Habana.

5. _______ There are more Puerto Ricans living in New York than in San Juan, Puerto Rico.

6. _______ Puerto Ricans are the only Hispanic group in New York of a significant population size.

¡A ESCRIBIR!

EL MUNDO VERDADERO The Spanish language television network **Telemundo** has just announced on the local Spanish TV station that they are going to produce a new show and are looking for participants. This show will bring together five people who have never met to live for six months in a house in Miami's South Beach. In order for your application to be considered, you must submit a paragraph in which you introduce yourself and describe your daily routine.

Strategy: Organizing your ideas

A good way to improve your writing is to organize the ideas you want to express before you actually begin composing your document.

ATAJO 4.0

Functions: Describing people; Introducing; Talking about the present

Vocabulary: Countries; Languages; Studies; Arts

Grammar: Verbs: **ser, tener;** Prepositions: **de;** Personal pronouns: **él, ella;** Articles: indefinite: **un, una;** Articles: definite: **el, la, los, las**

 For more information on ***ser* vs. *estar***, and ***tener* and *tener* expressions,** visit Heinle iRadio at www.cengage.com/spanish/viajes.

Paso 1 Start the paragraph by organizing your ideas before writing your first draft. Some of the following questions may help you do so:

- What will you say about yourself? Your name? Where you are from? How old you are? What you study in school?
- What will you say about your daily routine? What days of the week you attend classes? What times of the day you study? Where you study?

Paso 2 Now that you have all the ideas organized, write a first draft on a separate sheet of paper. Then, review and revise it, and write the final draft of your paragraph below.

Nombre ________________ Fecha ________________

Autoprueba

WB 1-18 | Los cursos Select the course that does not belong in the category.

1. Humanidades: **a.** literatura **b.** matemáticas **c.** filosofía
2. Lenguas: **a.** alemán **b.** inglés **c.** historia
3. Ciencias sociales: **a.** computación **b.** sicología **c.** economía
4. Arte: **a.** música **b.** pintura **c.** biología

WB 1-19 | ¿Qué hora es? What time is indicated on each digital display below?

1. 2:45 p.m. ________________
2. 1:22 p.m. ________________
3. 12:31 p.m. ________________
4. 5:15 a.m. ________________
5. 9:30 a.m. ________________

WB 1-20 | Está muy ocupada Roberto wants to get to know Nancy and wants you to find out when she is available to go out with him. Look at Nancy's busy study schedule below and explain to Roberto how busy she is. Tell him in Spanish what language she studies on each day of the week and at what time she studies. Follow the model.

Nancy's Study Schedule						
Monday	**Tuesday**	**Wednesday**	**Thursday**	**Friday**	**Saturday**	**Sunday**
Spanish 9:00 a.m.	German 3:45 p.m.	Chinese 12:45 p.m.	Russian 1:30 p.m.	Italian 5:15 p.m.	Portuguese 7:30 p.m.	Japanese 10:00 a.m.

Modelo *Los lunes Nancy estudia español a las nueve de la mañana.*

1. ________________
2. ________________
3. ________________
4. ________________
5. ________________
6. ________________

WB 1-21 | Los colores Write in Spanish the color that you associate with the following items.

1. a lemon ______________________________
2. Halloween ______________________________
3. blood ______________________________
4. dirt ______________________________
5. a snowman ______________________________
6. an American dollar bill ______________________________

WB 1-22 | Lupe y Lalo To learn about Lupe's and Lalo's lives at the university, complete the following paragraphs with either a definite or an indefinite article. **¡OJO!** Remember that these articles must agree in number and gender with the nouns they modify.

Lupe Zarzuela es **1.** ________ persona inteligente. Ella estudia economía, biología y arte en **2.** ________ UAG, que es **3.** ________ universidad prestigiosa (*prestigious*) de **4.** ________ ciudad de Guadalajara. Para Lupe, **5.** ________ clases no son difíciles. Sus clases favoritas son **6.** ________ pintura y **7.** ________ matemáticas.

Uno de **8.** ________ amigos de Lupe es Lalo Rodríguez. Lalo es estudiante de ciencias sociales. Para Lalo, **9.** ________ alemán es **10.** ________ lengua muy difícil. **11.** ________ clase de alemán es a **12.** ________ once de **13.** ________ mañana todos **14.** ________ días de **15.** ________ semana, excepto **16.** ________ sábados y domingos.

WB 1-23 | Las actividades del día Everyone who lives in Ramón's dorm has many activities and interests. Form sentences with the words provided to find out what everyone does each day.

1. Ramón / trabajar / todos los días

   ____

2. Teresa y Evelia / estudiar / matemáticas / por la tarde

   ____

3. yo / practicar / deportes / por la mañana

   ____

4. nosotros / descansar / a las cuatro de la tarde

   ____

5. tú / enseñar / ejercicios aeróbicos / por la noche

   ____

6. Uds. / regresar / a la casa / a las seis de la tarde

   ____

Nombre ______________________ Fecha ______________________

En una reunión familiar: México

VOCABULARIO 1 La familia

WB 2-1 | Familiares Unscramble the letters to reveal each pet and family-related term.

1. neory: ______________
2. soirbno: ______________
3. otag: ______________
4. jaropá: ______________
5. georsu: ______________

WB 2-2 | Buscapalabras Below are clues to six Spanish words you will find embedded in this word search. Can you find them? Can you find others? Circle the words that you find, and inside the circle write the number of the clue to which the word corresponds.

1. La madre de tu padre
2. El hijo de tu hermana
3. El nombre de la familia
4. Los hijos de tus hijos
5. La hermana de tu madre
6. Can you find other family-related vocabulary? Other Spanish words?

T	O	D	A	D	A	Ñ	C	R	E	O	J	E	D
A	L	O	I	N	I	A	S	O	L	T	E	R	O
N	O	Ñ	O	V	S	E	Ñ	E	I	I	T	I	E
U	T	A	H	A	O	C	U	Ñ	A	D	O	A	N
E	D	U	D	O	B	R	I	A	Z	E	G	P	E
R	I	O	C	T	R	E	C	U	U	F	A	E	R
A	V	E	S	T	I	A	S	I	N	P	E	L	O
L	A	P	A	C	N	R	T	R	A	A	L	L	A
E	N	I	E	T	O	S	B	E	U	D	U	I	T
U	H	E	R	M	A	N	A	S	T	R	O	D	A
B	O	R	J	E	S	O	T	T	O	I	B	O	M
A	R	A	Ñ	A	T	N	Y	E	R	N	O	F	A
J	O	B	A	R	U	A	R	B	I	O	D	I	O
O	R	T	E	R	A	S	U	O	P	S	A	R	A

WB 2-3 | La familia de Mariana Mariana is telling her coworkers all about her family members. Complete her story by supplying the appropriate words from the list below.

sobrinos hermana perro esposo hija hijos

En mi casa somos cinco personas y un animal. Mi **1.** ______________ se llama Paco. Tenemos dos **2.** ______________, se llaman Tomás y Miguelito, y tenemos una **3.** ______________, que se llama Carolina. El **4.** ______________ se llama Popeye. Yo tengo una **5.** ______________, Claudia. Su esposo se llama Jaime. Ellos tienen tres hijos, Carlos, Jesús y Mateo. Ellos son mis **6.** ______________. Paco no tiene hermanos.

WB 2-4 | La familia Herrera Castellanos Carlos Herrera Castellanos has just finished researching the paternal side of his family tree. Answer the following questions about his family members.

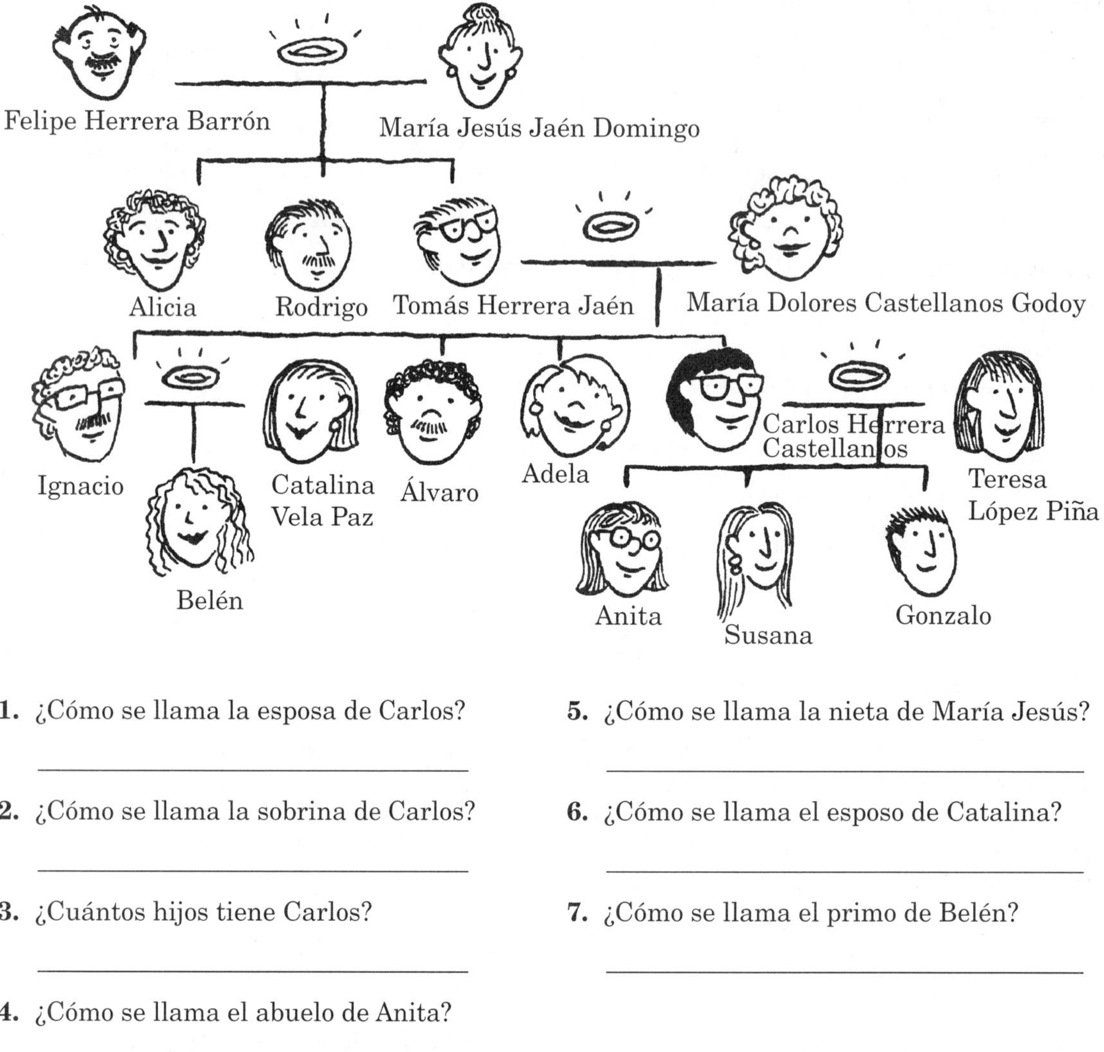

1. ¿Cómo se llama la esposa de Carlos?

   ____

2. ¿Cómo se llama la sobrina de Carlos?

   ____

3. ¿Cuántos hijos tiene Carlos?

   ____

4. ¿Cómo se llama el abuelo de Anita?

   ____

5. ¿Cómo se llama la nieta de María Jesús?

   ____

6. ¿Cómo se llama el esposo de Catalina?

   ____

7. ¿Cómo se llama el primo de Belén?

   ____

ESTRUCTURA Y USO I — Indicating ownership and possession: Possession with *de(l)* and possessive adjectives

WB 2-5 | Nuestras familias Francisco and his sister, Linda, are discussing families with their new friend, Antonio. Complete their conversation with the appropriate possessive forms. **¡OJO!** Pay attention to who is speaking to whom so that you will know which possessive form is necessary.

FRANCISCO: ¿Es grande **1.** __________ familia, Antonio?

ANTONIO: Sí, **2.** __________ familia es muy grande. Somos ocho personas. Y Uds., ¿es grande **3.** __________ familia?

FRANCISCO: No, **4.** __________ familia no es muy grande. Somos cinco.

LINDA: Pero **5.** __________ padres tienen familias grandes. Nuestra madre tiene seis hermanas y **6.** __________ padre tiene cuatro hermanos.

ANTONIO: Muy interesante, Linda. ¿De dónde es **7.** __________ madre?

LINDA: **8.** __________ madre es de México, de Zacatecas. Y tú, ¿de dónde son **9.** __________ padres?

ANTONIO: **10.** __________ padres son de Canadá, pero **11.** __________ padres (mis abuelos) son de España.

WB 2-6 | Compañeros You and your roommates clean house and find all kinds of things. Identify the owner of each of the following items. Follow the model.

Modelo ¿De quién son las fotos de Ricky Martin? (Mariana)
Son de Mariana. *Son sus* fotos.
¿De quién es esta mochila? (yo)
Es *mi* mochila.

1. ¿De quién es el disco compacto de los Maroon 5? (Juan)

   ______________ Juan. ______________ disco.

2. ¿De quién es la computadora? (ustedes)

   ______________ ustedes. ______________ computadora.

3. ¿De quién es el dinero? (nosotros)

   ______________ nosotros. ______________ dinero.

4. ¿De quién son las bicicletas? (Mariana)

   ______________ Mariana. ______________ bicicletas.

6. ¿De quién es la radio? (yo)

   ______________ radio.

ESTRUCTURA Y USO 2 Describing people and things: Common uses of the verb *ser*

WB 2-7 | ¡Mucho gusto! Aníbal and Jaime, two exchange students from Spain, are trying to get to know all the other Spanish speakers on their floor. Fill in the blanks with the appropriate form of the verb **ser** in their conversation.

ANÍBAL: ¿De dónde **1.** __________ vosotros?

CELIA: Nosotros **2.** __________ de Latinoamérica. Jesús **3.** __________ de Nicaragua. Felipe, Mabel y yo **4.** __________ de Cuba. Y tú, Aníbal, ¿de dónde **5.** __________?

ANÍBAL: Yo **6.** __________ de España, de Burgos.

MABEL: Y tú, Jaime, ¿de dónde **7.** __________?

JAIME: De España también. **8.** __________ de Córdoba.

CELIA: ¡Qué bueno! Y, ¿Uds. **9.** __________ hermanos?

JAIME: No, no **10.** __________ hermanos; **11.** __________ buenos amigos.

WB 2-8 | La vida de Elena Your pen pal from Guanajuato, Elena, has sent you the following letter telling you a little about her and her family and friends. Fill in the blanks with the appropriate form of the verb **ser** to read her letter.

Hola,

Yo **1.** ________ Elena. **2.** ________ de Guanajuato, México. En mi familia nosotros **3.** ________ cinco. Tengo dos padres, una hermana y un hermano. Mis padres **4.** ________ profesores en la universidad. Los dos **5.** ________ muy trabajadores. Mis hermanos **6.** ________ estudiantes. Mi hermano Jaime **7.** ________ alto y guapo, pero **8.** ________ un poco tímido. Mi hermana Linda **9.** ________ morena y muy bonita. Ella no **10.** ________ tímida; al contrario, **11.** ________ súper extrovertida. También tengo diez tíos y veinticinco primos. Nosotros **12.** ________ una familia grande, pero feliz. ¿Y tú?, ¿cómo **13.** ________ tu familia? ¿Cómo **14.** ________ tú?

ESTRUCTURA Y USO 3 Describing people and things: Agreement with descriptive adjectives

To learn more about **Adjectives,** visit Heinle iRadio at www.cengage.com/spanish/viajes.

WB 2-9 | ¡Qué familia tiene! Ángel has a large family with very different relatives. Write out complete sentences to describe each of these relatives shown below. Use the appropriate possessive form, as well as the adjective that best describes each person. Make sure the adjective agrees with the person/persons. Follow the model.

Modelo la mamá
Su mamá es artística.

1. el padre **2.** las hermanas, Marcela y Vanesa **3.** el hermano, Raúl **4.** los primos, Fabián, Anaís y Aldo **5.** la abuela

1. el padre

____

2. las hermanas, Marcela y Vanesa

____

3. el hermano, Raúl

____

4. los primos, Fabián, Anaís y Aldo

____

5. la abuela

____

WB 2-10 | ¿Cómo son? Describe each of the people listed by providing the correct form of the verb **ser** and an appropriate form of the adjective indicated.

Modelo Antonio Villaraigosa, alcalde *(mayor)* de Los Ángeles (liberal)
Antonio Villaraigosa *es liberal.*

1. Eric Chávez, jugador de béisbol profesional en Estados Unidos (atlético)

   Eric Chávez ______________________.

2. Gael García Bernal y Salma Hayek, actores (guapo)

   Gael García Bernal y Salma Hayek ______________________.

3. Dolores Huerta, cofundadora de los United Farm Workers (trabajador)

   Dolores Huerta ______________________.

4. Elena Poniatowska y Sandra Cisneros, escritoras (listo)

   Elena Poniatowska y Sandra Cisneros ______________________.

VOCABULARIO 2 Las nacionalidades

WB 2-11 | ¿De dónde son y qué lengua hablan? Describe each of the following people's nationality and native language. **¡OJO!** Nationalities agree with the number and gender of the person or people being described. Follow the model.

Modelo Alicia Ramos / España
Es española. Habla español.

1. Teresita Sedillo / Honduras

____

2. Tomás Romero / Puerto Rico

____

3. Beatriz y Nancy Ruiz / Costa Rica

____

4. Helmut Schmidig / Alemania

____

5. Steven Ensley / Canadá

____

6. Madeline Depuy / Francia

____

7. Alejandro y Luis Villegas / Paraguay

____

WB 2-12 | Cosas del mundo Test you worldliness. Write the origin of each of the items listed below. Choose from the list of countries. Follow the model.

Modelo Los gauchos *son argentinos.*

Argentina Cuba Rusia Puerto Rico Egipto Japón

1. El reggaetón *(type of music)* ________ ____________.
2. Las chicas Harajuku ________ ____________.
3. El vodka ________ ____________.
4. La esfinge *(sphynx)* ________ ____________.
5. Los cigarros Cohiba ________ ____________.

ESTRUCTURA Y USO 4 Describing daily activities at home or at school: Present tense of *-er* and *-ir* verbs

WB 2-13 | La vida universitaria David is a Mexican college student studying at the Universidad La Salle, a Catholic university in Mexico City. To find out how his life compares to yours, complete the sentences with the appropriate form of the verb in the present tense.

1. Mis amigos y yo ____________ (asistir) a la universidad.
2. Todos nosotros (vivir) ____________ con nuestros padres.
3. Ahora estudio ciencias religiosas *(religious)* y ____________ (aprender) sobre la historia de los franciscanos en México.
4. Yo ____________ (creer) en Dios y ____________ (asistir) a misa *(Mass)* con mis padres los domingos.
5. Mi novia ____________ (vivir) en Aguascalientes y no me visita mucho. Por eso yo ____________ (escribir) muchas cartas.
6. ____________ (beber) un café con mis amigos en el centro todos los días.

WB 2-14 | La vida de los estudiantes Tomás and Estela are students at the Universidad Autónoma de Guadalajara. See how similar their lives are to yours by writing the appropriate form of the verb provided.

Estela y su familia ____________ (vivir) en Guadalajara. Estela es estudiante y ____________ (aprender) mucho en sus clases de la UAG. Ella ____________ (comprender), ____________ (leer) y ____________ (escribir) tres lenguas: español, japonés e inglés. Después de la graduación, Estela quiere viajar por el mundo.

Nombre ______________________________ Fecha ______________________________

Tomás no ______________ (vivir) con su familia. Sus padres, sus dos hermanas y su hermano ______________ (vivir) en Mérida, la capital de Yucatán. Tomás le ______________ (escribir) a su familia frecuentemente y él ______________ (recibir) muchas cartas de ellos.

Tomás y Estela ______________ (aprender) psicología por la mañana. Él ______________ (deber) estudiar mucho porque es su especialidad (*major*). Por la tarde, Tomás y Estela ______________ (comer) en la cafetería de la UAG y después ______________ (beber) café juntos (*together*).

WB 2-15 | Actividades diarias To create a schedule of chores, you and your roommates need to know who is available at what time. Make a chart of everyone's routines by using one element from each of the categories below and writing logical sentences that describe what each roommate does on a regular basis. Follow the model and conjugate each verb properly in the present tense.

Modelo Magaly (beber café)
Magaly bebe café en el Café Roma por la mañana.

¿Dónde?	**¿Cuándo?**
en un restaurante	por la mañana
en el Café Roma	los domingos
en casa	todos los días
en el centro universitario	por la tarde
en la universidad	por la noche
en la biblioteca	los lunes
en la librería	los fines de semana

1. Mi familia y yo (comer) ______________________________.
2. Teresa (deber estudiar) ______________________________.
3. Yo (asistir a clases) ______________________________.
4. Esteban (escribir cartas) ______________________________.
5. Tú (leer libros) ______________________________.
6. Nancy (vender libros) ______________________________.

WB 2-16 | Una clase diferente Lorenzo's class is a bit strange today. To find out what is happening, fill in the blanks with the appropriate form of one of the verbs listed below. **¡OJO!** Not all verbs are used, but no verb is used twice.

abrir aprender asistir beber comprender creer comer

deber escribir leer recibir vender vivir

La profesora **1.** ______________ la puerta y entra en la sala de clase. Carlos y Héctor **2.** ______________ un libro cómico pero *(but)* ahora la profesora dice que ellos **3.** ______________ abrir su libro de texto. La profesora **4.** ______________

en la pizarra. Ahora Antonia y Mónica **5.** ________________ Coca-Cola y **6.** ________________ un burrito loco. ¡Y Javier! Él habla por teléfono y **7.** ________________ su computadora. Yo no **8.** ________________ esta clase hoy.

ESTRUCTURA Y USO 5 Expressing possession, age, and physical states: Common uses of the verb *tener*

To learn more about ***tener*** and ***tener*** **expressions,** visit Heinle iRadio at www.cengage.com/spanish/viajes.

WB 2-17 | Arte mexicano Form sentences with the following elements. Conjugate the verb **tener** in the present tense.

1. María y Tomás / tener / la famosa película mexicana *Y tu mamá también*

____

2. Yo / tener ganas de ver esa película

____

3. Los suegros de mi hermano / tener / una colección grande de arte de Diego Rivera

____

4. Mi familia y yo / tener / solamente un cuadro de Frida Kahlo

____

WB 2-18 | ¡Algo tienen! Alicia is talking about how strange her family is. Match each of her statements with the corresponding picture of her family members.

A.

B.

_______ **1.** Siempre tenemos mucha hambre.

_______ **2.** Mi hermano siempre tiene prisa.

_______ **3.** Mi hermanita siempre tiene sueño.

_______ **4.** Mi abuela siempre tiene sed.

_______ **5.** Alicia siempre tiene miedo.

_______ **6.** Álex y Alberto siempre tienen frío.

_______ **7.** La tía Silvia siempre tiene mucha paciencia con los niños.

Nombre ______________________ Fecha ______________________

C.

D.

E.

F.

G.

WB 2-19 | La familia Ortega To learn more about the Ortega family, complete the following sentences with the correct form of an appropriate **tener** expression.

1. María Elena es muy inteligente. Cuando hay una duda *(doubt)*, ella siempre ______________________________.
2. Chus y Lola son buenas estudiantes. Siempre ______________ en sus clases.
3. Carlos es un travieso *(rascal)*, pero su mamá ______________ mucha ______________ con él.
4. El abuelo nunca se quita *(takes off)* su suéter de lana *(wool sweater)* y por eso siempre ______________________________.

WB 2-20 | Una conversación Javier and Silvia are classmates who are getting to know each other better. Complete their conversation by using the appropriate form of the verb **tener.** **¡OJO!** Remember that Javier and Silvia are classmates and would use the **tú** form.

JAVIER: ¿Cuántos años **1.** ______________, Silvia?

SILVIA: **2.** ______________ 19 años. ¿Y tú?

JAVIER: Yo **3.** ______________ 24.

SILVIA: ¿Cuántos hermanos **4.** ______________?

JAVIER: **5.** ______________ seis: tres hermanas y tres hermanos.

SILVIA: ¡Qué bueno! Yo no **6.** ______________ hermanos. Pero mi mamá **7.** ______________ un pájaro.

JAVIER: Pues, en mi casa nosotros no **8.** ______________ mascotas. Pero mis abuelos **9.** ______________ tres gatos.

ESTRUCTURA Y USO 6 Counting to 100

WB 2-21 | Números Write the numerals that correspond to the following written numbers.

Modelo treinta y cinco
35

1. treinta y dos ______
2. cincuenta y cinco ______
3. cuarenta y nueve ______
4. noventa y nueve ______
5. ochenta y uno ______
6. setenta y siete ______
7. sesenta y ocho ______
8. cien ______

WB 2-22 | Más números Write out the words represented by the following numerals.

1. 66 ______________________________
2. 44 ______________________________
3. 83 ______________________________
4. 91 ______________________________
5. 37 ______________________________

WB 2-23 | Los gastos del mes How much did Jorge spend this month on the items listed? Write the numeric value of the prices written below.

1. café: treinta y tres dólares $________
2. comida: noventa y seis dólares $________
3. discos compactos: cuarenta y dos dólares $________
4. videojuegos: ochenta y cinco dólares $________
5. teléfono celular: setenta y cuatro dólares $________

VIAJEMOS POR MÉXICO

DVD In this video segment, you will learn about Mexico City and its cultural attractions.

WB 2-24 | Cognados In the video segment, you will hear a number of Spanish words that are cognates of English words. Try to pronounce each of the following Spanish words, and then match each with its meaning in English.

1. _____ capital	**a.** museum of anthropology
2. _____ catedral	**b.** cathedral
3. _____ centro político	**c.** history
4. _____ monumento	**d.** calendar
5. _____ museo de antropología	**e.** political center
6. _____ calendario	**f.** astronomical cycles
7. _____ ciclos astronómicos	**g.** monument
8. _____ templos	**h.** temples
9. _____ historia	**i.** capital

WB 2-25 | Cognados en contexto Watch the video segment, and listen for the following sentences, in which the cognates you just identified in activity **WB 2-24** appear. Fill in the blank with the cognate that you hear.

1. Sobre las ruinas de la ciudad azteca de Tenochtitlán, los españoles construyeron la ______________________ de la Guadalupe y el Palacio del Virrey.
2. En esta gran avenida está el ______________________ a la Independencia.
3. También sobre el Paseo de la Reforma está el ______________________.
4. Edificios, ______________________ y ______________________ se entremezclan para contar la ______________________ y un poco de la vida de los mexicanos de hoy.

WB 2-26 | Comprensión View the video segment again, and then select the phrase that best answers the following questions.

1. ¿Qué es el Zócalo?
   a. una de las plazas más grandes del mundo
   b. la capital de México
   c. un nombre para los aztecas
   d. una avenida *(avenue)*
2. ¿Qué es el Distrito Federal?
   a. el centro petrolero más grande de México
   b. la capital de México
   c. la capital de España
   d. la capital de Guatemala
3. ¿Qué hay en el Museo de Antropología?
   a. un ángel
   b. una catedral
   c. un monumento a la independencia
   d. un calendario para medir *(to measure)* los ciclos astronómicos

¡A ESCRIBIR!

Anuncios personales One of your good friends has been having trouble in the romance department lately and has asked you to help write a personal ad. He/She is very interested in meeting Spanish-speaking people and wants you to write the ad in Spanish. Write the personal ad that will help your friend meet the **amor de sus sueños** *(love of her / his dreams)*.

ATAJO 4.0

Functions: Introducing; Describing people
Vocabulary: Nationality; Numbers; University
Grammar: Verbs: **ser, tener;** Possession with **de;** Adjectives: agreement, position

Nombre ______________________ Fecha ______________________

Strategy: Learning Spanish word order

Word order refers to the meaningful sequence of words in a sentence. The order of words in Spanish sentences differs somewhat from that in English. Some common rules of Spanish word order that were presented to you in the textbook are these:

- Definite and indefinite articles precede nouns.
  Los gatos y **los perros** son animales.
  Tengo **un gato** y **un perro.**
- Subjects usually precede their verbs in statements.
  Mi gato es negro.
- Subjects usually follow their verbs in questions.
  ¿Tiene usted animales en casa?
- Adjectives of quantity usually precede nouns.
  ¿Cuántos animales tienes en casa?
- Adjectives of description usually follow nouns.
  El **perro pardo** *(brown)* se llama Bandido.
- Possession is often expressed by using **de** with a noun.
  Tigre es **el gato de Sara.**

Paso 1 Unscramble the words in the following sentences and then rewrite them in their correct sequence. Be sure to capitalize the first word of every sentence and to use a period or question marks where appropriate.

Modelo es Carlos Rodríguez de México
Carlos Rodríguez es de México.

1. es Ana López una madre

____

2. años tiene cuántos ella ¿?

____

3. chino es padre su

____

Paso 2 Now think of your ideas for your ad and write a first draft on a separate sheet of paper. Then, review it and write the draft of your paragraph below. Remember to check for correct word order.

____
____
____
____
____
____
____
____
____
____

Autoprueba

WB 2-27 | Los miembros de la familia Read the following statements and fill in the blanks with a family-related vocabulary word.

1. Mi mamá es la ______________________ de mi papá.
2. El hijo de mi tío es mi ______________________.
3. Me llamo Antonio Casagrande. Casagrande es mi ______________________.
4. La hija de mi hermano es mi ______________________.
5. Los hijos de mi hija son mis ______________________.

WB 2-28 | Descripciones Describe the following people by completing each sentence with the appropriate form of the verb **ser** and the appropriate form of the adjective in parentheses. Make any changes necessary so that the adjectives agree in number and gender with the person they are describing.

1. Salma Hayek ____________ una actriz ______________________ (mexicano).
2. David Letterman y yo ____________ personas ______________________ (simpático).
3. Ace Ventura y Austin Powers ____________ hombres ______________________ (tonto).
4. Tú ____________ una persona ______________________ (atlético).
5. Hillary Rodham Clinton ____________ una mujer bastante ______________________ (paciente).

WB 2-29 | Probablemente son... Your new friend, Andrés, is describing different friends and family members. Read his descriptions and then write the adjective that best matches each description. **¡OJO!** Do not use the same adjective more than once.

1. Iliana y Rafael trabajan diez horas al día. Probablemente son ______________________.
2. Eva estudia la filosofía de la ciencia. Estudia y lee libros todo el día. Probablemente es ______________________.
3. Carlos tiene mucho dinero, pero nunca gasta dinero. Probablemente es ______________________.
4. Belén usa mucho su tarjeta de crédito, pero nunca paga sus facturas *(pays her bills)*. Probablemente es ______________________.
5. Mi hija nunca limpia su cuarto y nunca estudia. Probablemente es ______________________.
6. Adán y Lupe comen mucho y nunca hacen ejercicio *(exercise)*. Probablemente son ______________________.

WB 2-30 | Los números Write out the numbers that correspond to the following numerals.

1. 32 ______________________
2. 99 ______________________
3. 24 ______________________
4. 12 ______________________

Nombre ________________________________ Fecha ________________________________

5. 15 ________________________________

6. 17 ________________________________

7. 46 ________________________________

8. 79 ________________________________

WB 2-31 | Una conversación Complete the following conversation with the appropriate forms of the verb **tener** and the appropriate possessive pronouns.

PILAR: ¿ **1.** ______________ tú una familia pequeña o grande, Lola?

LOLA: **2.** ______________ familia es grande. Yo **3.** ______________ cuatro hermanas.

PILAR: ¿No **4.** ______________ hermanos?

LOLA: No, **5.** ______________ padres **6.** ______________ cinco hijas.

PILAR: Pues, tus padres también **7.** ______________ un gato. ¿Cómo se llama **8.** ______________ gato?

LOLA: **9.** ______________ gato se llama Pipo.

PILAR: ¡Pipo! **10.** ______________ razón. ¡Qué gato más lindo!

LOLA: Oye, Pilar. Yo **11.** ______________ hambre. Vamos a *(Let's go)* comer algo. ¿**12.** ______________ hambre tú?

PILAR: No, pero **13.** ______________ sed. Yo voy contigo *(I will go with you)*.

WB 2-32 | En la universidad Complete the following conversation between Diana and Tomás with the appropriate verb form. Some verbs will be used more than once.

creer deber escribir recibir tener vivir

TOMÁS: ¿Dónde **1.** ______________, Diana?

DIANA: Yo **2.** ______________ con mi tía aquí en el Distrito Federal, pero mi familia **3.** ______________ en Guadalajara.

TOMÁS: ¿**4.** ______________ muchas cartas para tus padres?

DIANA: Sí, de vez en cuando *(once in a while)*. Y tú, Tomás, ¿**5.** ______________ muchas cartas para tus padres?

TOMÁS: No, pero yo **6.** ______________ muchas cartas de mis padres. Yo **7.** ______________ escribir más.

DIANA: Tú **8.** ______________ razón. ¡Yo **9.** ______________ en la importancia de la correspondencia escrita!

Nombre ______________________ Fecha ______________________

El tiempo libre: Colombia

VOCABULARIO 1 Los deportes y los pasatiempos

WB 3-1 | Juanjo el increíble Juanjo likes to do it all. Look at the pictures of Juanjo doing many of his favorite activities and write the letter of the picture that corresponds to each description.

_____ **1.** Le gusta patinar en línea.

_____ **2.** Le gusta montar a caballo.

_____ **3.** Le gusta ir a la discoteca.

_____ **4.** Le gusta esquiar.

_____ **5.** Le gusta el ciclismo.

_____ **6.** Le gusta caminar por las montañas.

_____ **7.** Le gusta jugar al golf.

_____ **8.** Le gusta hacer ejercicios.

_____ **9.** Le gusta visitar el museo.

_____ **10.** Le gusta ir de compras.

WB 3-2 | Buscapalabras Use the clues below to find the words related to sports and pastimes hidden in the puzzle.

A	C	A	T	B	E	D	T	O	F	U	C
C	E	A	R	A	Q	U	E	T	A	D	A
A	I	H	E	P	U	P	A	L	O	S	N
M	I	N	I	A	T	E	P	I	E	U	T
P	A	O	E	T	E	S	N	U	A	P	A
O	D	G	U	I	T	A	R	R	A	E	J
B	E	T	E	N	I	S	U	U	I	R	U
I	T	A	F	A	A	B	F	M	R	I	E
G	A	F	A	R	E	T	A	O	E	L	R
O	R	D	E	N	A	R	A	R	T	E	G
R	D	I	S	C	O	T	E	C	A	O	A
N	A	T	A	C	I	O	N	D	I	Y	S
O	K	L	O	B	T	U	F	A	R	O	X
N	O	T	R	R	I	C	N	O	C	I	N

Pistas:

1. Me gusta nadar; mi deporte favorito es la ________________.
2. Me gusta tocar la ________________.
3. Para *(in order to)* bailar, voy *(I go)* a la ________________.
4. Juegas al golf en un ________________.
5. Rafael Nadal juega al ________________.
6. Los 49ers son un equipo de ________________.
7. Arnold Schwarzenegger levanta ________________.
8. El fotógrafo saca ________________.
9. Para *(In order to)* escuchar música, voy a un ________________.
10. Necesitas patines para ________________.
11. Me gustan las películas; me gusta ir al ________________.

WB 3-3 | Actividades Amelia and her friends are always busy. Form sentences from the items below and then indicate if these activities are likely done indoors (**adentro**) or outdoors (**al aire libre**).

1. Amelia y sus amigos / mirar la tele / cada noche.

   ____

2. Nosotros / andar en bicicleta / los sábados.

   ____

3. Nancy y Pedro / levantar pesas / cada mañana.

   ____

4. Amelia / visitar el museo / los domingos y / sacar fotos / con su cámara digital.

   ____

Nombre ________________________ Fecha ________________________

ESTRUCTURA Y USO 1 Expressing likes and dislikes: *Gustar* + infinitive and *gustar* + nouns

WB 3-4 | ¿Qué les gusta? Colombian-born U.S. cycling champion Freddy Rodríguez discusses how he and his friends and family spend their free time. To find out what he says, form sentences by matching appropriate elements from each column.

1. ______ A mí	**a.** nos gusta hacer un picnic.
2. ______ A mi esposa y a mí	**b.** les gusta el ciclismo.
3. ______ A su hijo	**c.** me gusta andar en bicicleta por las montañas.
4. ______ A mis amigos	**d.** le gusta estar conectado en línea.
	e. te gusta correr.

WB 3-5 | Gustos famosos Alex Villalobos, manager for an exclusive hotel for the rich and famous, discusses the likes and dislikes of some of his most notorious guests. Use **me, te, le, nos, os,** or **les** to find out what he has to say.

Nuestro hotel sí es popular con la gente más conocida *(best known)* del mundo. A todos los famosos **1.** ________ gusta pasar por lo menos *(at least)* una semana aquí. Tenemos clientes políticos, como el vicepresidente Biden. A él **2.** ________ gusta bailar en la discoteca toda la noche. Pero él no es el único cliente político. El ex presidente Clinton visita también. A él no **3.** ________ gusta bailar en la discoteca, pues prefiere practicar los deportes. Por ejemplo, a Bill **4.** ________ gusta jugar al tenis.

A mí **5.** ________ gustan los clientes políticos, pero prefiero las estrellas de cine. A ellos **6.** ________ gusta hacer muchas actividades divertidas conmigo *(with me)*. Por ejemplo, a Angelina Jolie y a mí **7.** ________ gusta montar a caballo, andar en bicicleta, patinar en línea y pescar.

WB 3-6 | Mis preferencias Ignacio Casaverde is looking for a Spanish-speaking sports partner and has posted the following message on your gym billboard. Complete his message by selecting the correct verb form.

Hola, soy Iggi. En general, me **1.** (gusta / gustan) los deportes como el tenis y el baloncesto, pero me **2.** (gusta / gustan) más el ciclismo y el hockey. No me **3.** (gusta / gustan) la pesca porque es aburrida *(boring)*. Los viernes por la mañana a mi hermano y a mí nos **4.** (gusta / gustan) ir al gimnasio a levantar pesas. Los sábados por la mañana nos **5.** (gusta / gustan) jugar al fútbol. Por la tarde a mí me **6.** (gusta / gustan) jugar al billar. A mi hermano le **7.** (gusta / gustan) más las cartas *(cards)* y no juega conmigo. Los domingos no me **8.** (gusta / gustan) practicar ningún deporte porque a mi esposa le **9.** (gusta / gustan) ir de compras y no hay tiempo para jugar. ¿Qué te **10.** (gusta / gustan) hacer?

VOCABULARIO 2 Los lugares

WB 3-7 | Lugares revueltos Unscramble the letters to reveal different places in the city.

1. el emorcda: ______________________
2. la ientda: ______________________
3. la slegiai: ______________________
4. la cpisian: ______________________
5. el enic: ______________________
6. el suemo: ______________________

WB 3-8 | ¿Adónde va para...? Where in the city does one go to do the following activities? Choose the answers from the list provided. **¡OJO!** Use each response only once.

al museo	al centro comercial
al parque	a la discoteca
a la piscina	al supermercado
al café	al restaurante
al cine	al banco

1. Para ver una película: ______________________
2. Para nadar: ______________________
3. Para hacer las compras, hablar con amigos o tomar algo: ______________________
4. Para depositar dinero: ______________________
5. Para ver arte: ______________________
6. Para bailar: ______________________
7. Para comprar comida: ______________________
8. Para jugar al fútbol: ______________________
9. Para tomar café: ______________________
10. Para cenar con amigos: ______________________

Nombre ______________________ Fecha ______________________

ESTRUCTURA Y USO 2 Expressing plans with *ir: ir a* + destination, and *ir a* + infinitive

WB 3-9 | Entre amigos Gilberto and his girlfriend, Alejandra, run into Lola, Gilberto's ex-girlfriend. Does Gilberto still have a crush on her? Find out by filling in the blanks with the correct form of the verb **ir.**

GILBERTO: Hola, Lola, ¿cómo estás? ¿Qué tal el viaje *(how was the trip)*?

LOLA: Ay, muy bien, gracias. Bueno, ustedes, ¿qué **1.** ______________ a hacer aquí hoy?

GILBERTO: Nosotros **2.** ______________ al gimnasio aquí en el campus. Y tú, ¿adónde **3.** ______________ tan guapa *(looking so cute)*?

ALEJANDRA: ¡Gilberto!

LOLA: Yo **4.** ______________ a ver a mi compañero de clase, Cali Caretas. Nosotros **5.** ______________ a sacar fotos juntos *(together)*.

GILBERTO: ¿Con Cali? ¡Él no saca buenas fotos!

ALEJANDRA: ¡Gilberto! Yo me **6.** ______________ a ir de aquí. Mira Lola, Gilberto **7.** ______________ a hacer sus ejercicios ahora. Nos vemos.

LOLA: Pues, ¡hasta luego!

GILBERTO: ¡Hasta pronto!

ALEJANDRA: ¡Gilberto!

WB 3-10 | Compañeros de cuarto You and your roommates have busy lives. Based on the following calendar page, describe in complete sentences what everyone is going to do and when (day and time) they are going to do it. Follow the model.

Modelo Eugenia y Cati
Eugenia y Cati van a ir al cine el lunes a las tres de la tarde.

lunes 17 Eugenia y Cati: cine, 3 p.m. Carlos: sacar fotos con Silvia, 11 a.m.	**jueves** 20 Ángel, iglesia: 9 a.m.–1 p.m.	**sábado** 22 Carlos y yo: cenar y bailar, 9 p.m.
martes 18 Alberto: plaza, 8 p.m.	**viernes** 21 Eugenia: mercado al aire libre, 5 p.m.	**domingo** 23 Ángel, Carlos y Eugenia: jugar tenis, 2 p.m.
miércoles 19 Yo: comer con mis padres, 1 p.m.		

1. Carlos y Silvia

____

2. Alberto

____

3. Carlos y yo

____

4. Ángel, Carlos y Eugenia

____

5. Eugenia

____

6. Ángel

____

7. Yo

____

ESTRUCTURA Y USO 3 Describing leisure-time activities: Verbs with irregular *yo* forms

WB 3-11 | Conjugaciones Select the appropriate verb form for the persons listed.

1. yo / estar
   a. esta **b.** esté **c.** estoy **d.** estamos
2. Mario y Elena / poner
   a. pones **b.** pongo **c.** ponen **d.** pongan
3. nosotros / salir
   a. salimos **b.** salgamos **c.** salen **d.** sabemos
4. Julio / dar
   a. dan **b.** de **c.** da **d.** doy
5. Teresa y yo / hacer
   a. hagamos **b.** hacemos **c.** hacen **d.** hago
6. tú / conocer
   a. conozcas **b.** conoce **c.** conoces **d.** conocen
7. yo / saber
   a. salen **b.** sabe **c.** saber **d.** sé
8. Antonio, Jimena y su madre / ver
   a. ven **b.** ves **c.** vemos **d.** vean
9. yo / traer
   a. trae **b.** traen **c.** traes **d.** traigo

Nombre ______________________ Fecha ______________________

WB 3-12 | El profesor excéntrico Paco Empacanueces is the Colombian "Nutty Professor." Find out his strange habits by building sentences from the words below. **¡OJO!** Be careful to add prepositions where necessary. Follow the model.

Modelo yo / traer / comida / mis clases
Yo traigo comida a mis clases.

1. todos los días / yo / salir de la casa / cuatro de la mañana
____
2. yo / hacer ejercicios / el parque
____
3. allí *(there)* / yo / ver / a mis amigos
____
4. yo / traer / discos compactos / universidad
____
5. yo / poner / música de Metallica / mi oficina
____
6. yo / dar fiestas / por la mañana
____
7. yo / conocer / a todos mis colegas / la universidad
____
8. pero / yo / no saber / sus nombres
____

WB 3-13 | Los sábados Mercedes likes to spend her Saturdays with friends. Complete the following paragraph with the appropriate form of the verb in parentheses to find out what she does.

Los sábados por la mañana me gusta pasear por la ciudad. Normalmente yo **1.** ______________ (salir) de mi casa temprano para ir al mercado al aire libre. Allí **2.** ______________ (ver) a mis amigos y todos **3.** ______________ (hacer) las compras juntos. Mi amiga Lilián siempre **4.** ______________ (traer) a sus hermanos, Fabián y Santi. Ellos **5.** ______________ (conocer) a todos los vendedores *(vendors)* del mercado y por eso nosotros compramos a muy buenos precios. Después de ir al mercado mis amigos y yo **6.** ______________ (dar) una vuelta *(go around)* por el centro. Muchas veces vamos al museo de arte. Mi amiga Silvia **7.** ______________ (saber) mucho del arte y me gusta ir con ella. Otras veces vamos a un café muy especial que yo **8.** ______________ (conocer). En este café, el dueño *(owner)* siempre **9.** ______________ (poner) música reguetón y todos bailamos.

ESTRUCTURA Y USO 4 Expressing knowledge and familiarity: *Saber, conocer,* and the personal *a*

 To hear more about **saber** and **conocer**, visit Heinle iRadio at www.cengage.com/spanish/viajes.

WB 3-14 | ¿Cierto o falso? Read the following statements and indicate whether each is true by writing **cierto,** or false by writing **falso.** If you are not familiar with some of the people mentioned, you can look them up on the Internet.

_______________ **1.** Shakira sabe jugar al golf muy bien.

_______________ **2.** Alberto Contador conoce la ciudad de Madrid.

_______________ **3.** Gabriel García Márquez conoce a muchos escritores.

_______________ **4.** Juanes sabe tocar la guitarra.

_______________ **5.** Fernando Botero sabe cantar bien.

WB 3-15 | Y ahora... You are interviewing a future Spanish-speaking roommate from Colombia. Complete the following questions with the correct form of the verb **saber** or **conocer**. **¡OJO!** In many parts of Colombia the **usted** form is used instead of **tú.**

1. ¿_______________ a muchas personas aquí?

2. ¿_______________ jugar al tenis?

3. ¿_______________ cocinar bien?

4. ¿_______________ a los dueños del apartamento?

5. ¿_______________ qué tiendas están cerca *(close by)*?

WB 3-16 | Los abuelos de Camila To find out what Camila's grandparents are like, complete the phrases with the correct form of **saber** or **conocer.**

CAMILA: Diego, usted **1.** _______________ tocar muy bien la guitarra.

DIEGO: Gracias, Camila, pero también usted **2.** _______________ tocar el piano y cantar muy bien.

CAMILA: ¡Gracias! Oiga, ¿quiere **3.** _______________ a mis abuelos? Mi abuela toca el tambor en una banda de rock metálico y mi abuelo canta con un grupo de música punk.

DIEGO: Sí, con mucho gusto. Yo **4.** _______________ que ellos tienen como 80 años, ¿no?

CAMILA: Sí, es cierto, ¡pero todavía *(still)* **5.** _______________ vivir!

DIEGO: Bueno, quiero **6.** _______________ a sus abuelos. ¡Voy a aprender mucho de ellos!

Nombre ______________________ Fecha ______________________

ESTRUCTURA Y USO 5 Talking about the months, seasons, and the weather

WB 3-17 | Estaciones y meses Write the season and the months of that season (in the Northern Hemisphere) represented in each drawing. Then, using the prompts, indicate the weather conditions.

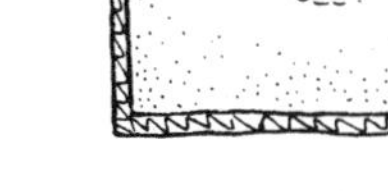

1. Estación: ______________________

Meses de la estación: ______________________

El tiempo: Hace ______________________,

hace ______________________

y está ______________________.

2. Estación: ______________________

Meses de la estación: ______________________

El tiempo: Hace ______________________

y hace ______________________.

3. Estación: ______________________

Meses de la estación: ______________________

El tiempo: Hace mucho ______________________

y ______________________.

¡Hace ______________________!

4. Estación: ______________________

Meses de la estación: ______________________

El tiempo: Está ______________________

y ______________________. Probablemente

hace ______________________.

WB 3-18 | Las condiciones en Tolima Consult the following weather report for El Tolima, Colombia, and answer the questions in complete sentences.

CONDICIONES ACTUALES: EL TOLIMA, COLOMBIA	
Temperatura	77°F
Humedad	84%
Viento	0–6 mph
Condiciones	Neblina
Visibilidad	6 millas

1. ¿Qué tiempo hace hoy en El Tolima?

____

____

2. ¿Hace mucho viento hoy en El Tolima?

____

3. ¿Es un buen día para esquiar? ¿Por qué sí o por qué no?

____

WB 3-19 | ¿Cuándo...? Provide the appropriate information about when the following events occur.

Modelo Es el primer día de primavera en Santa Fe, Nuevo México. ¿En qué mes estamos?
Estamos en marzo.

1. Es el veinticinco de diciembre en Nueva York. ¿Qué estación es?

____

2. Es el cuatro de julio en la Patagonia, Argentina. ¿Qué estación es?

____

3. Es el quince de septiembre en la Ciudad de México. ¿Qué estación es?

____

4. La gente esquía en el agua en Minnesota. ¿Qué estación es?

____

5. Es el primer día de verano en Ohio. ¿En qué mes estamos?

____

Nombre ______________________ Fecha ______________________

VIAJEMOS POR COLOMBIA

DVD In this video you will learn about the Colombian capital city, Bogotá.

WB 3-20 | Cognados In the video you will hear a number of Spanish words that are cognates of English. Before viewing, try to pronounce each of the following Spanish words and phrases, and then try to match each with its meaning in English.

1. _____ centro cultural	**a.** monastery
2. _____ exportación	**b.** cultural center
3. _____ esmeraldas	**c.** teleferic / tram
4. _____ contemplar	**d.** emeralds
5. _____ monasterio	**e.** exportation
6. _____ teleférico	**f.** contemplate
7. _____ zona residencial	**g.** hero
8. _____ balcones	**h.** residential zone
9. _____ héroe	**i.** textiles
10. _____ textiles	**j.** balconies

WB 3-21 | Cognados en contexto Watch the video and listen for the following sentences, in which some of the cognates you just identified in activity **WB 3-20** will appear. Fill in the blanks with the cognate you hear.

1. Bogotá, situado en el centro del país, es la capital y el ______________ principal del país.
2. La ______________ de ______________ y flores forma una parte importante de la economía del país.
3. La Candelaria, una ______________, es el centro histórico de Bogotá.
4. La artesanía colombiana es muy variada, desde los ______________ hasta la bisutería *(costume jewelery)*.

WB 3-22 | Comprensión View the video again, and then answer the following questions.

1. ¿Qué influencias culturales hay en Colombia? *(Select all that apply.)*

   a. africanas — **c.** indígenas *(indigenous)*

   b. chinas — **d.** hondureñas

2. ¿A qué lugares de Bogotá va la gente para la recreación? *(Select all that apply.)*

   a. los parques — **c.** Cartagena

   b. El Cerro de Montserrate — **d.** los circos

3. ¿A qué parte de la ciudad va uno si quiere aprender de la historia de Colombia? *(Select all that apply.)*

   a. las discotecas — **c.** La Candelaria

   b. La Avenida El Dorado — **d.** La Avenida 19

¡A ESCRIBIR!

Mis planes para el verano Your friend Carlos wrote to tell you about his summer vacation plans, and he wants to know what you are doing. Write him back and tell him about all of your summer plans.

Strategy: Combining sentences

Learning to combine simple sentences into more complex ones can help you improve your writing style immensely. In Spanish, there are several words you can use as connectors to combine sentences and phrases.

y	and (**y** becomes **e** before **i** or **hi**)
que	that, which, who
pero	but
o	or (**o** becomes **u** before **o** or **ho**)
porque	because

Before you begin to write, follow these steps.

Paso 1 Write a few basic sentences about your plans for summer. Follow the model

Modelo Este verano (yo) ir a
Este verano voy a ir a Nueva York.

Este verano (yo) querer
Este verano quiero visitar a mis abuelos.

1. Este verano (yo) ir a
____

2. Este verano (yo) no ir a
____

3. Este verano (yo) querer
____

4. Este verano (yo) no querer
____

Paso 2 Connect some of these phrases you have just written with **y, o, pero,** or **porque** to form more complex, logical sentences. Follow the model.

Modelo *Este verano voy a ir a Nueva York porque quiero visitar a mis abuelos.*

____
____
____
____
____
____
____
____

Nombre ______________________ Fecha ______________________

Paso 3 Now that you have your ideas organized, write a first draft on a separate sheet of paper. Then, review it and write the final draft of your letter with complete sentences. You can begin with ***Querido Carlos.***

Functions: Writing a letter (informal); Describing people; Talking about the present

Vocabulary: Sport; Leisure; Board games; Family members; Domestic; University

Grammar: Verbs: **ser, tener, conocer,** and **saber;** Verbs: Future with **ir;** Article: contractions **al, del**

Autoprueba

WB 3-23 | Los meses y las estaciones In the first column write the Spanish names for the months in which the following U.S. holidays are celebrated. In the second, write the season in which the holiday falls.

	Mes	Estación
1. Christmas	________________	________________
2. Valentine's Day	________________	________________
3. New Year's Day	________________	________________
4. Halloween	________________	________________
5. Memorial Day	________________	________________
6. Thanksgiving	________________	________________

WB 3-24 | En la ciudad Write the letter of the description next to the place where you would most likely do that activity.

_____	**1.** un museo	**a.** aprender historia
_____	**2.** una plaza	**b.** comprar comida
_____	**3.** el mercado	**c.** mandar una carta
_____	**4.** un banco	**d.** sacar dinero
_____	**5.** la oficina de correos	**e.** comer algo
_____	**6.** la piscina	**f.** nadar
_____	**7.** el restaurante	**g.** hablar con los amigos

WB 3-25 | Los pasatiempos State your pastimes by matching a verb from the first column with an appropriate phrase from the second column. Begin each sentence with **Me gusta** and form a complete sentence.

Modelo hacer + ejercicio
Me gusta hacer ejercicio.

1. ver	fotos
2. sacar	la guitarra
3. jugar	al tenis
4. tocar	a mis abuelos
5. bailar	con la música rock
6. visitar	películas en video

1. ____

2. ____

3. ____

4. ____

Nombre ______________________ Fecha ______________________

5. ______________________

6. ______________________

WB 3-26 | Entre amigos Complete the following conversation with the appropriate forms of the verb **ir**.

IRENE: ¿Adónde **1.** ____________ tú este fin de semana?

CARLOS: **2.** ____________ al parque para estudiar. ¿Por qué no **3.** ____________ conmigo?

IRENE: No, gracias. Mi mamá y yo **4.** ____________ de compras.

CARLOS: ¿No **5.** ____________ tu papá con Uds.?

IRENE: No, porque mi papá, Raúl y Sara **6.** ____________ al cine.

WB 3-27 | Un joven contento Complete the paragraph with the **yo** form of the appropriate verb from the list.

conocer saber ver dar salir estar hacer ir poner

Yo **1.** ____________ mucho con mis amigos y **2.** ____________ muchas cosas con ellos. Normalmente **3.** ____________ a fiestas con estos amigos y a veces **4.** ____________ fiestas en mi casa con ellos. En las fiestas **5.** ____________ mucha música rock y todo el mundo baila. **6.** ____________ a muchas personas y **7.** ____________ que a todos les gusta estar en mis fiestas. Los domingos **8.** ____________ a mis abuelos y comemos juntos. La verdad es que *(the truth is that)* **9.** ____________ muy contento.

WB 3-28 | ¿Saber o conocer? Choose between the appropriate form of **saber** or **conocer** to complete the following sentences.

1. Sergio García ____________ jugar al golf.
2. Juanes y Carlos Vives ____________ a Shakira.
3. Los colombianos ____________ bailar el vallenato.
4. Yo no ____________ al presidente de Colombia.

WB 3-29 | **¿Qué vas a hacer?** Match a verb from the first column with an appropriate phrase from the second column to form complete sentences with **ir + a** + infinitive. Follow the model.

Modelo visitar un museo
Yo voy a visitar un museo.

practicar	al tenis
jugar	a caballo
nadar	en la piscina
montar	pesas
levantar	deportes

1. ______________________________
2. ______________________________
3. ______________________________
4. ______________________________
5. ______________________________

WB 3-30 | **¿Qué tiempo hace?** Describe the weather depicted in each of the following scenes.

A. ______________________________
B. ______________________________
C. ______________________________
D. ______________________________
E. ______________________________
F. ______________________________

Nombre ______________________ Fecha ______________________

En la casa: España

VOCABULARIO 1 La casa

WB 4-1 | Sopa *(Soup)* de letras Unscramble the letters to reveal the name of a household item. Then write where in the house that item is typically found. Follow the model.

Modelo MACA
Palabra **Lugar de la casa**
cama *dormitorio*

	Palabra	Lugar de la casa
1. MRRAIOA	______________	______________
2. ORDONIO	______________	______________
3. SEMA	______________	______________
4. ÁFSO	______________	______________
5. REBAÑA	______________	______________
6. NÓLISL	______________	______________
7. DAHUC	______________	______________
8. AMÓDOC	______________	______________

WB 4-2 | En la agencia de bienes raíces *(real estate)* Which house will you rent? Match the letter of each picture with its description. Then, in each drawing write the names of the items mentioned in its description.

A.

B.

C.

______ **1.** Esta casa tiene tres dormitorios, un baño y una sala que están en el segundo piso. La sala tiene un sofá y un estante para libros. En el primer piso, hay una cocina grande con una puerta muy elegante que da a un patio grande. La casa también tiene un jardín pequeño que está al lado del garaje.

______ **2.** Esta casa de dos pisos tiene tres dormitorios, un baño, una cocina y una sala. La sala está en el primer piso. Tiene dos sillones, un sofá, una lámpara y una alfombra. Una de las paredes de la sala tiene un espejo pequeño. También en la sala hay una escalera elegante para llegar al segundo piso. Los dormitorios y el cuarto de baño están en el segundo piso. La casa no tiene garaje, pero tiene un patio grande.

______ **3.** Esta casa tiene tres dormitorios, una cocina y un cuarto de baño con inodoro y lavabo. La casa también tiene una sala grande con tres sillones y una lámpara. Esta casa tiene muchas ventanas que dan al (*look out on the*) patio pequeño. Al lado del *(Next to the)* patio hay un jardín grande con muchas flores. La casa también tiene un sótano y un garaje pequeño.

Nombre ______________________ Fecha ______________________

WB 4-3 | ¿Para qué es esto? Select the name of the appliance described in each statement.

_____ **1.** Es para preparar la comida rápidamente.

a. la estufa **b.** el horno de microondas **c.** la tostadora

_____ **2.** Es para limpiar la alfombra.

a. la aspiradora **b.** la plancha **c.** la secadora

_____ **3.** Es para quitar arrugas *(wrinkles)* de la ropa.

a. el despertador **b.** el refrigerador **c.** la plancha

_____ **4.** Es necesario usarla después de lavar la ropa.

a. el lavaplatos **b.** el horno de mircroondas **c.** la secadora

WB 4-4 | Una venta Stella and José are moving in together and trying to organize their things. They will sell those items that they will have two of, so help them decide what needs to be sold by writing the name of these items under the appropriate category. Follow the model.

Cosas que tienen...

para la cocina

una estufa

____

____

para la habitación

____

para la limpieza *(cleaning)*

____

____

Cosas que tienen que vender...

para la cocina

una tostadora

____

____

para la habitación

____

para la limpieza *(cleaning)*

una aspiradora

____

WB 4-5 | ¿Dónde? Where in the home do you usually find the following items? Follow the model.

Modelo el horno de microondas
En la cocina.

1. el lavabo

____

2. el lavaplatos

____

3. la alfombra

____

4. la cama

____

5. el inodoro

____

ESTRUCTURA Y USO 1 Describing household chores and other activities: Present tense of stem-changing verbs *(e → ie; o → ue; u → ue; e → i)*

WB 4-6 | Una nueva casa Teresa wants to move to a bigger house and is talking with her real estate agent about what she is looking for. To find out what they discuss, fill in the spaces with the appropriate verb form.

AGENTE: ¿Qué tipo de casa **1.** ______________ (preferir) usted?

TERESA: Ay, por favor, trátame de tú *(use the **tú** form with me)*.

AGENTE: Vale *(Ok)*. Pues ¿qué **2.** ______________ (querer) tú en una casa?

TERESA: Bueno, yo **3.** ______________ (querer) una casa con tres habitaciones porque tengo un hijo y una hija y todos nosotros **4.** ______________ (querer) nuestro propio *(own)* dormitorio. La casa que yo **5.** ______________ (tener) ahora, solamente **6.** ______________ (tener) dos dormitorios. Es demasiado *(too)* pequeña.

AGENTE: Vale, yo **7.** ______________ (entender) tu situación. **8.** ¿ ______________ (preferir) vosotros vivir en el centro o fuera de la cuidad?

TERESA: Nosotros no **9.** ______________ (tener) coche y por eso *(for that reason)* nosotros **10.** ______________ (pensar) que es mejor vivir en el centro.

AGENTE: Y, ¿cuándo **11.** ______________ (pensar) vosotros mudaros *(move)*?

TERESA: Bueno, mis hijos **12.** ______________ (preferir) mudarse *(move)* cuanto antes *(as soon as possible)*, y yo también **13.** ______________ (tener) prisa.

AGENTE: Vale, yo **14.** ________________ (empezar) a buscar casas para vosotros mañana.

TERESA: Muchísimas gracias.

AGENTE: De nada.

WB 4-7 | ¡Qué compañeros! Paqui lives in a **colegio mayor** *(dorm)* in Madrid and is always complaining about her roommates. To find out what she says, complete the following sentences with an appropriate form of a verb from the list below.

cerrar   comenzar   pedir   perder   regar   venir

1. Tomás siempre ____________________ favores.
2. El día de Santi ____________________ a las 3:00 de la mañana.
3. Lola y Eva siempre ____________________ sus llaves *(keys)*.
4. Carlos nunca ____________________ las plantas.
5. Los amigos de Amparo ____________________ a visitar muy tarde.
6. Belén nunca ____________________ la boca *(mouth)*.

WB 4-8 | La familia Addams The **familia Addams** is the Spanish version of the Addams family—a little creepy and kooky. Today the daughter, Miércoles, is giving an oral report on her family life. Form complete sentences with the words below to find out what she says.

1. mi papá / siempre / jugar / con una espada *(sword)*

   ____

2. mi tío Fétido / dormir / en una cama de clavos *(nails)*

   ____

3. mi madre Morticia / siempre / volver a casa / con plantas muertas *(dead)*

   ____

4. nosotros / almorzar / a las 2:00 de la mañana

   ____

5. mi hermano Pugsley / poder / dormir con los ojos abiertos

   ____

VOCABULARIO 2 Los quehaceres domésticos *(Household chores)*

WB 4-9 | Entrevista Mariana is talking to her friend about her chores. Look at her answers and write the question that Mariana most likely asked. **¡OJO!** Remember some of the question words you have already learned. Follow the model.

Modelo *¿Cuándo te gusta barrer el piso?*
Me gusta barrer el piso por la mañana.

1. ¿ ____?

   Sí, pongo la mesa todos los días.

2. ¿ ____?

   No, no me gusta planchar la ropa.

3. ¿ ____?

Mi hermano riega las plantas.

4. ¿ ____?

No, no tenemos que lavar las ventanas.

5. ¿ ____?

Sí, hago mi cama todos los días.

WB 4-10 | ¿Qué hacen? Find out what the **Servicio de limpieza** can do for you. Form sentences with the elements listed. Follow the model.

Modelo Ana María / lavar / los platos
Ana María lava los platos.

1. Juan Carlos y Ana María / pasar la aspiradora

____

2. Yo / regar / las plantas

____

3. Todos nosotros / lavar / las ventanas

____

4. Juan Carlos / barrer / el piso

____

5. Ana María / hacer / las camas

____

WB 4-11 | De vacaciones Pedro asked you to house-sit for him while he is on vacation, but he left you with an incomplete list of chores. Complete the list with the chores that he most likely wants you to do in each place indicated. Follow the model.

En la cocina	**En toda la casa**
Barrer el piso.	______________
______________	______________
En la habitación	**En el jardín**
______________	______________
______________	______________

Nombre ______________________ Fecha ______________________

ESTRUCTURA Y USO 2 — Expressing preferences and giving advice: Affirmative *tú* commands

WB 4-12 | Las reglas Ana has just moved into the sorority house and her house mother is telling her the rules of the house. To find out what she says, make **tú** commands with the following phrases.

Modelo Llegar a casa antes de las once de la noche.
Llega a casa antes de las once de la noche.

1. Leer los anuncios del día.

   ____

2. Limpiar tu habitación una vez a la semana.

   ____

3. Hablar con tus hermanas.

   ____

4. Regar las plantas del jardín cada lunes.

   ____

5. Cantar nuestra canción con tus hermanas.

   ____

WB 4-13 | Mari Mandona Mari Mandona always has advice for all of her friends. For each of her friend's problems listed in the left-hand column, write the letter of Mari's advice listed in the right-hand column.

_____ **1.** Tengo que limpiar toda la casa hoy.

_____ **2.** No me gusta estar en casa.

_____ **3.** No me gusta mi nuevo compañero de casa.

_____ **4.** No tengo comida en la casa.

_____ **5.** Quiero visitarte.

_____ **6.** Soy muy mala.

_____ **7.** La universidad ya no tiene habitaciones disponibles *(available)* en la residencia.

_____ **8.** Tengo un secreto.

a. Ven a mi casa.

b. Dime tu secreto.

c. Haz un buen trabajo.

d. Pon tu nombre en la lista de espera *(waiting list)*.

e. Sé buena.

f. Sal de la casa.

g. Ve al supermercado.

h. Ten paciencia con él.

WB 4-14 | Y tú, ¿qué dices? You have just been hired to write the advice column of your university's newspaper. What advice will you give to the following people? For each situation, write a different **tú** command. Follow the model.

Modelo Una mujer mayor que quiere conocer a hombres jóvenes.
Ve a muchos partidos de fútbol.

1. Una chica que quiere vivir en la residencia estudiantil.

____

2. Un chico que quiere vivir en Argentina.

____

3. Un chico que quiere saber cómo sacar buenas notas.

____

4. Una chica que no sabe qué llevar a una fiesta latina.

____

5. Un chico que nunca dice la verdad.

____

ESTRUCTURA Y USO 3 Talking about location, emotional and physical states, and actions in progress: The verb *estar*

WB 4-15 | ¿Dónde está? Based on the pictures below, state where the indicated items are located by supplying the appropriate prepositional phrase from the list. Do not use the same phrase more than once. Follow the model.

Modelo El sillón está *al lado de* la mesa.

al lado de	debajo de	en	lejos de
cerca de	delante de	encima de	sobre
con	detrás de	entre	

1. La aspiradora está ______________________ los estantes.
2. El baño está ______________________ el dormitorio y la sala.
3. El espejo está ______________________ la mesa.
4. La cómoda está ______________________ la sala.
5. La lámpara está ______________________ la mesa.
6. Los estantes están ______________________ la aspiradora.

Nombre ______________________ Fecha ______________________

WB 4-16 | Pobre Antonio Antonio Banderas is in Spain to film a movie without his wife, Melanie Griffith. Help Antonio complete the following imaginary letter to Melanie by filling in the blanks with the appropriate form of the verb **estar.**

Mi querida Melanie,

¿Cómo **1.** ______________ tú? ¿Cómo **2.** ______________ mi hija, Stella? Yo, pues, **3.** ______________ muy triste porque tú no **4.** ______________ aquí. Ahora **5.** ______________ en las islas Canarias para filmar una escena de mi película, «Dos noches de amor». Penélope Cruz **6.** ______________ aquí también y nosotros dos **7.** ______________ muy ocupados. Nosotros **8.** ______________ en la playa para filmar nuestra escena. Mañana voy a **9.** ______________ en las islas Baleares con Victoria Abril. Ella **10.** ______________ muy guapa estos días. Como puedes notar, yo **11.** ______________ muy ocupado. Bueno, me tengo que ir, pero espero verte a ti *(see you)* y a Stella muy pronto. Cuando vosotras no **12.** ______________ conmigo no puedo vivir.

Un beso, Antonio

WB 4-17 | Todos están trabajando When you arrive to your friend's house you find that everyone is working but one person. Describe what each person is doing in the pictures using the verb **estar** + the progressive form.

1. Patricio ____.
2. Paula ____.
3. Angelita ____.
4. Esteban ____.
5. Carlos ____.
6. Francisco y Stella ____.

WB 4-18 | ¡Solo en los sueños *(dreams)*! Imagine that you are watching a movie of your ideal life. Write complete sentences to describe what is happening in this movie. Use an appropriate form of the present progressive.

Modelo Mis amigos *están bailando en un club famoso.*

1. Yo ____.
2. Mis padres ____.
3. Mis amigos y yo ____.
4. Mis profesores ____.

ESTRUCTURA Y USO 4 Counting from 100 and higher: Los números de 100 a 1,000,000

WB 4-19 | Matemáticas Solve the following math problems. Write out the numbers in words. Follow the model.

Modelo doscientos cincuenta + tres = *doscientos cincuenta y tres*

1. trescientos cuarenta y ocho + quinientos setenta y nueve = ____________________
2. doscientos cincuenta y ocho + mil cuatrocientos y tres = ____________________
3. mil ochocientos catorce + cinco mil noventa y siete = ____________________

WB 4-20 | Pagando las facturas Luis Ángel, an exchange student from Burgos, Spain, is leaving for a long vacation. Because he is such a shopaholic, he's got a lot of big bills that will come due and needs you to help him keep current with them. Following the notes he left for you, write out the checks to pay his bills.

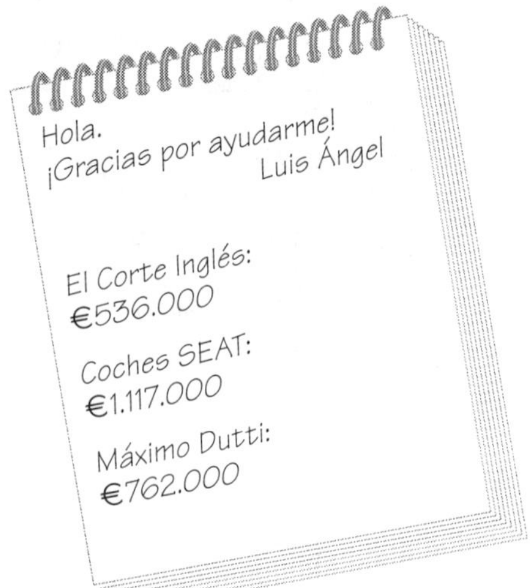

Nombre ______________________ Fecha ______________________

Luis Ángel Martín Elordieta **102**
c/ Altamirano 9
Burgos, España Fecha ______________________

Páguese por este cheque a: ______________________

______________________ euros.

002659870002687 6698 9897598 7889 *Luis Ángel Martín Elordieta*

Luis Ángel Martín Elordieta **103**
c/ Altamirano 9
Burgos, España Fecha ______________________

Páguese por este cheque a: ______________________

______________________ euros.

002659870002687 6698 9897598 7889 *Luis Ángel Martín Elordieta*

Luis Ángel Martín Elordieta **104**
c/ Altamirano 9
Burgos, España Fecha ______________________

Páguese por este cheque a: ______________________

______________________ euros.

002659870002687 6698 9897598 7889 *Luis Ángel Martín Elordieta*

WB 4-21 | El costo de la vida Your Spanish pen pal wants to know how much it costs to be a university student in the United States. Answer his questions using words in place of numerals.

1. ¿Cuánto es la matrícula universitaria, cada trimestre o semestre, en tu universidad?

____

2. ¿Cuánto gastas *(do you spend)* en libros cada trimestre o semestre?

____

3. ¿Cuánto es el alquiler *(rent)* por un apartamento en tu ciudad?

____

4. ¿Cuánto gastas en comida cada mes?

____

VIAJEMOS POR ESPAÑA

In these video segments you will learn about the many cultural treasures of the two Spanish cities of Madrid and Toledo.

WB 4-22 | ¿Dónde está ubicada España? Circle Spain on the map of Western Europe below.

WB 4-23 | Cognados In the video segments you will hear a number of Spanish words that are cognates of English. Before viewing, try to pronounce each of the following Spanish words, and then try to match each with its meaning in English.

_______	**1.** península ibérica	**a.** ham
_______	**2.** habitantes	**b.** dynamic
_______	**3.** dinámica	**c.** Iberian Peninsula
_______	**4.** jamón	**d.** European Union
_______	**5.** área de recreo	**e.** innumerable
_______	**6.** Unión Europea	**f.** inhabitants
_______	**7.** centro financiero	**g.** financial center
_______	**8.** innumerables	**h.** prestigious
_______	**9.** prestigiosos	**i.** recreation area
_______	**10.** sinagoga	**j.** celebrated painter
_______	**11.** cristianos	**k.** Christians
_______	**12.** célebre pintor	**l.** synagogue

Nombre ______________________ Fecha ______________________

WB 4-24 | Cognados en contexto Watch the video and listen for the following sentences, in which some of the cognates you just identified in activity **WB 4-23** will appear. Fill in the blanks with the cognates.

from segment 1 (Madrid)

1. Madrid, la capital de España, se sitúa en el centro de la ______________________.
2. Es una ciudad ______________________ y una de las ciudades de mayor población de la ______________________.
3. También es un ______________________ y cultural importante.
4. En sus grandes ______________________ la gente va a caminar, o simplemente a descansar bajo el sol brillante de Madrid.

from segment 2 (Toledo)

5. Dentro de las murallas de Toledo, encontramos monumentos, iglesias, ______________________ y museos.
6. La Casa Museo de El Greco exhibe la obra de este ______________________, que vivió en Toledo en el siglo dieciséis.

WB 4-25 | Comprensión Decide whether the following statements are **cierto** *(true)* or **falso** *(false)* according to what you learn from the video segments.

1. __________ En la Plaza Mayor de Madrid hay restaurantes muy buenos.
2. __________ Hay una estación de metro en la Gran Vía.
3. __________ En los Museos de Jamón ves el arte del célebre pintor español El Greco.
4. __________ El Retiro es un museo grande de Madrid.
5. __________ Toledo está muy lejos de Madrid.
6. __________ Hay influencias judías *(Jewish influences)* en la cultura de Toledo.

¡A ESCRIBIR!

LAS VIVIENDAS ESTUDIANTILES You have been asked to write a short article on student residences in the United States for a magazine for international students. Before you begin to write, reflect on the writing strategy you learned in your text.

Strategy: Writing topic sentences

The first step in writing a well-structured paragraph is to formulate a clear, concise topic sentence. A good topic sentence has the following characteristics.

- It comes at the beginning of a paragraph.
- It states the main idea of the paragraph.
- It focuses on only one topic of interest.
- It makes a factual or personal statement.
- It is neither too general nor too specific.
- It attracts the attention of the reader.

Paso 1 Think about the types of questions you might answer in this article. For example:

- Where do the majority of students choose to live?
- What options are available for students?
- How much does each type of living arrangement cost?

Paso 2 On a separate piece of paper write a sentence about the most important idea you would want to communicate to international students about student living arrangements in the United States. This will be your topic sentence. Then, write several sentences that support the point you make in your topic sentence. Organize these sentences and complete the first draft of your brief article.

Paso 3 Check over your paragraph, focusing on the characteristics of a good topic sentence and its relationship to the rest of the paragraph. You may use the following checklist questions as a guide: Does the topic sentence . . .

1. come at the beginning of the paragraph? _____ yes _____ no
2. state the main idea of the paragraph? _____ yes _____ no
3. focus on only one topic of interest? _____ yes _____ no
4. make a factual or personal statement? _____ yes _____ no
5. seem neither too general nor too specific? _____ yes _____ no
6. attract the attention of the reader? _____ yes _____ no

Paso 4 Make any necessary changes to your paragraph and write the final version below:

ATAJO 4.0

Functions: Writing an introduction; Describing objects

Vocabulary: House: bathroom, bedroom, furniture, kitchen, living room

Grammar: Verbs: **estar, tener;** Progressive tenses; Position of adjectives

Nombre ______________________ Fecha ______________________

Autoprueba

WB 4-26 | Los muebles Complete the sentences with the names of the appropriate household items from the following list.

un armario mi cama un escritorio el inodoro el jardín

1. Escribo mis cartas en ______________________.
2. Pongo toda la ropa en ______________________.
3. Duermo bastante bien en ______________________.
4. Limpio ______________________ en el baño.
5. Miro las plantas en ______________________.

WB 4-27 | Los electrodomésticos Complete the sentences with the names of the appropriate appliances from the following list.

la nevera una lavadora un despertador un horno de microondas una aspiradora

1. Para llegar a clase a tiempo uso ______________________.
2. Preparo la comida rápida en ______________________.
3. Siempre lavo mi ropa en ______________________.
4. Limpio las alfombras con ______________________.
5. Pongo la comida en ______________________.

WB 4-28 | En la casa Complete the following sentences with the names of the places where the chores described are normally done.

la cocina el comedor el jardín la sala

1. Lavo los platos en ______________________.
2. Paso la aspiradora en ______________________.
3. Corto el césped en ______________________.
4. Pongo la mesa en ______________________.

WB 4-29 | Carlos y Eva Complete the following conversation with the appropriate present-tense form of the verbs listed. **¡OJO!** You must use each of the verbs at least once.

comenzar pensar preferir querer tener

CARLOS: ¿Qué **1.** ______________ hacer hoy, Eva?

EVA: **2.** ______________ ganas de ir al cine. ¿Qué **3.** ______________ hacer tú?

CARLOS: Yo no **4.** ______________ ir al cine. **5.** ______________ ver videos en casa esta noche. Pero, dime *(tell me)*, ¿a qué hora **6.** ______________ la película en el cine?

EVA: **7.** ______________ a las 6:00. Mi hermana y yo no **8.** ______________ ver videos en casa, **9.** ______________ ir al cine.

CARLOS: ¿Tu hermana va con nosotros? Yo **10.** ______________ que no voy con Uds.

WB 4-30 | Con mi familia Complete the following paragraph with an appropriate present-tense form of the verbs listed.

almorzar decir dormir jugar servir volver
comenzar pensar preferir querer tener

Normalmente, yo **1.** __________ con mi familia a las 2:00 durante la semana. Mis padres preparan la comida, luego mi padre **2.** __________ la comida. Siempre como dos porciones y mi padre siempre **3.** __________ que voy a estar gordo. Después de **4.** __________, yo **5.** __________ la siesta por media hora. Después, mis padres **6.** __________ a su trabajo y yo **7.** __________ a la universidad. A veces, mis amigos y yo **8.** __________ al fútbol después de nuestras clases. Yo no **9.** __________ muy bien, pero me gusta mucho practicar ese deporte.

WB 4-31 | ¿Qué hago? Tell your friend how to get along better with his roommates. Use the following verb phrases to form ***tú*** commands.

1. hacer tu cama todos los días

____

2. quitar la mesa después de comer

____

3. sacar la basura todos los días

____

4. ir al supermercado todos los sábados

____

WB 4-32 | ¿Cuántos son? Solve these mathematical problems using words, not numerals.

1. doscientos treinta y cinco + mil quinientos tres = __________

2. seiscientos setenta y nueve + cuatrocientos ochenta y uno = __________

3. dos mil trescientos cincuenta y dos – novecientos treinta y seis = __________

Nombre ________________________________ Fecha ________________________________

La salud: Bolivia, Ecuador y Perú

VOCABULARIO 1 Las partes del cuerpo

WB 5-1 | El cuerpo humano Escribe los nombres de las partes del cuerpo del dibujo *(drawing)*.

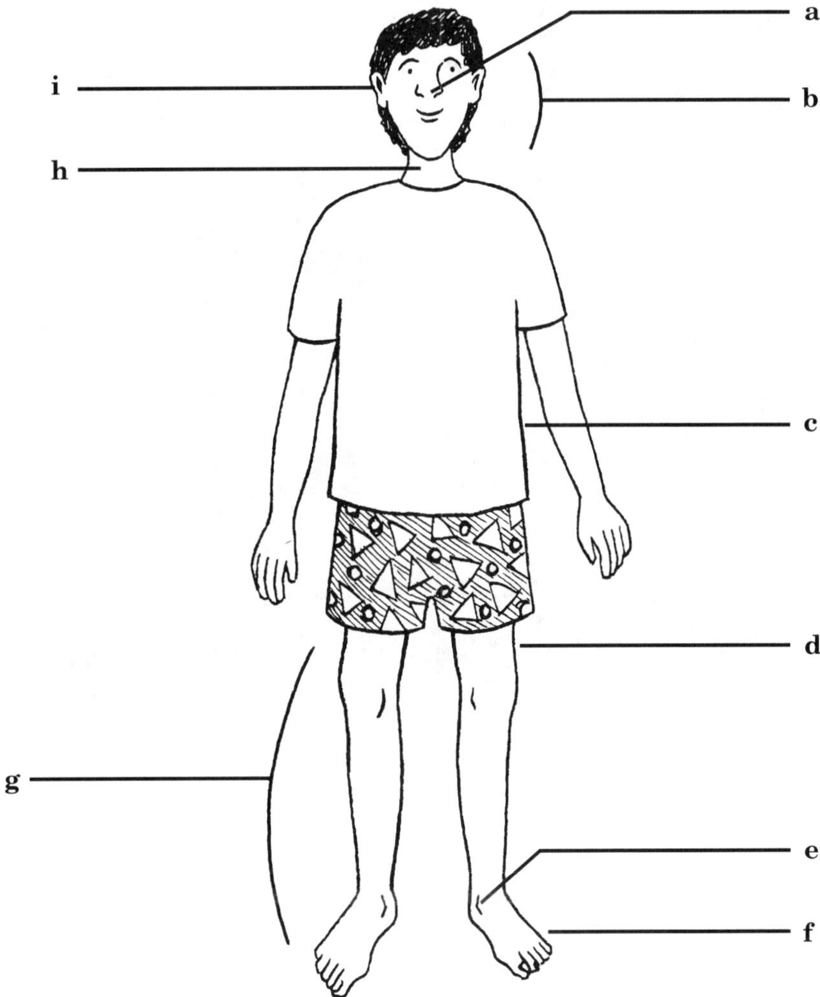

WB 5-2 | Crucigrama Soluciona el siguiente crucigrama rellenando los espacios en blanco con la palabra indicada en cada pista *(clue)*. Todas las palabras son partes del cuerpo humano.

Vertical

1. Dumbo tiene ______ muy grandes.
2. Señalas *(You point)* con el ______.
3. Michael Jordan no tiene ______.
4. Ves con los ______.
5. La ______ tiene cinco dedos.
7. Cuando tomas algo, el líquido pasa por la ______.
9. La ______ es parte de la cara.
10. Comes con la ______.
12. El ______ está conectado con la mano.

Horizontal

2. Tienes ______ en la boca.
6. Jessica Alba tiene una ______ muy bonita.
8. Si comes mucho, te duele *(hurts)* el ______.
11. El ______ es el símbolo del amor.
13. En medio del brazo está el ______.
14. Respiras con los ______.

Nombre ______________________ Fecha ______________________

WB 5-3 | El cuerpo revuelto Estas palabras son partes del cuerpo. Pon sus letras en orden para revelar *(reveal)* qué parte es.

Modelo gualen: *lengua*

1. anreip: ______________
2. sodde: ______________
3. rizan: ______________
4. dooc: ______________
5. ózarnoc: ______________

ESTRUCTURA Y USO 1 Talking about routine activities: Reflexive pronouns and present tense of reflexive verbs

WB 5-4 | La familia Soriana La casa Soriana es un lugar de mucha actividad. Todos los miembros tienen rutinas distintas. ¿Cómo son? Para saberlo *(to find out)* forma oraciones completas con los elementos dados *(given)*. Sigue el modelo.

Modelo Mari Pepa / acostarse / las 6:30 / la mañana
Mari Pepa se acuesta a las seis y media de la mañana.

1. Carmen / despertarse / 6:30 / la mañana

____

2. don Carlos y Miguel / afeitarse / en la noche

____

3. yo / lavarse / y después / cepillarse / los dientes

____

4. los niños / bañarse / en la mañana

____

5. doña Lucía y Luisita / maquillarse / y después / peinarse

____

6. Miguel / quitarse / la ropa / y acostarse / las 8:00 de la noche

____

WB 5-5 | **¿Compañeros?** Jerry piensa compartir *(share)* su apartamento con tres estudiantes hispanos: Elena, de Bolivia; Jorge, de España; y Lola, de Miami. Ahora están hablando de sus rutinas diarias para ver si van a poder compartir el apartamento pequeño de Jerry. Para saberlo, rellena los espacios en blanco con la forma apropiada del verbo. **¡OJO!** Jorge es español y usa la forma **vosotros.**

JERRY: Debemos hablar de cómo vamos a compartir el apartamento, ¿no?

JORGE: Pues, yo **1.** ____________________ (despertarse) a las 5:00 de la mañana porque trabajo muy temprano. **2.** ____________________ (Bañarse) en seguida *(right away)* y después **3.** ____________________ (secarme) y **4.** ____________________ (ponerme) la ropa. ¿Y vosotras? ¿A qué hora **5.** ____________________ (levantarse)?

ELENA: Yo, aunque *(although)* **6.** ____________________ (dormirse) tarde, **7.** ____________________ (despertarse) a las 7:00 de la mañana porque tengo clase a las 8:00. ¿Y tú, Lola? **8.** ____________________ (acostarse) tarde y **9.** ____________________ (despertarse) temprano también, ¿no?

LOLA: Sí. Y **10.** ____________________ (ducharse), **11.** ____________________ (vestirse) y **12.** ____________________ (maquillarse) en el baño, así que paso mucho tiempo allí en la mañana.

ELENA: Ah, ¡no te preocupes! A mí me gusta **13.** ____________________ (pintarse) en mi cuarto. No paso mucho tiempo en el baño en la mañana. Parece que todo está bien entonces, ¿no?

JERRY: Un momento, por favor. Yo también **14.** ____________________ (levantarse) temprano, a las 7:30. Necesito **15.** ____________________ (bañarse) inmediatamente para **16.** ____________________ (despertarse). Después **17.** ____________________ (cepillarse) los dientes, **18.** ____________________ (peinarse) y **19.** ____________________ (afeitarse). Finalmente, **20.** ____________________ (ponerse) la ropa y salgo del baño a las 8:30.

JORGE: Este hombre **21.** ____________________ (cuidarse) bien, ¿no?

Nombre ______________________ Fecha ______________________

WB 5-6 | ¿Qué está pasando? ¿Qué va a pasar? Mira los dibujos y contesta las preguntas. Escoge *(choose)* un verbo apropiado de la lista y escribe las dos posibles maneras de contestar. **¡OJO!** No todos los verbos son necesarios. Sigue el modelo.

cepillarse	ducharse	levantarse	peinarse	vestirse
dormirse	lavarse	maquillarse	quitarse	

Modelo ¿Qué está haciendo Nuria?
Nuria está cepillándose el pelo / Nuria se está cepillando el pelo.

1. ¿Qué está haciendo José María?

____

____

2. ¿Qué está haciendo Carlos?

____

____

3. ¿Qué va a hacer Pablo?

____

____

4. ¿Qué va a hacer Susana?

____

____

ESTRUCTURA Y USO 2 Talking about things you have just finished doing: *Acabar de* + infinitive

WB 5-7 | ¡Hecho! Forma oraciones con la estructura ***acabar de + infinitivo.*** Sigue el modelo.

Modelo Tú / bañarse: *Acabas de bañarte.*

1. Yo / maquillarse: ______________________________.
2. Elio / cepillarse los dientes: ______________________________.
3. Miguel / dar un paseo: ______________________________.
4. Belén / sacar fotos: ______________________________.

WB 5-8 | La vida sana El doctor Ruiz, un médico de España, está conversando con la familia Bodega sobre una vida sana. Les hace *(He asks them)* varias preguntas sobre su estilo de vida. Escribe sus respuestas usando la construcción ***acabar + de + el infinitivo.*** Sigue el modelo.

Modelo A los niños: ¿Os cepilláis los dientes todos los días?
Sí, acabamos de cepillarnos los dientes.

1. A toda la familia: ¿Coméis vosotros el desayuno todos los días?

____

2. A la señora Bodega: ¿Descansa Ud. durante el día?

____

3. A Juanito: ¿Te bañas todos los días?

____

4. A la señora Bodega: ¿Toman mucha agua los niños?

____

WB 5-9 | ¿Qué acaban de hacer? Escribe lo que estas personas acaban de hacer en cada situación. Escoge los verbos de la lista. Sigue el modelo.

acostarse andar comer comprar despertarse dibujar
dormirse levantarse maquillarse quitarse secarse

Modelo Silvia y Gabriela / Son las seis y media de la mañana.
Acaban de despertarse.

1. Nosotros / No tenemos hambre.

____

2. Tú / Estás seco.

____

3. Antonio / Se va a dormir.

____

4. Yo / No llevo ropa.

____

Nombre ______________________ Fecha ______________________

VOCABULARIO 2 La salud

WB 5-10 | Bienvenidos Dolores Castellanos les da un tour de la clínica a unos voluntarios en la Clínica de Salud Rural Andina. Completa su descripción de la clínica con una palabra apropiada de la lista. **¡OJO!** No vas a usar todas las palabras, y no puedes usar la misma palabra más de una vez.

ambulancia antibiótico catarro enfermedad enfermero(a) farmacia
gripe jarabe mareado médico pacientes pastillas
receta sala de emergencia sala de espera síntomas

Empezamos en la **1.** ______________________, donde los **2.** ______________________ esperan su cita *(appointment)* con el **3.** ______________________. Antes de ver al doctor Dardo Chávez, ellos comentan sus síntomas con el (la) **4.** ______________________. Durante el invierno, muchos de ellos tienen **5.** ______________________ y sus **6.** ______________________ son fiebre, escalofríos y dolores del cuerpo. En estos casos el doctor Dardo Chávez les da una **7.** ______________________ para antibióticos, y los pacientes tienen que ir a la **8.** ______________________. Pero en otros casos los pacientes simplemente tienen **9.** ______________________, pues tosen y estornudan mucho. En estos casos el doctor Dardo Chávez les da **10.** ______________________ y **11.** ______________________. Ahora, Uds. pueden venir conmigo para ver la **12.** ______________________. Allí es donde esperan los pacientes que vienen en la **13.** ______________________.

WB 5-11 | ¿Qué pasa? Describe a los siguientes pacientes. Empareja *(match)* las descripciones de la columna de la derecha con los dibujos de la izquierda.

1.

2.

3.

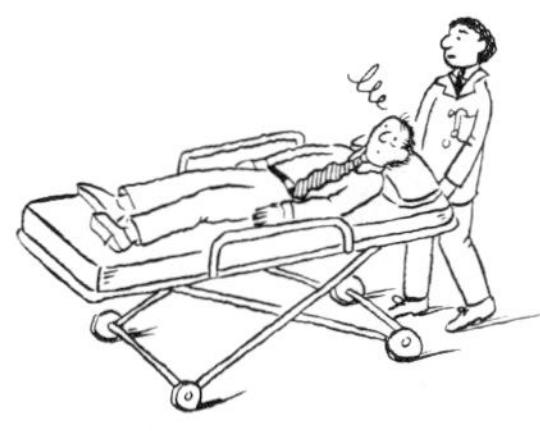

a. Le duele el estómago.

b. Está mareado.

c. Tiene escalofríos.

d. Tiene alergias.

e. Le duele la cabeza.

f. Tiene fiebre.

g. Está con el enfermero.

h. Estornuda.

WB 5-12 | ¿Loco por las medicinas? ¿Para qué son las medicinas que tiene David? Empareja las medicinas de la columna de la izquierda con sus usos de la columna de la derecha.

	La usas cuando...
1. Alka Seltzer®	**a.** te duele la piel
2. Solarcane®	**b.** te duele el cuerpo
3. Vicks®	**c.** te duele la garganta
4. Epsom salts	**d.** te duele el estómago

WB 5-13 | ¿Qué les duele? Tú y tus amigos acaban de subir a El Capitán en el parque Yosemite. Forma oraciones completas para indicar qué partes del cuerpo les duelen. Sigue el modelo.

Modelo Alberto / los pies: *A Alberto le duelen los pies.*

1. Alicia / los brazos: ______________________________.
2. Tomás / el tobillo: ______________________________.
3. Cara y Nidia / las rodillas: ______________________________.
4. Yo / la espalda: ______________________________.

ESTRUCTURA Y USO 3: Describing people, things, and conditions: *Ser* vs. *estar*

 To hear more about **ser** and **estar**, visit Heinle iRadio at www.cengage.com/spanish/viajes.

WB 5-14 | El nuevo médico Ángela y Roberto están hablando del nuevo doctor en la clínica. Escoge la forma apropiada del verbo para completar sus oracaiones.

1. El nombre del nuevo doctor (es / eres / está / somos) Juan José Valerio.
2. (Están / Son / Es / Está) de Copacabana, Bolivia.
3. Copacabana (están / son / es / está) cerca del Lago Titicaca.
4. Creo que el doctor Valerio y la doctora Vargas (son / estás / están / somos / eres) en la sala de espera ahora.
5. Ahora (es / está / están / son) las dos de la tarde; el doctor Vargas (es / somos / está / estamos) comiendo el almuerzo.

WB 5-15 | ¿Cuánto sabes? Las siguientes oraciones son sobre gente, lugares o eventos de Bolivia y Paraguay. Reescribe cada oración con la forma apropiada del verbo **ser** o **estar.**

Modelo El boliviano Jaime Escalante (ser / estar) muy inteligente.
El boliviano Jaime Escalante es muy inteligente.

1. Santa Cruz de la Sierra (ser / estar) en el este de Bolivia.

____

2. El parque Carlos Antonio López (ser / estar) en Asunción.

____

Nombre ______________________ Fecha ______________________

3. La Paz y Sucre (ser / estar) las capitales de Bolivia.

____

4. El guaraní (ser / estar) la moneda oficial de Paraguay.

____

5. La celebración de Achocalla (ser / estar) en La Paz.

____

WB 5-16 | La doctora Reyes La doctora Reyes está revisando *(reviewing)* sus apuntes *(notes)* sobre una de sus pacientes. Completa sus apuntes con la forma apropiada de los verbos **ser** o **estar.**

Hoy **1.** ______________ viernes, 22 de febrero y **2.** ______________ las 2:00 de la tarde.

La paciente **3.** ______________ Aracelia Itzapú. Ella **4.** ______________ casada y **5.** ______________ madre de tres hijos. Ella **6.** ______________ de Asunción y **7.** ______________ paraguaya, pero su esposo **8.** ______________ boliviano. Aracelia **9.** ______________ baja y delgada. Hoy día Aracelia **10.** ______________ muy enferma. **11.** ______________ congestionada, **12.** ______________ tosiendo y estornudando mucho. Dice que **13.** ______________ muy cansada también. Además, dice que **14.** ______________ un poco deprimida *(depressed)* por varias razones: acaba de morir su padre y su esposo no **15.** ______________ aquí. Él **16.** ______________ en La Paz y **17.** ______________ buscando trabajo. Creo que **18.** ______________ necesario para Aracelia dormir más y tomar vitaminas. La próxima cita para Aracelia va a **19.** ______________ el primero de marzo.

ESTRUCTURA Y USO 4 Pointing out people and things: Demonstrative adjectives and pronouns

WB 5-17 | ¿Cómo funciona? Hoy es el primer día de trabajo en la clínica para Leticia y tiene muchas preguntas. Completa sus preguntas con la forma correcta del pronombre demostrativo: ***este, esta, estos, estas.*** Sigue el modelo.

Modelo ¿Ayudo a *este* señor?

1. ¿Hablo con __________ mujer?
2. ¿Trabajo en __________ sala?
3. ¿Escribo sobre __________ síntomas?
4. ¿Todos los pacientes son de __________ pueblo?
5. ¿Tratamos aquí todas __________ enfermedades?

WB 5-18 | ¡Pobre Leticia! No está haciendo bien su trabajo. Para saber cómo la corrige su jefe *(how her boss corrects her)*, completa sus comentarios con el adjetivo demostrativo correcto: ***ese, esa, esos, esas.*** Sigue el modelo.

Modelo No, ayuda a *ese* señor.

1. No, habla con _________ mujer.
2. No, trabaja en _________ sala.
3. No, escribe sobre _________ problemas.
4. No, los pacientes son de _________ dos pueblos.
5. No, aquí solamente tratamos a _________ pacientes.

WB 5-19 | Más preguntas de Leticia Leticia todavía tiene más preguntas. Ayuda a completarlas. Sigue el modelo.

Modelo ¿Es *esa (that one there)* mujer la que tiene catarro o es *aquella (that one way over there)*?

1. ¿ _______ hombre *(this man right here)* tiene náusea o es _______ *(that one way over there)*?
2. ¿ Son _______ niños *(these boys right here)* los que necesitan jarabe o son _______ *(those over there)*?
3. ¿A quién le duele el estómago? ¿a _______ muchacha *(that one way over there)* o a _______ *(this one right here)*?
4. Doctor, ¿necesita _______ pastillas *(these pills right here)* o _______ *(those over there)*?

VIAJEMOS POR BOLIVIA, ECUADOR Y PERÚ

En estos tres segmentos de video, vas a aprender un poco sobre las ciudades principales de Bolivia, Ecuador y Perú.

WB 5-20 | Geografía Identifica los países de Bolivia, Ecuador y Perú en el mapa.

1. _________ Escribe la letra del mapa que corresponde a Bolivia.
2. _________ Escribe la letra del mapa que corresponde a Ecuador.
3. _________ Escribe la letra del mapa que corresponde a Perú.

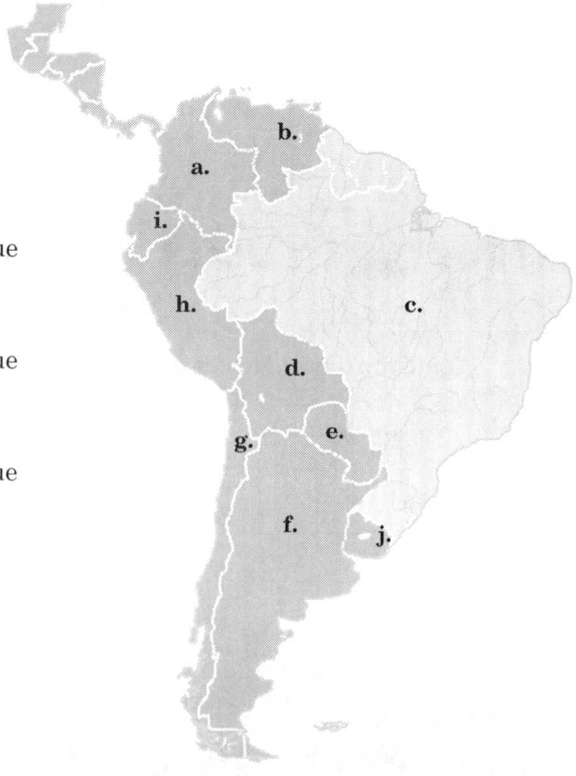

a.
b.
i.
h.
c.
d.
e.
g.
f.
j.

Nombre ______________________ Fecha ______________________

WB 5-21 | Cognados En los videos vas a escuchar muchos cognados *(cognates)* que pueden facilitar *(facilitate)* tu comprensión del video. Algunos de estos cognados aparecen aquí. Antes de ver los segmentos, trata de pronunciar cada palabra o frase y luego empareja *(match)* los cognados con su definición en inglés.

1. ____ gubernamental	**a.** volcanoes
2. ____ escultura	**b.** adoration
3. ____ animadas	**c.** governmental
4. ____ indígena	**d.** abundance
5. ____ volcanes	**e.** animated
6. ____ adoración	**f.** indigenous
7. ____ acelerada	**g.** sculpture
8. ____ abundancia	**h.** accelerated
9. ____ artesanía	**i.** topography
10. ____ diversidad	**j.** artisan *(handmade)* crafts
11. ____ topografía	**k.** contrasts
12. ____ turismo ecológico	**l.** small part
13. ____ parte menor	**m.** ecotourism
14. ____ contrastes	**n.** diversity

WB 5-22 | Cognados en contexto Mira los segmentos de video y trata de rellenar los espacios en blanco con el cognado apropiado de la actividad **WB 5-21.**

del segmento sobre Bolivia

1. En La Paz se ven grandes ______________ sociales.
2. La mayoría de los bolivianos son ______________ aymaras y quechuas.

del segmento sobre Ecuador

3. La diversidad de su ______________ — costa, montañas y selva amazónica— es excelente para el ______________.

del segmento sobre Perú

4. Otras atracciones de Lima son el mercado de ______________, las plazas e iglesias, las playas, el barrio chino y el maravilloso "circuito mágico del agua", un conjunto de fuentes de agua ______________ con luz y sonido.

WB 5-23 | **Comprensión** Mira los tres segmentos otra vez y luego, indica si las siguientes oraciones son **ciertas** (C) o **falsas** (F).

1. ______ La Paz es la capital de Ecuador.
2. ______ En los mercados de La Paz puedes comprar artesanía indígena.
3. ______ La gente de origen europeo forma la parte menor de la población boliviana.
4. ______ Los limeños son las personas que viven en Lima.
5. ______ En el Parque del Amor de Lima puedes ver una escultura de dos personas que se están bañando.
6. ______ En Quito puedes ver el monumento de José de San Martín, el héroe de la independencia ecuatoriana.
7. ______ En Ecuador hay muchos volcanes.
8. ______ Los quiteños son personas que viven en Bolivia.

¡A ESCRIBIR!

Escribir por Internet You have just made a new Paraguayan friend through the Internet. Her name is Alicia Veraní and she wants to know all about you. Write her an e-mail and tell her all about yourself.

Strategy: Using a bilingual dictionary

A bilingual dictionary is a useful tool that, when used properly, can enhance the quality, complexity, and accuracy of your writing in Spanish. It is very important, however, that you learn to use it correctly. Here are some suggestions to help you use your bilingual dictionary properly.

1. When you look up the Spanish equivalent of an English word, you will often find several meanings for the same word, often appearing like this:
   cold: *n.* frío, catarro, resfriado
   adj. frío
2. In larger dictionaries, additional information may be given that will clarify meanings and uses.
   cold: *n.* frío *(low temperature)*; catarro *(illness)*; resfriado *(illness)*
   adj. frío
3. Pay attention to certain abbreviations in your dictionary that will tell you what type of word you have found. Notice the abbreviations *n.* and *adj.* in the examples above, indicating that the word is a noun or an adjective. Some of the more common abbreviations you will find are listed below. Their Spanish equivalents are in parentheses.
   n. noun *(sustantivo)*
   adj. adjective *(adjetivo)*
   adv. adverb *(adverbio)*
   conj. conjunction *(conjunción)*
   prep. preposition *(preposición)*
   v. verb *(verbo)*
4. Looking up a lot of different words in a bilingual dictionary when you are writing is inefficient. If you insist on looking up too many words as you write, you may become frustrated or feel like you want to give up altogether. It is wiser and faster to use the phrases you already know in Spanish as much as possible, rather than trying to translate too many new words you don't know from English to Spanish. You will learn more and more new words as you continue reading and listening to the language.

Nombre ______________________ Fecha ______________________

Paso 1 Add to the following list at least 5 important aspects of describing yourself.

- where you and your family are from
- your nationality
- your marital status
- where your house is located
- your personality traits and your family members' personality traits

____

____

____

____

____

Paso 2 Choose 4 aspects from above and write several sentences to describe each aspect chosen. If you need to use the dictionary, remember the strategy you have learned for looking up words.

Paso 3 Write a first draft of your e-mail letter and review this draft to make sure your ideas are clearly stated and that your vocabulary usage is correct.

Paso 4 Write the final draft below.

____

____

____

____

____

____

____

____

____

____

ATAJO 4.0

Functions: Describing people, talking about the present

Vocabulary: Countries, studies, leisure, family members, university

Grammar: Verbs: **ser, estar**

Autoprueba

WB 5-24 | El cuerpo humano Escribe los nombres de las partes del cuerpo indicadas *(indicated)* en el dibujo.

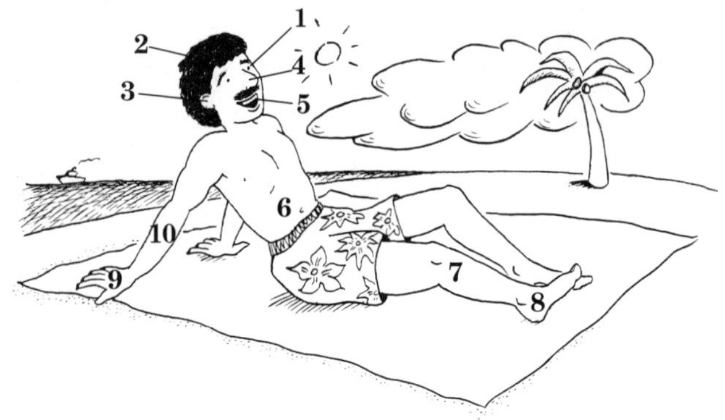

1. ______________________
2. ______________________
3. ______________________
4. ______________________
5. ______________________
6. ______________________
7. ______________________
8. ______________________
9. ______________________
10. ______________________

WB 5-25 | Los problemas médicos Completa las oraciones con las palabras de la lista. **¡OJO!** Usa cada palabra solamente una vez. Tienes que conjugar *(conjugate)* algunos verbos.

alergia	enfermo(a)	fiebre	síntomas
catarro	escalofríos	guardar cama	tomar la temperatura
congestionado(a)	estornudar	náuseas	toser
enfermedad	examinar	sano(a)	

1. En la primavera las flores me dan una ______________________ y yo ______________________ mucho.
2. Cuando alguien tiene ______________________, tose mucho.
3. El SIDA *(AIDS)* puede ser una ______________________ fatal.
4. Cuando alguien tiene alergia, a veces está ______________________.
5. El dolor del cuerpo y los ______________________ son ______________________ de la gripe.
6. Alguien que no está ______________________ está ______________________ muy seguido *(often)*.
7. El médico ______________________ a sus pacientes antes de darles una receta.

8. Para saber si alguien tiene ______________________, el médico le ______________________.

9. Si alguien está mareado, puede tener ______________________ y por eso debe ______________________ para sentirse mejor.

WB 5-26 | La rutina diaria Mira los dibujos de la rutina diaria de Beti Villalobos y describe lo que hace todos los días. **¡OJO!** Vas a usar verbos reflexivos y no reflexivos.

1. ______________________
2. ______________________
3. ______________________
4. ______________________
5. ______________________
6. ______________________
7. ______________________
8. ______________________

WB 5-27 | ¡Cómo vuela el tiempo! Son las ocho de la mañana en la vida de Beti Villalobos. Mira los dibujos otra vez *(again)* y escribe todo lo que acaba de hacer.

1. ______________________
2. ______________________
3. ______________________
4. ______________________
5. ______________________
6. ______________________
7. ______________________
8. ______________________

WB 5-28 | Lorena Bobada Completa el párrafo con la forma apropiada de los verbos ***ser*** y ***estar***.

Lorena Bobada **1.** ______________ de Sucre, Bolivia. **2.** ______________ estudiante de medicina y por eso **3.** ______________ ahora en La Paz, donde **4.** ______________ la universidad. Lorena ya no **5.** ______________ casada; **6.** ______________ divorciada y no tiene novio. **7.** ______________ soltera. Lorena **8.** ______________ una mujer inteligente y **9.** ______________ bastante ocupada con sus estudios. Un día ella quiere **10.** ______________ cirujana *(surgeon)*. Para ella una carrera **11.** ______________ muy importante y por eso ahora la vida académica **12.** ______________ la única para ella.

WB 5-29 | Gemelos distintos Roberto y Gustavo son gemelos, pero tienen opiniones muy diferentes. Si Roberto quiere una cosa, Gustavo quiere la otra. Para saber más de ellos, forma oraciones usando los pronombres demostrativos. Sigue el modelo.

Modelo Quiero ir a esta clínica.
No quiero esta, prefiero esa clínica.

1. Prefiero esta medicina.

 ____

2. Quiero ver a este médico.

 ____

3. Prefiero guardar esta cama.

 ____

4. Voy a pedir estos jarabes.

 ____

5. Prefiero esto.

 ____

Nombre ______________________ Fecha ______________________

¿Quieres comer conmigo esta noche? Venezuela

VOCABULARIO 1 La comida

WB 6-1 | Sopa de letras Todas de las siguientes palabras forman parte de una cena completa. Identifica las letras que faltan *(are missing)* de las siguientes *(following)* palabras. Después, pon en orden *(in order)* todas las letras señaladas *(signaled)* con * en los espacios debajo del dibujo *(drawing)* para revelar la expresión idiomática *(idiom)* que el dibujo representa.

1. _*_ N _*_ A L ___ D A
2. C H ___ L ___ _*_ ___ _*_
3. ___ C E ___ _*_ E
4. A ___ _*_ P A S
5. ___ _*_ A N
6. C _*_ ___ É
7. ___ E R D U ___ A _*_
8. V ___ N _*_
9. ___ A P _*_ S

Frase idiomática: ¿Qué piensa esta mujer de su admirador?

¡___ ___ ___Á HA___ ___A ___N ___ ___ ___ ___P ___!

WB 6-2 | En la cafetería Luis habla de la cafetería de su trabajo donde siempre come. Para saber qué come, rellena cada espacio en blanco con una palabra apropiada de la lista. **¡OJO!** No tienes que usar todas las palabras, pero solo puedes usar una palabra una vez.

agua mineral	jamón	sal
almuerzo	lechuga	sándwich
azúcar	pan	verduras
camarones	pavo	vinagre
cerveza	pimienta	vino
desayuno	queso	

La cafetería de la compañía es muy conveniente y a la una siempre como el **1.** ____________ allí con mis compañeros. Muchos días como un **2.** ____________ de **3.** ____________ y **4.** ____________. Me gusta mucho, sobre todo *(especially)* cuando le pongo *(I put on it)* **5.** ____________ y **6.** ____________. Mi amigo Jorge no come carne, así que él siempre come **7.** ____________. Pero los miércoles la cafetería no sirve mariscos y Jorge tiene que comer **8.** ____________ con **9.** ____________.

A mí también me gusta comer las papas fritas con mucha **10.** __________ y a veces les pongo **11.** __________. Jorge no come las papas fritas porque es un poco gordo. Después de comer, siempre tomamos algo. Por lo general, yo tomo una **12.** __________, pero Jorge toma **13.** __________ porque no puede tomar bebidas alcohólicas.

WB 6-3 | ¿Cómo come la gente? ¿Qué tipo de comida sirven en el restaurante *Como* en Maracaibo? Para saberlo, mira el menú y contesta las preguntas que siguen.

1. Si quieres comida del océano, ¿qué puedes pedir?

   ____

2. ¿Tienen bebidas de fruta?

   ____

3. ¿Qué bebidas alcohólicas sirven?

   ____

4. ¿Qué platos de carne ofrecen?

   ____

5. ¿Qué bebidas no alcohólicas sirven?

   ____

6. ¿Qué platos ofrecen para los que no comen carne roja?

   ____

7. ¿Qué sirven de postre?

   ____

Nombre ______________________ Fecha ______________________

ESTRUCTURA Y USO 1 Making comparisons: Comparatives and superlatives

WB 6-4 | Opiniones Lupe y Lalo tratan de decidir en dónde van a comer esta noche. Lee su conversación y rellena los espacios en blanco con la forma comparativa apropiada de **tan, tanto, más** o **menos**. **¡OJO!** Recuerda que **tan** y **tanto** usan la palabra **como** para hacer la comparación, mientras que **más** y **menos** usan **que.**

LUPE: ¡Vamos a El Caracól! Me encantan los mariscos allí. Son los mejores.

LALO: Sí, pero no sirven **1.** ____________ carne como El Asador. Y los platos no son **2.** ____________ grandes como los platos de Mar Abierto.

LUPE: Tienes razón, pero El Asador no tiene **3.** ____________ meseros como El Caracol, así que *(so)* su servicio no es **4.** ____________ bueno como el servicio en El Caracol.

LALO: Bueno, ¿por qué no vamos a Salicome? Tienen **5.** ____________ meseros que todos los otros restaurantes, sirven **6.** ____________ carne como mariscos y los precios no son **7.** ____________ altos como los otros restaurantes.

LUPE: Pero no me gusta su comida. Sus mariscos tienen **8.** ____________ sabor *(taste)* que los mariscos de El Caracol.

LALO: ¿Sabes qué? ¡Creo que debemos comer en casa!

WB 6-5 | Lo más... Una compañía de marketing publicó *(published)* los siguientes datos *(data)* sobre las opiniones de los estadounidenses hoy. Escribe los resultados en forma de comparaciones usando **más**, **menos**, **mejor**, **peor** y el adjetivo. **¡OJO!** Recuerda que los adjetivos tienen que concordar *(agree)* con el sustantivo *(noun)*. Sigue el modelo.

Modelo más nutritivo: la hamburguesa / la ensalada *
La ensalada es más nutritiva que la hamburguesa.

peor equipo: los Leones de Detroit* / los Raiders de Oakland
Los Leones de Detroit son peor equipo que los Raiders de Oakland.

1. más cómico: Carlos Mencía* / Steve Carell
____
2. mejor: Round Table / Pizza Hut*
____
3. menos guapo: Paris Hilton* / Jessica Simpson
____
4. rico: el chocolate puro* / el caramelo
____
5. menos dulce: la manzana* / la naranja
____

WB 6-6 | ¿Cómo se comparan? Tu amigo quiere llevarte *(bring you)* a El Toro Loco, un restaurante nuevo, pero tu quieres ir a tu restaurante favorito, El Pollo Loco. Le preguntas a tu amigo si el restaurante nuevo es tan bueno como tu restaurante favorito. Escribe sus respuestas usando comparaciones de igualdad *(comparisons of equality)*. Sigue los modelos.

Modelo ¿Es bonito el El Toro Loco?
Sí. *El Toro Loco es tan bonito como El Pollo Loco.*

Modelo ¿Hay mucha gente en El Toro Loco?
No. *No hay tanta gente en el Toro Loco como en El Pollo Loco.*

1. ¿Es barato El Toro Loco?
   Sí. ______________________________
2. ¿Sirven mariscos en El Toro Loco?
   Sí. ______________________________
3. ¿Sirven muchas ensaladas en El Toro Loco?
   Sí. ______________________________
4. ¿Es grande El Toro Loco?
   No. ______________________________

WB 6-7 | La nueva novia Roberto describe a la familia de su nueva novia Alicia, cuya *(whose)* familia tiene un restaurante en Venezuela. Para saber lo que dice, forma oraciones con el superlativo. Sigue el modelo.

Modelo Alicia / simpática / todas mis novias
Alicia es la más simpática de todas mis novias.

1. Alicia / menor / hijas
   ____
2. José / mayor / hijos
   ____
3. Tomás / alto / familia
   ____
4. la familia / conocida / Maracaibo
   ____
5. su restaurante / mejor / Maracaibo
   ____

Nombre ______________________ Fecha ______________________

WB 6-8 | Preferencias Rafa actualiza *(is updating)* su página de Facebook. Ayúdale *(help him)* a escribir oraciones completas con una forma superlativa de los adjetivos. **¡OJO!** Los adjetivos tienen que concordar con los sustantivos. Sigue el modelo.

Modelo *U2* y *Black Eyed Peas* / grupo musical / chévere *(cool)* / de todos
U2 y Black Eyed Peas son los grupos musicales más chéveres de todos.

1. ciclismo / deporte / divertido / de todos

____

2. jamón serrano / comida / deliciosa / de todas (las comidas)

____

3. *Star Wars* y *Lord of the Rings* / película / mejor / de todas (las películas)

____

4. Justin Timberlake / cantante / peor / de todos

____

5. Ferrari y Porsche / coche / interesante / de todos

____

VOCABULARIO 2 El restaurante

WB 6-9 | ¿Cómo lo dicen? Tu amiga sale con unos amigos latinos a un restaurante venezolano, pero no sabe hablar español. Ayúdala *(Help her)* a entender lo que está pasando con la selección de la mejor opción.

_____ **1.** Camarero, el menú por favor.

a. Te invito. **b.** Sí, ¡cómo no! **c.** Gracias.

_____ **2.** ¿Cuál es la especialidad de la casa?

a. Está muy fresca esta noche. **b.** El menú. **c.** Arepas, ¡por supuesto!

_____ **3.** ¿Qué les apetece?

a. No, gracias. **b.** Para mí las arepas. **c.** Estoy a dieta.

_____ **4.** ¿Desean ver la lista de postres?

a. ¡Ay, no! ¡No puedo comer más! **b.** Te invito. **c.** ¡Buen provecho!

_____ **5.** Yo invito.

a. ¡Salud! **b.** Está muy rica. **c.** Gracias, voy a dejar una propina.

WB 6-10 | Ah, *El Venezolano* Otro amigo conoce el restaurante adonde va tu amiga y le cuenta sobre una tradición latina. Para saber lo que es, completa el párrafo con una palabra apropiada de la lista. **¡OJO!** Usa la forma correcta del verbo en el presente.

a dieta camarero cuenta desear ligero lista de postres
menú pedir picar propina recomendar rico

¡Me encanta ese restaurante! Tienen de todo y el servicio es excelente. Cuando voy, nunca tengo que ver el **1.** ______________ porque sé bien lo que voy a **2.** ______________. Si no tienes

mucha hambre, es decir *(that is to say),* cuando solo quieres algo para **3.** ____________,
puedes pedir algo **4.** ____________. Yo **5.** ____________ la sopa de chipichipi. No está para nada pesada. Pero si realmente tienes mucha hambre y **6.** ____________ algo muy **7.** ____________, tienes que pedir el pabellón. ¡Está para chuparse los dedos! Siempre pido el pabellón. Después de comer, el **8.** ____________ te pregunta que si deseas ver la **9.** ____________. ¡Tienen helados y tortas muy, pero muy, ricos! Siempre estoy **10.** ____________, pero no me importa *(it doesn't matter to me):* en ese restaurante siempre pido un helado. Ahora, los restaurantes latinos son un poco diferentes de los restaurantes norteamericanos. Uds. tienen que pedir la **11.** ____________ cuando todos estén listos para salir. Los camareros no la traen *(bring it)* a la mesa automáticamente. Sé que te va a gustar mucho este restaurante. A propósito, el servicio es tan bueno que tienes que dejar una buena **12.** ____________, ¿sabes?

13. ¿Qué consejo le da a tu amiga?

a. No debe ir al restaurante porque la comida es malísima.

b. No debe pagar la cuenta. Los hombres latinos siempre la pagan.

c. Tiene que decirle al mesero que está lista para ver la cuenta.

d. Solo van los ricos a ese restaurante así que los precios son muy altos.

WB 6-11 | ¿Qué se dice? Indica qué se debe *(one should)* decir en las siguientes situaciones. Selecciona la mejor opción.

1. Estás en un restaurante con un amigo y van a tomar vino. Levantan sus copas y antes de tomar dicen: ______

a. ¡Bueno provecho!

b. ¡Dios mío!

c. ¡Salud!

2. Le dices al mesero que quieres ver el menú. El mesero contesta: ______

a. ¡Cómo no! En seguida.

b. ¿Está fresca la langosta?

c. Te invito.

3. Acabas tu cena y el mesero te pregunta si quieres algo más. Tú contestas: ______

a. ¿Desean ver el menú de postres?

b. ¿Está fresca la langosta?

c. Estoy satisfecho(a), gracias.

4. Cenas con una amiga y ella dice que va a pagar la cuenta, pero tú quieres pagar la cuenta. Dices: ______

a. La especialidad de la casa es el flan casero.

b. Te invito.

c. Estoy a dieta.

Nombre ______________________ Fecha ______________________

ESTRUCTURA Y USO 2 — Describing past events: Regular verbs and verbs with spelling changes in the preterite

 To hear more about the **preterite**, visit Heinle iRadio at www.cengage.com/spanish/viajes.

WB 6-12 | Palabra escondida Conjuga los verbos indicados en el pretérito para revelar las letras de la palabra escondida. Después de conjugar todos los verbos, ordena las letras en las cajas *(boxes)* para descubrir esta palabra misteriosa. **¡OJO!** La palabra escondida es a la vez *(at the same time)* algo que hicimos *(we did)* ayer y que hacemos todas las mañanas.

Verbos

1. buscar (ellos)
2. comprender (nosotros)
3. creer (usted)
4. salir (tú)
5. deber (ella)
6. comenzar (yo)
7. tocar (yo)
8. ayudar (ellas)
9. comer (ellos)
10. recibir (ustedes)
11. escribir (ella)

1. _ _ _ _ [ ] _ _ _
2. _ _ _ _ _ _ _ _ _ [ ] _ _
3. _ _ _ [ ] _
4. [ ] _ _ _ _ _ _
5. [ ] _ _ _ _
6. _ [ ] _ _ _ _ _
7. _ _ _ [ ] _
8. _ _ _ _ [ ] _ _ _
9. _ _ _ _ [ ] _ _ _
10. _ _ _ _ _ _ _ _ _ [ ]
11. _ [ ] _ _ _ _ _ _

La palabra escondida es ______________.

WB 6-13 | Una fiesta de sorpresa Doña Carmen le cuenta a un amigo de una fiesta de sorpresa que le dio *(gave to her)* su familia. Para saber lo que dice, rellena los espacios en blanco con la forma apropiada del pretérito de los verbos indicados.

1. Amalia ______________ (comprar) toda la comida.
2. Carlos y Lupe ______________ (preparar) las empanadas.
3. Enrique ______________ (invitar) a todos mis amigos.
4. Los invitados ______________ (llegar) a las 8:30.
5. Yo ______________ (llegar) a las 9:00 y ______________ (empezar) a bailar inmediatamente.
6. Nosotros ______________ (comer) las empanadas y otras cosas.

WB 6-14 | Una pachanga ***(wild party)*** Maricarmen y Verónica hablan de la fiesta de cumpleaños de Paco de anoche. Rellena los espacios en blanco con la forma apropiada del verbo en el pretérito para saber lo que dicen. **¡OJO!** Tienes que prestar atención para saber cuál es el sujeto del verbo.

MARICARMEN: Pues, ¡qué buena fiesta anoche!, ¿no?

VERÓNICA: Sí, sí, y yo **1.** ______________ (comer) un montón en esa fiesta. Pero tú no **2.** ______________ (comer) nada. ¿Por qué?

MARICARMEN: Bueno, ayer a la 1:00 yo **3.** ______________ (almorzar) con mi novio, Jorge. Él me **4.** ______________ (invitar) a ese restaurante italiano que tanto me gusta. Yo **5.** ______________ (decidir) pedir el pescado frito y él **6.** ______________ (decidir) pedir los camarones al ajillo. Después, nosotros **7.** ______________ (decidir) pedir un postre y no **8.** ______________ (salir) del restaurante hasta las 3:30 de la tarde.

VERÓNICA: Ah, ahora entiendo. Bueno, no solamente comí mucho, sino que *(but)* también (yo) **9.** ______________ (beber) tres cervezas anoche.

MARICARMEN: ¡Ay, mujer, eso no es nada! Tú no **10.** ______________ (beber) nada comparada con el pobre Paco. Yo **11.** ______________ (oír) que él **12.** ______________ (tomar) muchas cervezas..

VERÓNICA: Ya lo sé. Mi novio y yo **13.** ______________ (llevar) a Paco a su casa. ¡Qué suerte que tengo!

MARICARMEN: ¿Ustedes **14.** ______________ (llevar) a Paco a casa? Ahhh, ¡por eso! A las 2:00 de la mañana yo **15.** ______________ (decidir) salir para mi casa y yo **16.** ______________ (buscar) a Paco para llevarlo a su casa, pero no lo **17.** ______________ (encontrar) en ningún lado. ¿A qué hora **18.** ______________ (volver) a sus casas?

VERÓNICA: Pues, Paco **19.** ______________ (llegar) a su casa a la 1:30, pero yo no **20.** ______________ (llegar) a mi casa hasta las 4:00 de la mañana.

MARICARMEN: ¡Vero! ¿Hasta las 4:00? ¿Por qué?

VERÓNICA: Pues, porque a la 1:30, cuando todos **21.** ______________ (llegar) a la casa de Pablo, él **22.** ______________ (comenzar) a hacer tonterías *(silly things)*. **23.** ______________ (leer) y **24.** ______________ (cantar) poesía medieval en voz alta *(loudly)*. Claro, yo **25.** ______________ (comenzar) a gritarle *(yell at him)*, pero él no me **26.** ______________ (oír) y **27.** ______________ (salir) de la casa.

MARICARMEN: Vero, pobrecita. ¿Cuándo **28.** ______________ (regresar) Paco a la casa?

VERÓNICA: Una hora más tarde.

MARICARMEN: ¡Qué increíble!

Nombre ______________________ Fecha ______________________

WB 6-15 | Sobre la pachanga ¿Cuánto comprendiste de la conversación entre Maricarmen y Verónica en la actividad **WB 6-14**? Selecciona la mejor respuesta a cada pregunta.

1. Maricarmen didn't eat a lot at the party because...

a. She didn't like the fried fish.

b. She ate a big lunch.

c. She drank too much and forgot to eat.

2. Last night...

a. Maricarmen lost her boyfriend at the party.

b. Paco stayed home and never went to the party.

c. Verónica drank several beers.

3. Vero got home late because...

a. Her boyfriend yelled at her and wouldn't drive her home.

b. She had to take care of Paco.

c. Maricarmen drove her home late.

ESTRUCTURA Y USO 3 Giving detailed descriptions about past events: Verbs with stem changes in the preterite

To hear more about the **preterite,** visit Heinle iRadio at www.cengage.com/spanish/viajes.

WB 6-16 | Formas verbales Escribe la forma indicada del pretérito de cada verbo. **¡OJO!** No te olvides *(Don't forget)* de poner los acentos donde sea necesario *(wherever necessary)*.

1. servir / yo: ______________

2. servir / tú: ______________

3. preferir / él: ______________

4. reírse / nosotros: ______________

5. sentirse / ustedes: ______________

6. divertirse / yo: ______________

7. divertirse / ella: ______________

8. vestirse / usted: ______________

9. vestirse / yo: ______________

10. morir / tú: ______________

11. pedir / nosotros: ______________

12. dormir / él: ______________

13. dormir / yo: ______________

WB 6-17 | ¿Qué pasó? Lee lo que los Sepúlveda hacen a veces y después escribe lo que hicieron en el pasado. Sigue el modelo.

Modelo A veces, Susana María duerme más de diez horas.
Anoche Susana María durmió más de diez horas.

1. A veces, yo me visto y luego visito a mi hija Susana María.

Esta mañana ______________ y luego ______________ a mi hija Susana María.

2. A veces, Juan Carlos pide una Coca-Cola, pero su papá le sirve jugo.

El otro día Juan Carlos ______________ una Coca-Cola, pero su papá le ______________ jugo.

3. A veces, Gloria se divierte mucho con su hijo.

   El jueves pasado Gloria ________________ mucho con su hijo.

4. A veces, el bebé se duerme rápidamente cuando se acuesta.

   Anoche el bebé ________________ rápidamente cuando se acostó.

5. A veces, Julio y Tomás prefieren ver *Hermanos y hermanas* en la televisión.

   Anoche Julio y Tomás ________________ ver *Hermanos y hermanas* en la televisión.

6. A veces, nosotros nos morimos de risa *(we die of laughter)* al contar chistes.

   Ayer ________________ de risa al contar chistes.

WB 6-18 | ¿Una cita divertida? Patricio habla con Silvina sobre su cita de anoche con Laura. Completa su conversación con la forma apropiada del pretérito de los verbos indicados.

SILVINA: Dime, Patricio, ¿**1.** ________________ (divertirse) anoche con Laura?

PATRICIO: Bueno, sí y no. Ella sí **2.** ________________ (divertirse) conmigo, pero no sé si yo realmente **3.** ________________ (divertirse) con ella, ¿sabes?

SILVINA: Pues, cuéntame, ¿qué pasó?

PATRICIO: Mira, yo **4.** ________________ (conseguir) mi primera tarjeta de crédito y para impresionar bien a Laura yo **5.** ________________ (sugerir) que fuéramos *(that we go)* a ese restaurante muy caro del centro. Ella dijo que sí. Esa noche yo **6.** ________________ (vestirme) muy elegantemente y…

SILVINA: ¿También **7.** ________________ (vestirse) Laura elegantemente?

PATRICIO: Sí, Laura estuvo muy linda. Bueno, llegamos al restaurante y el mesero nos **8.** ________________ (servir) unos vasos de vino tinto. Pero entonces Laura **9.** ________________ (pedir) una botella de champán muy caro.

SILVINA: ¿Qué hiciste?

PATRICIO: Pues, en ese momento **10.** ________________ (preferir) no decir nada así que simplemente **11.** ________________ (sonreír) y no dije nada.

SILVINA: ¿Qué **12.** ________________ (pedir) tú para comer?

PATRICIO: Yo **13.** ________________ (pedir) el pollo asado, pero ella **14.** ________________ (preferir) comer la langosta y el bistec.

SILVINA: ¿La langosta y el bistec? Esa chica sí tiene gustos muy caros ¿no? ¿Y hablaron mucho durante la cena?

PATRICIO: Sí, hablamos mucho y ella **15.** ________________ (reírse) mucho. Yo diría *(would say)* que durante la cena nosotros sí **16.** ________________ (divertirse) mucho. Pero cuando el mesero me trajo la cuenta, yo casi **17.** ________________ (morirse) de miedo.

SILVINA: ¿Cuánto costó la cena?

PATRICIO: ¡1.200 pesos!

SILVINA: ¡Caray!

PATRICIO: Sí, y después de pagar la cena, Laura **18.** ______________ (sugerir) ir a tomar copas y escuchar música en algún bar. Pero cuando yo le dije que mi tarjeta de crédito ya no podía más *(couldn't take it anymore)*, ella dijo que se sentía *(she felt)* enferma.

SILVINA: ¡No me digas!

PATRICIO: Sí. Es la pura verdad. Entonces, nosotros **19.** ______________ (despedirse) y yo fui a casa y **20.** ______________ (dormirse) en seguida.

SILVINA: ¿Y la pobre tarjeta de crédito?

PATRICIO: ¡Yo creo que la pobre tarjeta ya **21.** ______________ (dormirse) para siempre!

WB 6-19 | ¿Se divirtieron? Indica si las siguientes oraciones son **ciertas** (C) o **falsas** (F) sobre la cita de Patricio de la actividad **WB 6-18.**

1. ______ Patricio invited Laura to an elegant restaurant.

2. ______ Patricio got dressed up, but Laura didn't dress very nicely.

3. ______ Patricio ordered a cheap bottle of wine.

4. ______ Patricio and Laura had fun during dinner.

5. ______ Patricio was surprised at how inexpensive the dinner was.

6. ______ Laura said she was sick at the end of the evening.

7. ______ Patricio wants to have more dates like this with Laura.

VIAJEMOS POR VENEZUELA

En este video, vas a aprender un poco sobre la ciudad de Caracas, la capital de Venezuela.

WB 6-20 | ¿Dónde se ubica Venezuela?
Identifica el país de Venezuela en el mapa.

______ Escribe la letra del mapa que corresponde con Venezuela.

WB 6-21 | Cognados En el video vas a escuchar muchos cognados que pueden facilitar tu comprensión del video. Algunos de estos cognados aparecen aquí. Antes de ver el segmento, trata de pronunciar cada palabra o frase y luego trata de emparejar *(match)* los cognados con su definición en inglés.

1. ______ petróleo	**a.** observatory
2. ______ exportación	**b.** producer
3. ______ productor	**c.** legendary liberator
4. ______ legendario libertador	**d.** colonial architecture
5. ______ urbano	**e.** mausoleum
6. ______ mausoleo	**f.** urban
7. ______ arquitectura colonial	**g.** exportation
8. ______ pirámide	**h.** pyramid
9. ______ observatorio	**i.** petroleum
10. ______ meteorológico	**j.** meteorological

WB 6-22 | Cognados en contexto Mira el video y trata de rellenar los espacios en blanco con el cognado apropiado de la actividad **WB 6-21.**

1. La base de la economía venezolana es el ________________.
2. El ________________ ________________ de América, Simón Bolívar, nació en Caracas.
3. La Plaza Bolívar, un espacio ________________ para grandes y chicos, es el centro histórico de la ciudad.
4. Los restos del Libertador reposan en este ________________, que se encuentra en el Panteón Nacional.
5. En Caracas encontramos edificaciones de ________________ ________________, como la Catedral de Caracas.
6. El Calvario es un santuario moderno en forma de ________________ maya.

WB 6-23 | Comprensión Después de ver el video, indica si las siguientes oraciones son **ciertas** (C) o **falsas** (F).

1. ______ Venezuela es uno de los principales países productores de petróleo del planeta.
2. ______ Hay un observatorio en el Centro Simón Bolívar.
3. ______ Caracas es una ciudad pequeña y colonial.
4. ______ Hay un metro en la ciudad de Caracas.
5. ______ Los caraqueños son ejemplos de arquitectura colonial.
6. ______ El Observatorio Cagigal ofrece información sobre el clima.

Nombre ______________________ Fecha ______________________

¡A ESCRIBIR!

Strategy: Adding details to a paragraph

In Chapter 4, you learned how to write a topic sentence for a paragraph. The other sentences in the paragraph should contain details that develop the main idea stated in the topic sentence. The following procedure will help you develop a well-written paragraph in Spanish:

1. Write a topic sentence about a specific subject.
2. List some details that develop your topic sentence.
3. Cross out any details that are unrelated to the topic.
4. Number the remaining details in a clear, logical order.
5. Write the first draft of a paragraph based on your work.
6. Cross out any ideas that do not contribute to the topic.
7. Write the second draft of your paragraph as clearly as possible.

Task: Writing about a typical student diet

One of your favorite Spanish websites is soliciting short essays about the typical diet of American college students. Write a short paragraph on this topic to submit to this site.

Paso 1 List a series of questions that people in Spanish-speaking countries might ask about the diet of an American college student. Some possibilities are **¿Es una dieta equilibrada? ¿Es una dieta variada? ¿Es una dieta de comida rápida?**

Paso 2 Now, choose the most interesting of the questions you listed and answer it. Your answer will serve as the topic sentence for your paragraph.

Paso 3 Write a list of details that support the opinion (the answer to your question) you present in your topic sentence. For example, if your topic sentence is **La dieta del estudiante estadounidense no es muy equilibrada,** some examples of supporting details include, **Los estudiantes comen mucha comida rápida. La comida de las residencias universitarias es muy mala.**

Paso 4 Now write the first draft of your paragraph, incorporating your topic sentence and the sentences you wrote with supporting details. Include only details that truly demonstrate the point you make in your topic sentence.

Paso 5 Read over your first draft and correct any errors; then write a second draft below.

____

____

____

____

____

____

____

____

ATAJO 4.0

Functions: Appreciating food; Describing objects; Stating a preference

Vocabulary: Food; Food: restaurant

Grammar: Verbs: **gustar, ser, tener;** Present tense of verbs

Autoprueba

WB 6-24 | La comida Pon *(put)* los nombres de las comidas en las categorías más apropiadas.

aceite	queso	naranja	calamares
cerveza	banana	sal	jugo
lechuga	flan	café	pavo
pollo	manzana	jamón	vinagre
agua mineral	res	papas	leche
chuletas de cerdo	bistec	té helado	pimienta
mantequilla	helado	camarones	vino

Carnes:

____

Pescado/Mariscos:

____

Bebidas:

____

Postres:

____

Frutas:

____

Verduras:

____

Condimentos:

____

WB 6-25 | En el restaurante Indica la letra de la palabra o frase que mejor completa cada oración.

_____ **1.** Antes de pedir la comida, el camarero nos trae...

a. la cuenta. **b.** la propina. **c.** el menú.

_____ **2.** Antes de comer con otros amigos, les decimos...

a. ¡Cómo no! **b.** ¡Estoy a dieta! **c.** ¡Buen provecho!

_____ **3.** Antes de tomar una bebida con nuestros amigos, les decimos...

a. ¡Salud! **b.** ¡Estoy satisfecho! **c.** ¡Está para chuparse los dedos!

_____ **4.** Si no tienes mucha hambre, pides algo...

a. para picar. **b.** para chuparse los dedos. **c.** pesado.

______ **5.** Si alguien te ofrece más comida y ya no quieres comer más, puedes decir...

a. No gracias, deseo ver la lista de postres. **b.** No gracias, estoy satisfecho(a). **c.** ¡Buen provecho!

______ **6.** Si quieres pagar la cuenta de tu amigo, puedes decir...

a. te invito. **b.** voy a dejar una propina. **c.** la cuenta, por favor.

WB 6-26 | ¡Viva la igualdad! Beti y su primo Martín tienen mucho en común. Usa la información dada para comparar a los dos primos usando **tan, tanto, tanta, tantos** y **tantas.**

Modelo tener años / *Beti tiene tantos años como Martín.*
ser inteligente / *Beti es tan inteligente como Martín.*

1. comer verduras
____
2. almorzar en restaurantes
____
3. pedir arepas
____
4. ser amable
____
5. tomar café
____

WB 6-27 | El más... Escribe oraciones usando el superlativo. Sigue el modelo.

Modelo dos hermanas: Beti (22 años) / Lorena (19 años) / menor
Lorena es la menor.

1. dos hijos: Tomás (8 años) / Guillermo (10 años) / mayor
____
2. dos primos: Alejandro (muy paciente) / Alberto (paciente) / paciente
____
3. dos bebidas: la leche (no es dulce) / el jugo (muy dulce) / dulce
____
4. dos jugadores: Kobe Bryant (muy bueno) / Jason Kidd (bueno) / mejor
____

WB 6-28 | ¿Qué hicimos? Completa la siguiente conversación usando el pretérito de los verbos indicados.

TONI: Alicia, ¿ya **1.** ________________ (almorzar) Ignacio?

ALICIA: Sí, yo **2.** ________________ (almorzar) con él a las 2:00. Nosotros **3.** ________________ (comer) un sándwich y una ensalada. Yo **4.** ________________ (tomar) un café y él **5.** ________________ (beber) jugo. ¿Ya **6.** ________________ (terminar) tu novela?

TONI: Sí, **7.** ________________ (terminar) esa y **8.** ________________ (comenzar) otra. En la última hora **9.** ________________ (leer) 40 páginas.

ALICIA: Ah, esa es la novela que Luis **10.** ________________ (leer) el mes pasado. Yo **11.** ________________ (buscar) ese libro la semana pasada para ti.

TONI: Pues, yo **12.** ________________ (comprar) este libro esta mañana.

WB 6-29 | Padre e hijo Completa el párrafo con la forma correcta del pretérito de los siguientes verbos.

dormirse divertirse pedir servir

Anoche Julio y Juan Carlos **1.** ________________ mucho mirando un video de Disney. Mientras lo miraban, el niño **2.** ________________ un refresco y su padre le **3.** ________________ una Coca-Cola. Más tarde el niño **4.** ________________ en el sofá.

Nombre ______________________ Fecha ______________________

De compras: Argentina, Paraguay y Uruguay

VOCABULARIO 1 La ropa

WB 7-1 | ¿Qué se necesita? Lee cada descripción de las prendas de ropa y selecciona de la lista la palabra o frase apropiada. **¡OJO!** No vas a usar todas las palabras, pero no puedes usar una palabra más de una vez.

abrigo	chaleco	guantes	traje de baño
bolsa	cinturón	impermeable	vaqueros
bufanda	corbata	paraguas	zapatos
calcetines	cuero	sombrero	
cartera	gafas de sol	suéter	

1. Para nadar en una piscina te pones un ______________.

2. Usas un ______________ con los pantalones.

3. Cuando llueve te pones un ______________ y usas un ______________.

4. Te pones unos ______________ en las manos.

5. Muchos llevan ______________ de la marca Levis.

6. Guardas dinero en una ______________.

7. Muchas mujeres guardan sus cosas en una ______________.

8. Para proteger los ojos del sol te pones unas ______________.

9. Te llevas un ______________ en la cabeza.

WB 7-2 | La ropa apropiada Selecciona la prenda *(clothing item)* más apropiada para las siguientes actividades.

________	**1.** ir a clase	**a.** un traje de baño
________	**2.** ir a un concierto de música ranchera *(country)*	**b.** unas botas de cuero
________	**3.** ir a una boda *(wedding)*	**c.** un vestido de seda
________	**4.** esquiar	**d.** un suéter de lana
________	**5.** pasar el día en la playa	**e.** una camisa de algodón

WB 7-3 | **¡Emergencia de moda!** María Inés y Francisco Javier tienen problemas para coordinar bien su ropa. Describe su estilo único seleccionando las mejores opciones de la lista.

1. María Inés lleva *(selecciona todas las opciones posibles)*:
   a. un abrigo
   b. una falda de rayas
   c. una chaqueta de lunares
   d. zapatos de tacón alto
   e. medias
   f. un reloj

2. Francisco Javier lleva *(selecciona todas las opciones posibles)*:
   a. una gorra de béisbol
   b. una corbata de rayas
   c. un traje de cuadros
   d. un suéter de lunares
   e. una pulsera
   f. sandalias con calcetines

ESTRUCTURA Y USO 1 Talking about singular and/or completed events in the past: Irregular verbs in the preterite

To hear more about the **preterite**, visit Heinle iRadio at www.cengage.com/spanish/viajes.

WB 7-4 | **Formas verbales** Conjuga los verbos indicados en el pretérito.

1. dar / yo: ______________________
2. dar / ella: ______________________
3. hacer / nosotros: ______________________
4. hacer / ustedes: ______________________
5. poder / tú: ______________________
6. poder / yo: ______________________
7. tener / yo: ______________________
8. tener / tú: ______________________
9. tener / él: ______________________
10. estar / usted: ______________________
11. estar / yo: ______________________

Nombre ________________ Fecha ________________

12. estar / nosotros: ________________

13. ser / yo: ________________

14. ser / ella: ________________

15. ir / ellos: ________________

WB 7-5 | Una fiesta Gloria te cuenta todos los chismes de la fiesta que te perdiste anoche. Para saber lo que dice, completa las oraciones con la forma apropiada del verbo en el pretérito.

1. Muchas personas ________________ (venir) a la fiesta.

2. ________________ (haber) casi 70 personas en mi casa.

3. Marcos y su novia ________________ (traer) mucho vino.

4. Yo ________________ (ponerse) borracha y ________________ (ser) la reina de la fiesta.

5. Antonio le ________________ (dar) un beso a la novia de Óscar.

WB 7-6 | El viaje a Argentina Bea hizo un viaje a Argentina con su novio. Le escribió esta carta a su amiga, Eva, para contarle de un pequeño problema que tuvieron durante su viaje. Para saber cuál fue el problema y cómo lo solucionaron, rellena los espacios en blanco con la forma apropiada del verbo indicado en el pretérito.

Querida Eva, Pues, ¿qué te puedo decir? **1.** ¡ ________________ (Ser) un viaje maravilloso! Yo **2.** ________________ (ir) primero a Buenos Aires y **3.** ________________ (estar) sola allí cuatro días. Mi novio, Rafael, **4.** ________________ (venir) el quinto (*fifth*) día y nosotros **5.** ________________ (hacer) varias cosas juntos, pues **6.** ________________ (haber / hay) muchísimas actividades para hacer en Buenos Aires. Después nosotros **7.** ________________ (ir) a Mendoza. Tú **8.** ________________ (decir) una vez que tu madre nació allí, ¿verdad? Bueno, nosotros **9.** ________________ (estar) en Mendoza tres días y el último día yo le **10.** ________________ (dar) a Rafa una sorpresa. Yo **11.** ________________ (hacer) reservaciones para ir a Bariloche para esquiar. Rafa no **12.** ________________ (saber) de mis planes hasta la última noche en Mendoza. Yo le **13.** ________________ (traer) los boletos (*tickets*) de avión esa noche en el hotel. Pero, Eva, ¿sabes qué? Rafa no **14.** ________________ (querer) ir. Él **15.** ________________ (decir) que los boletos costaron demasiado. Yo le **16.** ________________ (decir) que no costaron mucho, pero él **17.** ________________ (ponerse) enojado (*angry*). Yo no **18.** ________________ (poder) creerlo. Yo **19.** ________________ (hacer) todo lo posible para convencerlo, pero nada. Pero después de dos horas de discusión, yo **20.** ________________ (saber) por qué. Él también me **21.** ________________ (dar) una sorpresa: él había comprado (*had bought*) boletos para visitar las cataratas (*falls*) del Iguazú. ¡Qué romántico! Pues, tú sabes, ¡al final nosotros **22.** ________________ (tener) que ir a los dos sitios!

Bueno, ya te cuento más en otro momento.

Un beso,

Bea

WB 7-7 | Sobre el viaje a Argentina Contesta las preguntas sobre el viaje de la actividad **WB 7-6.**

1. ¿Qué problema tuvieron Bea y Rafa en este viaje?

  a. Rafa left Bea alone in Mendoza, Argentina.

  b. Rafa was upset because Bea spent too much money on this vacation.

  c. Rafa and Bea secretly planned to visit two different parts of Argentina.

  d. Bea broke her leg skiing.

2. ¿Cómo solucionaron este problema?

  a. They took both side trips that each planned.

  b. They visited Eva's mother in Mendoza.

  c. Eva decided to cancel part of the trip to save some money.

  d. Bea flew home early.

VOCABULARIO 2 De compras

WB 7-8 | ¡De compras! Belén es una profesional en las compras. Ahora describe sus estrategias. Completa sus siguientes oraciones con una palabra o un término *(term)* de la lista.

barato descuento efectivo ganga liquidación número ofertas

por ciento talla tarjeta de crédito usar

1. Nunca pago el precio de la etiqueta *(tag)*. Siempre busco las ________________.

2. No compro una prenda si el ________________ es menos del veinte ________________.

3. Nunca pago en ________________ cuando puedo usar mi ________________. Así tengo más tiempo para pagar la factura *(bill)*.

Nombre ______________________ Fecha ______________________

WB 7-9 | En la tienda Escribe la letra de la palabra o frase que mejor describe cada dibujo indicado.

_________ 1. **a.** la talla
b. un descuento del 20 por ciento
c. el cheque

_________ 2. **a.** una rebaja
b. la talla de Shaquille O'Neal
c. el número que usa Shaquille O'Neal

_________ 3. **a.** Es una ganga.
b. Es muy cara.
c. Está de última moda.

_________ 4. **a.** No le quedan bien.
b. Cuestan mucho.
c. Hacen buen juego.

_________ 5. **a.** una tarjeta de crédito
b. un cheque
c. dinero en efectivo

WB 7-10 | ¡Qué buena ganga! Ángela está de compras y quiere comprar algo para su novio. Para saber lo que es, ordena las oraciones del diálogo.

1. _________ Bueno, este traje es del estilo «retro», de los años 60. En su momento estuvo de última moda.
2. _________ ¡Me parece bárbaro! ¡Qué buena ganga!
3. _________ Quisiera comprar un traje nuevo para mi novio.
4. _________ No, gracias. Aquí está mi tarjeta de crédito.
5. _________ ¡Qué bueno! ¿Cuánto cuesta ese traje?

6. __________ No sé su talla, pero creo que esa talla que Ud. tiene por allí le va a quedar muy bien.

7. __________ Bien, ¿necesita algo más, señorita?

8. __________ Sí, señorita, es una ganga. ¿Sabe Ud. qué talla necesita su novio?

9. __________ Pues, normalmente ese traje cuesta unos 2.000 pesos, pero le puedo hacer un pequeño descuento. ¿Qué le parece un descuento del 30 por ciento?

10. __________ Buenas tardes, señorita, ¿en qué puedo servirle?

ESTRUCTURA Y USO 2 Simplifying expressions: Direct object pronouns

WB 7-11 | La vida de una supermodelo Mientras lees el periódico argentino *El Clarín,* encuentras la siguiente entrevista con la supermodelo argentina Carolina Peleritti. Completa la entrevista seleccionando la respuesta más apropiada a cada una de las preguntas. Presta atención al uso de los pronombres de objeto directo. Sigue el modelo.

Modelo ¿Levantas pesas con frecuencia?

______ Sí, los levanta con frecuencia.

__*X*__ Sí, las levanto con frecuencia.

______ Sí, me levanto con frecuencia.

1. ¿Tienes que hacer muchos ejercicios todos los días?

__________ No, no las tengo que hacer.

__________ Sí, tengo que hacerla todos los días.

__________ Sí, los tengo que hacer todos los días.

2. ¿Te llama todos los días tu entrenador personal?

__________ Sí, me llama todos los días.

__________ Sí, te llama todos los días.

__________ Sí, te llamo todos los días.

3. ¿Compras la ropa de última moda?

__________ No, no las compro.

__________ Sí, me compran siempre.

__________ Sí, la compro cada mes.

4. ¿Conoces a Donna Karan?

__________ Sí, me conocen.

__________ Sí, lo conozco.

__________ Sí, la conozco.

5. ¿Puedes tomar muchas vacaciones?

__________ Sí, las puedo tomar cada año.

__________ Sí, lo puedo tomar cada verano.

__________ No, la podemos tomar mucho.

6. ¿Te invitan a muchas fiestas los diseñadores famosos?

______ Sí, los invito a muchas fiestas.

______ Sí, me invitan a muchas fiestas.

______ Sí, nos invitan a muchas fiestas.

WB 7-12 | Planes Amalia y Elvia hablan de las cosas que quieren comprar. Completa su conversación con el pronombre de objeto directo apropiado.

1. AMALIA: Elvia, ¿vas a comprar esa blusa?
   ELVIA: Sí, ______ voy a comprar.
2. ELVIA: Amalia, ¿tienes ahí tu tarjeta de crédito?
   AMALIA: No. No ______ tengo.
3. AMALIA: Elvia, ¿quieres comprar esas bufandas?
   ELVIA: Sí, ______ quiero comprar.
4. ELVIA: Amalia, ¿conoces estos diseñadores?
   AMALIA: No. No ______ conozco.
5. AMALIA: Elvia, ¿vas a gastar tanto dinero?
   ELVIA: Sí, voy a gastar______.

WB 7-13 | Un año en el extranjero Antonio regresó de un año en Argentina y ahora Carmen le hace varias preguntas sobre su viaje. Completas sus respuestas con el pronombre de objeto directo.

1. CARMEN: ¿Visitaste la Patagonia?
   ANTONIO: Sí, ______ visité tres veces.
2. CARMEN: ¿Aprendiste a jugar al fútbol?
   ANTONIO: Sí, aprendí a jugar______.
3. CARMEN: ¿Probaste los famosos asados argentinos?
   ANTONIO: Sí, ______ probé mucho.
4. CARMEN: ¿Pudiste ver muchas películas argentinas?
   ANTONIO: Sí, pude ver______ todas.

WB 7-14 | Cambio de opinión Antonia fue de compras pero no le gusta lo que compró. Completa su conversación con su esposo con la forma apropiada del pronombre de objeto directo.

CARLOS: **1.** ¿______ llamaste, Antonia?

ANTONIA: Sí, Carlos. **2.** ______ necesito ver. ¿Puedes venir aquí un rato?

CARLOS: Aquí estoy. ¿Qué pasa?

ANTONIA: No puedo encontrar mi tarjeta de crédito. **3.** ¿______ tienes tú?

CARLOS: No, mi amor. No **4.** ______ tengo. ¿Por qué **5.** ______ necesitas?

ANTONIA: Porque no me gustan los pantalones que compré ayer y **6.** ______ quiero devolver a la tienda.

CARLOS: Pero, Antonia, ayer me dijiste que **7.** ____________ tuviste que comprar porque te quedaron muy bien y eran súper bonitos.

ANTONIA: Sí. Es cierto. Pero cambié de opinión.

CARLOS: ¡Antonia, tú **8.** ____________ vas a matar con tus cambios de opinión!

ESTRUCTURA Y USO 3 Describing ongoing and habitual actions in the past: The imperfect tense

To hear more about the **imperfect,** visit Heinle iRadio at www.cengage.com/spanish/viajes.

WB 7-15 | Investigación A las 6:00 de la tarde ayer, hubo un robo *(robbery)* en De moda, una tienda de ropa de Rosario. ¿Qué hacía cada empleado a las seis de la tarde cuando ocurrió el robo? Rellena el espacio en blanco con la forma correcta del verbo en el imperfecto. Sigue el modelo.

Modelo María ___ (limpiar) el patio.
María limpiaba el patio.

¿Qué hacía… a las 6:00 de la tarde?

1. Luis Miguel ____________ (estar) en el baño.
2. Teresa ____________ (probarse) un vestido nuevo.
3. Amalia y yo ____________ (pagar) las facturas en la oficina.
4. Guillermo y Santi ____________ (conversar) con un cliente.
5. Francisco ____________ (dormir) una siesta.

WB 7-16 | Cómo cambiaron los tiempos Ana María está hablando con su nieto y recordando el pasado y cómo eran las cosas. Para completar sus recuerdos, escribe la forma correcta de los verbos en el **imperfecto.**

1. En el pasado los jóvenes ____________ (comer) más en casa.
2. En el pasado tú nunca ____________ (llevar) la ropa de última moda.
3. En el pasado la ropa no ____________ (costar) mucho dinero.
4. En el pasado nosotros ____________ (ir) al cine para ver películas.
5. En el pasado tus padres ____________ (trabajar) solo ocho horas al día.
6. En el pasado la gente joven ____________ (leer) más.

WB 7-17 | Cuando yo era niña Ana María habla de cómo era de niña. Rellena los espacios en blanco con la forma apropiada del imperfecto para saber su historia.

Los sábados yo **1.** ________________________ (levantarse) a las 8:00 y luego **2.** ________________________ (ir) al baño. A veces, **3.** ________________________ (tener) mucho sueño. Después, **4.** ________________________ (desayunar) mientras **5.** ________________________ (mirar) la televisión por media hora. Entonces

Nombre ______________________ Fecha ______________________

6. ______________ (bañarse) y me 7. ______________ (vestirse). Luego 8. ______________ (jugar) un poco en casa o, si 9. ______________ (ver) a mis amigos en la calle, 10. ______________ (jugar) juntos. Yo 11. ______________ (tener) muchos amigos y 12. ______________ (ser) muy unidos. A veces 13. ______________ (ir) todos a la plaza para hablar con otros amigos y otras veces 14. ______________ (ir) al cine. (Nosotros) Nunca 15. ______________ (gastar) mucho dinero, pero siempre 16. ______________ (divertirse) mucho.

WB 7-18 | Una experiencia emocionante La semana pasada, Elena fue a la plaza central para hacer las compras. Para saber lo que pasó, rellena los espacios en blanco con la forma apropiada de los verbos. Tienes que escoger entre el pretérito y el imperfecto. **¡OJO!** Repasa las reglas sobre el uso de estos tiempos antes de hacer esta actividad.

1. ______________ (llover) mucho ese día y, por eso, 2. ______________ (decidir) buscar un taxi. Claro, 3. ______________ (haber) muchas otras personas que también 4. ______________ (buscar) taxis por el mal tiempo que 5. ______________ (hacer). Por fin, (yo) 6. ______________ (encontrar) un taxi y subí. Le dije al taxista adónde 7. ______________ (querer) ir cuando de repente 8. ______________ (recordar) que mi bolsa 9. ______________ (estar) en una de las tiendas de la plaza. Bajé del taxi y 10. ______________ (ir) corriendo hacia el mercado. Cuando 11. ______________ (llegar) al mercado, 12. ______________ (ver) mi bolsa. Yo 13. ______________ (estar) muy contenta.

VIAJEMOS POR ARGENTINA, PARAGUAY Y URUGUAY

En estos segmentos del video vas a aprender un poco sobre las ciudades de Buenos Aires, Asunción y Montevideo, las capitales de Argentina, Paraguay y Uruguay, respectivamente.

WB 7-19 | ¿Dónde se ubican estos países? Escribe las letras del mapa que corresponden a Argentina, Paraguay y Uruguay.

____________ Argentina

____________ Paraguay

____________ Uruguay

WB 7-20 | Cognados En el video vas a escuchar muchos cognados que pueden facilitar tu comprensión del video. Algunos de estos cognados aparecen aquí. Antes de ver los segmentos, trata de pronunciar cada palabra o frase. Luego trata de emparejar *(match)* los cognados con su definición en inglés.

1. ____________ conmemora	**a.** bay
2. ____________ centenario	**b.** influences
3. ____________ fundación	**c.** gastronomic (culinary)
4. ____________ influencias	**d.** descendants
5. ____________ bahía	**e.** commemorate
6. ____________ ruinas	**f.** founding
7. ____________ arpa	**g.** tomb
8. ____________ bilingüe	**h.** centennial
9. ____________ descendientes	**i.** bilingual
10. ____________ campeonatos	**j.** harp
11. ____________ tumba	**k.** ruins
12. ____________ gastronómica	**l.** champions

Nombre ______________________ Fecha ______________________

WB 7-21 | Cognados en contexto Mira los segmentos de video y rellena los espacios en blanco con el cognado apropiado de la actividad **WB 7-20.**

del segmento sobre Buenos Aires:

1. El famoso Obelisco ______________ el cuarto ______________ de la ______________ de la ciudad.
2. Los casi 3 millones de argentinos que viven en Buenos Aires, y los turistas que visitan, disfrutan de una ciudad latinoamericana con marcadas ______________ culturales europeas.

del segmento sobre Asunción:

3. Asunción, la capital del país, situada en la ______________ del río Paraguay, conserva ______________ y construcciones coloniales.
4. La vida artística de Paraguay está relacionada con el ______________ paraguaya.

del segmento sobre Montevideo:

5. Un punto importante en la capital uruguaya es el Estadio ______________, sede de la Copa Mundial de fútbol de 1930, y de grandes ______________ sudamericanos.
6. La especialidad ______________ uruguaya es la carne a la parilla.

WB 7-22 | Comprensión Mira los segmentos de video otra vez y luego selecciona la frase correcta para completar las siguientes oraciones.

1. ______ La parte de Buenos Aires donde se originó el tango se llama...
   a. la Plaza de Mayo. **b.** el Obelisco. **c.** la Boca.
2. ______ A la ciudad de Buenos Aires se le dice *(it is called)*...
   a. Casa Rosada. **b.** Bonaerense. **c.** el París de Sudamérica.
3. ______ El arpa...
   a. llegó a Paraguay con los conquistadores. **b.** es una palabra guaraní. **c.** es el instrumento preferido de Argentina.
4. ______ Paraguay...
   a. significa "bahía". **b.** es un país bilingüe. **c.** tiene playas bonitas.
5. ______ Otro nombre para los uruguayos es...
   a. montevideanos. **b.** charrúas. **c.** ramblas.
6. ______ La tumba del General Artigas, un héroe uruguayo, está en...
   a. la Ciudad Vieja. **b.** el Parque Rodó. **c.** la Plaza Independencia.

¡A ESCRIBIR!

Strategy: Editing your writing

Editing your written work is an important skill to master when learning a foreign language. You should plan on editing what you write several times. When checking your compositions, consider the following areas:

1. **Content**
   - **a.** Is the title of your composition captivating? Would it cause readers to want to read further?
   - **b.** Is the information you wrote pertinent to the established topic?
   - **c.** Is your composition interesting? Does it capture reader interest?
2. **Organization**
   - **a.** Does each paragraph in the composition have a clearly identifiable main idea?
   - **b.** Do the details in each paragraph relate to a single idea?
   - **c.** Are the sentences in the paragraph ordered in a logical sequence?
   - **d.** Is the order of the paragraphs correct in your composition?
3. **Cohesion and style**
   - **a.** Does your composition as a whole communicate what you are trying to convey?
   - **b.** Does your composition "flow" easily and smoothly from beginning to end?
   - **c.** Are there transitions between the different paragraphs you included in your composition?
4. **Style and accuracy**
   - **a.** Have you chosen the precise vocabulary words you need to express your ideas?
   - **b.** Are there grammatical errors in your composition (that is, subject-verb agreement; adjective-noun agreement; errors with verb forms or irregular verbs, and so on)?
   - **c.** Are there spelling errors in your composition (including capitalization, accentuation, and punctuation)?

If you consider these points as you edit your written work, the overall quality of your compositions will improve drastically!

Task: Reporting on changing fashion habits

You will write a short report to describe what fashion was like when you were younger and how it has changed over time in your opinion.

ATAJO 4.0

Functions: Talking about past events; Talking about recent events

Vocabulary: Clothing; Fabrics; Colors; Stores and products

Grammar: Verbs: irregular preterite, regular preterite; Personal pronouns: direct, indirect

Nombre ____________________ Fecha ____________________

Paso 1 Before you begin to write, answer the following questions in Spanish. How has fashion changed since you were in high school? How has fashion changed since your parents were in high school? What clothes did people wear that they don't wear now? What shops and designers were popular then that are not now?

Paso 2 Now write a first draft on a separate piece of paper; then revise it using the strategy you have just learned.

Paso 3 Write your revised draft below.

Autoprueba

WB 7-23 | La ropa Para cada categoría escribe el nombre de la(s) prenda(s) apropiada(s).

Modelo Para las manos: *los guantes*

las botas	la falda	las sandalias	el traje de baño
la blusa	el impermeable	el sombrero	el vestido
los calcetines	las medias	el traje	los zapatos
la corbata	los pantalones		

1. Para nadar: ______________________________

2. Para la cabeza: ______________________________

3. Para los pies: ______________________________

4. Para las mujeres: ______________________________

5. Para los hombres: ______________________________

6. Para la lluvia: ______________________________

WB 7-24 | En la tienda Completa la conversación con la palabra o frase apropiada de la lista. **¡OJO!** No tienes que usar todas las palabras y frases.

en qué puedo servirle	le debo	probarme	talla
ganga	moda	queda bien	tarjeta de crédito
hace juego	número	rebaja	

DEPENDIENTE: Buenas tardes, señor. **1.** ¿______________________?

CLIENTE: Buenas tardes. Busco un traje nuevo. ¿Puedo **2.** ______________________ este traje?

DEPENDIENTE: Sí, por aquí.

CLIENTE: Ay, este traje no es mi **3.** ______________________. No me **4.** ______________________.

DEPENDIENTE: Lo siento, señor. Aquí está otro.

CLIENTE: Sí, este es mejor. Y esta camisa, ¿qué opina? **5.** ¿______________________ con el traje?

Nombre ______________________ Fecha ______________________

DEPENDIENTE: Sí, es un juego perfecto. Además, es de última **6.** ______________________.

CLIENTE: Muy bien, ¿cuanto **7.** ______________________?

DEPENDIENTE: En total son 200 dólares.

CLIENTE: ¡Qué **8.** ______________________! ¿Puedo pagar con **9.** ______________________?

DEPENDIENTE: ¡Claro que sí!

WB 7-25 | ¡Fin de semana! Completa la conversación con el pretérito de los verbos indicados.

DELIA: ¿Adónde **1.** ______________________ (ir) tú este fin de semana?

NORA: (Yo) **2.** ______________________ (Ir) con mi familia a Santa Fe.

DELIA: ¿Qué **3.** ______________________ (hacer) Uds. allí?

NORA: **4.** ______________________ (Tener) que ir a una fiesta con nuestros amigos.

DELIA: Ah, **5.** ¿______________________ (venir) muchas personas a la fiesta?

NORA: Sí, y todos **6.** ______________________ (traer) algo distinto para comer. ¡La comida **7.** ______________________ (estar) riquísima! ¿Y tú? ¿Qué **8.** ______________________ (hacer) este fin de semana?

DELIA: Bueno, para mí el fin de semana no **9.** ______________________ (ser) muy bueno. No **10.** ______________________ (hacer) nada. El viernes quería ir a una fiesta, pero a mi novio no le gusta la persona que hacía la fiesta y él no **11.** ______________________ (querer) ir. El sábado había una exposición de arte en el museo, pero yo no **12.** ______________________ (saber) que el museo estaba abierto hasta demasiado tarde.

NORA: ¡Qué pena!

WB 7-26 | ¡A comer! Completa la conversación con el pronombre de objeto directo apropiado.

1. "Preparaste una cena muy buena, Marcos. ¡Qué amable!"
   "Gracias, Elena. ______________ preparé porque sé que estás enferma."
2. "Beto, ¿ya comiste tu postre?"
   "Pues… no, papá. Mi hermanito ______________ está comiendo."
3. "Mamá, tú ¿______________ quieres a mí?"
   "Sí, tu papá y yo ______________ queremos mucho, Beto."
4. "Quiero una de esas manzanas, papá."
   "Bien, Beto. Acabo de comprar______________ ayer."

WB 7-27 | Mi niñez Completa la narración sobre la niñez de Héctor usando el imperfecto de los verbos apropiados de la lista.

comer comprar gustar ir limpiar sacar tener vivir

De joven, yo **1.** ______________________ cerca de Asunción. (Yo)

2. ______________________ algunos quehaceres en casa. Por ejemplo,

3. ______________________ la basura y **4.** ______________________ las habitaciones de la casa.

Cada sábado mi mamá y yo **5.** ______________________ de compras al centro. A veces ella no

6. ______________________ nada, pero nos **7.** ______________________ mirar las cosas de las tiendas. Por la tarde nosotros **8.** ______________________ un pequeño almuerzo en un café.

WB 7-28 | ¡Y ahora baila! Completa la conversación con la forma apropiada del **pretérito** o el **imperfecto** de los verbos que están entre paréntesis.

PACA: Anoche mientras nosotras **1.** ______________________ (trabajar) en la cocina, Marcos me **2.** ______________________ (llamar) por teléfono.

PECA: ¿Marcos? Sabes que él y yo no nos llevamos bien. Cuando nosotros **3.** ______________________ (ser) jóvenes, él siempre **4.** ______________________ (burlarse) *(made fun)* de mí.

PACA: ¿Sí? Bueno, ahora es una persona muy simpática. De hecho *(in fact),* él me **5.** ______________________ (invitar) a salir a bailar el próximo sábado.

PECA: ¡Qué curioso! De joven él nunca **6.** ______________________ (bailar) con nadie. Bueno, **7.** ¿______________________ (aceptar) (tú) su invitación?

PACA: Sí, la **8.** ______________________ (aceptar). ¡Y vamos a salir mañana!

Nombre ______________________ Fecha ______________________

8 Fiestas y vacaciones: Guatemala y El Salvador

VOCABULARIO 1 Fiestas y celebraciones

WB 8-1 | Las celebraciones Completa cada frase con la palabra apropiada.

anfitrión brindis cohetes disfraz máscara pastel velas

1. Se oyen muchos ______________ durante la celebración de la Independencia de los Estados Unidos.
2. El ______________ es la persona que da la fiesta.
3. Para celebrar Mardi Gras en Nueva Orleans, mucha gente se pone una ______________.
4. Se ponen las ______________ en el ______________ de cumpleaños.
5. En los Estados Unidos la gente se pone un ______________ para celebrar el día 31 de octubre.
6. Al hacer el ______________ la gente dice "¡salud!".

WB 8-2 | ¿Qué pasó en la fiesta? Paulino no fue a la fiesta de sorpresa de Luci anoche, pero escuchó los siguientes detalles sobre lo que pasó. Empareja los detalles con los dibujos y luego pon la lista de los detalles en orden.

	Orden		Letra del dibujo
1.	______	Juan Carlos le gritó a Javi y Javi se asustó.	______
2.	______	Todos lo pasaban bien, menos su novio, Juan Carlos.	______
3.	__1__	Anoche se reunió toda la familia de Luci.	__D__
4.	______	Juan Carlos reaccionó mal cuando vio que Javi, el ex novio de Luci, estaba en la fiesta.	______
5.	______	Luci cumplió 20 años y su familia le dio una fiesta de sorpresa.	______
6.	______	Luci lloró y le dijo a Juan Carlos que se portaba muy mal.	______
7.	______	Todos los invitados le trajeron regalos.	______

WB 8-3 | ¡Qué dramáticos! Carlos habla de cómo reaccionan los miembros de su familia en los días festivos. Para saberlo, forma oraciones con una forma apropiada de **ponerse** + el adjetivo dado. Recuerda que los adjetivos tiene que concordar en número y género con la persona que describen. Sigue el modelo.

Modelo El cumpleaños: Teresa y Gabriel / triste
Teresa y Gabriel se ponen tristes.

1. El Día de los Reyes Magos: Carolina / enojado

____

2. El Día de los Muertos: Javier y Silvia / asustado

____

3. El Día de la Raza: yo (Carlos) / emocionado

____

4. La Noche Vieja: nosotros / cansado

____

WB 8-4 | Nuestras costumbres Para saber lo que hace Normita y su familia en los días festivos, rellena los espacios en blanco con la palabra o frase apropiada de la lista. No vas a usar todas las palabras, pero ninguna palabra se usa *(is used)* más de una vez. **¡OJO!** Tienes que conjugar los verbos según el sujeto *(subject)*.

cumpleaños cumplir años hacer una fiesta olvidar
pasarlo reaccionar recordar reunirse

Cuando alguien en mi familia **1.** ______________________, nosotros siempre **2.** ______________________. Nosotros **3.** ______________________ con todos los miembros de la familia y siempre **4.** ______________________ bien. Cuando celebramos el **5.** ______________________ de mi madre, ella siempre se pone molesta porque mi padre nunca **6.** ______________________ la fecha y no le compra un regalo.

Nombre ______________________ Fecha ______________________

ESTRUCTURA Y USO 1 Inquiring and providing information about people and events: Interrogative words

To hear more about **question words,** visit Heinle iRadio at www.cengage.com/spanish/viajes.

WB 8-5 | Una llamada a mamá Mónica llama a su mamá en El Salvador y, como siempre, su mamá tiene muchas preguntas. Completa su conversación con las palabras interrogativas apropiadas. **¡OJO!** Recuerda que estas palabras siempre llevan un acento escrito.

SEÑORA LÓPEZ: ¡Bueno!

MÓNICA: ¡Hola, mamá! Soy yo, Mónica.

SEÑORA LÓPEZ: ¡Mónica! **1.** ¿______________ estás, hija?

MÓNICA: Bien, mami, bien.

SEÑORA LÓPEZ: Me alegro. Oye, **2.** ¿______________ estás ahora? ¿Estás en la residencia?

MÓNICA: Sí, mami. ¿Y papi, **3.** ¿______________ está? ¿Está en casa?

SEÑORA LÓPEZ: Sí, pero ya se durmió. **4.** ¿______________ hora es allí?

MÓNICA: Son las once. Dentro de poco voy a una fiesta.

SEÑORA LÓPEZ: Mónica, **5.** ¿______________ quieres ir a una fiesta tan tarde? ¿No tienes clases mañana?

MÓNICA: Ay, mami. Sí, tengo clases, pero está bien. No pasa nada.

SEÑORA LÓPEZ: **6.** ¿______________ vas? ¿Con **7.** ______________ vas?

MÓNICA: Mami, no te preocupes. No vamos a salir de la residencia. Voy con mi amiga Carola.

SEÑORA LÓPEZ: **8.** ¿______________ es Carola? **9.** ¿______________ es ella? ¿Es de Nueva York? **10.** ¿______________ tiempo hace que la conoces?

MÓNICA: ¡Mami! Tranquila. Es mi amiga y es de Manhattan, pero habla español muy bien. Es muy buena gente *(a good person)* y vamos a estar bien. Dime, mami, **11.** ¿______________ pasa allí? ¿Alguna novedad?

SEÑORA LÓPEZ: Pues, sí. ¡Nació *(was born)* tu primera sobrina!

MÓNICA: ¿De verdad? **12.** ¿______________ nació?

13. ¿______________ se llama?

SEÑORA LÓPEZ: Se llama Verónica y nació anoche.

MÓNICA: **14.** ¿______________ pesa?

SEÑORA LÓPEZ: Unas ocho libras. Es grande.

MÓNICA: ¡Qué alegría, mami! Mira, voy a tener que ir, pero quería preguntarte, ¿te acuerdas *(do you remember)* del libro que me recomendaste la semana pasada?

SEÑORA LÓPEZ: **15.** ¿____________________ libro?

MÓNICA: El libro de cuentos. **16.** ¿____________________ era el título?

SEÑORA LÓPEZ: Ay, mi amor, ya soy tan vieja que no puedo recordar.

MÓNICA: Bueno, mami. Tal vez la próxima vez. Mira, ya me tengo que ir. Un beso para papi y dos para mi nueva sobrina. Chao.

SEÑORA LÓPEZ: Te quiero mucho. Chao, Mónica.

ESTRUCTURA Y USO 2 Narrating in the past: The preterite and the imperfect

To hear more about the **preterite** and the **imperfect**, visit Heinle iRadio at www.cengage.com/spanish/viajes.

WB 8-6 | Una pachanga Anoche Lupe asistió a una fiesta con sus colegas *(coworkers)* de trabajo y ella dice que pasaron algunas cosas muy extrañas *(strange)*. Ahora le cuenta a Eva sobre la fiesta. Selecciona la forma correcta de los verbos indicados.

Eva, anoche (yo) **1.** (vi / veía) algo muy raro en la fiesta del trabajo. Cuando **2.** (llegué / llegaba) a la fiesta ya **3.** (hubo / había) un ambiente *(atmosphere)* muy extraño. Por ejemplo, Ofelia **4.** (bailó / bailaba) en la mesa mientras que Ledia **5.** (recitó / recitaba) poesía en un rincón *(corner)* y Kati le **6.** (habló / hablaba) a Miguel sobre su esposo famoso. De repente *(all of a sudden)*, Samuel, **7.** (corrió / corría) medio desnudo por la sala recitando palabra por palabra episodios del *Quijote*.

Eva, yo creo que tus colegas se han vuelto locos *(they've gone crazy)*. ¿Recuerdas que el año pasado ellos **8.** (fueron / iban) a la fiesta y no **9.** (se divirtieron / se divertían) para nada?

WB 8-7 | Traducciones Traduce *(Translate)* las siguientes oraciones al español. **¡OJO!** Cada oración requiere un verbo en el pretérito y otro en el imperfecto.

1. My grandmother was preparing food when the guests arrived.

____

2. My little brother was behaving poorly and he had to go to his bedroom.

____

3. My girlfriend called while I was watching television.

____

4. Teri and Juan remembered the party while they were at the office.

____

5. It began to rain as Santi was leaving the house.

____

Nombre ______________________________ Fecha ______________________________

WB 8-8 | Un cuento de hadas *(fairy tale)* Rellena los espacios en blanco con la forma apropiada del verbo en el pretérito o el imperfecto. Lee la historia una vez antes de rellenar los espacios para comprender el contexto y luego escoge *(choose)* la forma apropiada del verbo. Al final, adivina *(guess)* qué cuento de hadas es.

1. ____________________ (Haber) una vez un rey que **2.** ____________________ (tener) cinco hijas. De todas ellas, la más joven **3.** ____________________ (ser) la más bonita. La princesa **4.** ____________________ (tener) una pelota y siempre **5.** ____________________ (ir) a jugar a solas con esta pelota al lado de un estanque *(pond)* cerca del castillo. Un día la princesa **6.** ____________________ (perder) su pelota en el agua del estanque. La pobre princesa no **7.** ____________________ (saber) nadar y por eso no **8.** ____________________ (poder) recoger su pelota favorita. La princesa **9.** ____________________ (estar) muy triste y **10.** ____________________ (empezar) a llorar. De repente la princesa **11.** ____________________ (oír) una voz. La voz le decía: «Princesa, ¿qué **12.** ____________________ (pasar) aquí? ¿Por qué lloras?» La princesa no **13.** ____________________ (saber) de dónde **14.** ____________________ (venir) la voz, pero pronto ella **15.** ____________________ (ver) un sapito *(little frog)*. En este momento el sapo **16.** ____________________ (volver) a hablar y **17.** ____________________ (decir): «Yo te puedo devolver *(return)* tu querida pelota si me haces un favor». La princesa **18.** ____________________ (preguntar) cuál **19.** ____________________ (ser) el favor y el sapo le **20.** ____________________ (contestar) que él **21.** ____________________ (querer) un beso. La princesa **22.** ____________________ (tener) que pensar un minuto: ella **23.** ____________________ (querer) su pelota, pero no **24.** ____________________ (saber) si **25.** ____________________ (poder) darle un beso al sapo. Al final **26.** ____________________ (decidir) que sí. Ella **27.** ____________________ (ir) a darle un beso al sapo.

En ese momento el sapo se zambulló *(dove)* en el agua y le **28.** ____________________ (devolver) la pelota a la princesa. Ahora la princesa **29.** ____________________ (tener) que besarlo. Ella **30.** ____________________ (cerrar) los ojos y lo **31.** ____________________ (besar). Un segundo después la princesa **32.** ____________________ (saber) por qué el sapo quería el beso.

¿Cómo se llama el cuento? **33.** ____________________

a. "Caperucita Roja" *(Little Red Riding Hood)*
b. "La princesa y el sapo" *(The Frog Prince)*
c. "Los tres cerditos" *(The Three Little Pigs)*

VOCABULARIO 2 La playa y el campo

WB 8-9 | Activos Javi y sus amigos son muy deportistas y activos. Escribe una oración completa para describir las actividades que hacen en cada dibujo. Sigue el modelo.

Modelo Javi *pasea en canoa.*

1. Nadia ______________________________

2. Carlos ______________________________

3. Alicia ______________________________

4. Javi y Ángela______________________________

5. Rafa ______________________________

WB 8-10 | De vacaciones Luis y Jorge fueron de vacaciones con sus amigos. Para saber cómo lo pasaron, completa el párrafo con las palabras apropiadas de la siguiente lista.

balneario	canoa	olas
broncearse	crema bronceadora	parrillada
caminar por las montañas	lago	playa
camping	mar	tomar el sol

La semana pasada Luis, Jorge y algunos amigos decidieron tomar las vacaciones. A Jorge le gusta mucho estar en las montañas así que él quería hacer **1.** ______________________. Jorge dijo que conocía un lugar precioso donde podían **2.** ______________________

y nadar en un **3.** ______________________. Pero a los otros les gusta más estar cerca del mar y decidieron ir a un **4.** ______________________.

Encontraron un hotel que estaba justo al lado *(right along side)* del **5.** ______________________. El primer día de sus vacaciones salieron del hotel temprano y fueron a la **6.** ______________________ para **7.** ______________________. Para protegerse contra el sol, se aplicaron la **8.** ______________________. Después de **9.** ______________________ lo suficiente *(sufficiently)*, decidieron hacer algunas actividades acuáticas. Primero corrieron las **10.** ______________________ y después decidieron pasear en **11.** ______________________. Esa noche, para comer, todos hicieron una **12.** ______________________. Se divirtieron mucho y hasta *(even)* Jorge estaba muy contento.

ESTRUCTURA Y USO 3 Stating indefinite ideas and quantities: Affirmative and negative expressions

WB 8-11 | Conversaciones en el café Estás en un café en San Salvador y escuchas partes de diferentes conversaciones. Lee las preguntas y respuestas y luego selecciona la palabra afirmativa o negativa apropiada para rellenar el espacio. **¡OJO!** No es necesario que uses todas las palabras y algunas de las palabras las puedes usar más de una vez.

algo alguien nada nadie ni... ni nunca o... o siempre

1. ¿Quieres tomar algo más?

   No, no quiero tomar ______________________.
2. ¿Tomas café con leche?

   No, ______________________ tomo café con leche.
3. ¿Conoces a ______________________ de esa compañía?

   Sí, conozco a varias personas.
4. ¿Quieres hacer camping este fin de semana o prefieres correr las olas?

   Este fin de semana ______________________ quiero hacer camping ______________________ quiero correr las olas. Prefiero quedarme en casa.
5. ¿Viste ______________________ interesante en la tele anoche?

   No. No vi ______________________ interesante anoche.

WB 8-12 | Bienvenida, abuela La abuela de Rafa acaba de llegar y Rafa piensa que ella le trajo un regalo. Para saber si lo hizo, rellena los espacios en blanco con la palabra afirmativa o negativa apropiada.

algo algún algunas algunos ningún ninguna siempre tampoco

RAFA: ¿Me trajiste **1.** ____________ regalo, abuela?

ABUELA: ¡Claro! **2.** ____________ te traigo regalos, ¿verdad?

RAFA: Sí. ¿Me trajiste **3.** ____________ tarjetas de iTunes?

ABUELA: No, Rafa. No te traje **4.** ____________ tarjeta.

RAFA: ¿Me trajiste **5.** ____________ para comer?

ABUELA: **6.** ____________, Rafa.

RAFA: Pues, ¿qué me trajiste, abuela?

ABUELA: Te traje **7.** ____________ libros de historia.

RAFA: ¡Ay, no quiero **8.** ____________ libro de historia!

ABUELA: ...y un juego electrónico.

RAFA: ¡Eres mi abuela favorita!

WB 8-13 | Opuestos Forma una oración con el significado opuesto sustituyendo las palabras afirmativas con palabras negativas.

1. Hay algunas canoas para alquilar en el balneario.

   ____

2. Todos en nuestro grupo saben pescar.

   ____

3. Talía también sabe bucear.

   ____

4. Pati o quiere nadar o quiere broncearse.

   ____

Nombre ______________________ Fecha ______________________

VIAJEMOS POR GUATEMALA Y EL SALVADOR

En estos segmentos de video, vas a aprender un poco sobre los países de Guatemala y El Salvador.

A B
D C
E
F
G
H
I
South America
J

WB 8-14 | ¿Dónde se ubican? Identifica los países de Guatemala y El Salvador en el mapa.

1. __________ Escribe la letra del mapa que corresponde a Guatemala.
2. __________ Escribe la letra del mapa que corresponde a El Salvador.

WB 8-15 | Cognados En los segmentos de video vas a escuchar muchos cognados que pueden facilitar tu comprensión del video. Algunos de estos cognados aparecen aquí. Antes de ver los segmentos, trata de pronunciar cada palabra o frase y luego trata de emparejar *(match)* los cognados con su definición en inglés.

1. _____ descendientes **a.** eruptions
2. _____ ritos **b.** descendants
3. _____ volcanes **c.** tomb
4. _____ erupciones **d.** rituals
5. _____ tumba **e.** volcanoes
6. _____ extinto **f.** extinct

WB 8-16 | Cognados en contexto Mira el video otra vez y trata de rellenar los espacios en blanco con el cognado apropiado de la actividad **WB 8-15.**

from the segment about Guatemala

1. Las costumbres religiosas de sus habitantes, que son __________________ de los mayas, son una mezcla de __________________ mayas y cristianos.
2. Desde el lago, se ven los __________________ Atitlán, Tolimán y San Pedro.

from the segment about El Salvador

3. El Salvador, el país más pequeño de Centroamérica, tiene una historia larga de __________________ volcánicas.
4. El Cerro Verde es un volcán __________________.

WB 8-17 | Comprensión Después de ver el video, indica si las siguientes oraciones son **ciertas** (C) o **falsas** (F).

	cierto	falso
1. Chichicastenango es una ciudad turística de El Salvador.	☐	☐
2. Los huipiles son blusas tradicionales indígenas típicas de Guatemala.	☐	☐
3. Los guatemaltecos son descendientes de los mayas.	☐	☐
4. San Salvador es un pueblo pequeño.	☐	☐
5. Muchos visitan la Catedral Metropolitana de San Salvador para ver la tumba del arzobispo Óscar Romero.	☐	☐

¡A ESCRIBIR!

Strategy: Writing a summary

A good summary tells the reader the most important information about an event. The following is a list of important data that one should include in a summary:

- An interesting title or topic sentence
- Description of the setting: when and where the action took place, who was involved, any special conditions that were in existence
- What made the situation interesting or unique
- What actions took place, expected or unexpected
- How the event or situation ended or was resolved

Task: Writing a summary of a favorite holiday or celebration

Paso 1 When you were young, what was your favorite holiday or celebration? How long has it been since you last celebrated? How did you celebrate? Did something special / funny / interesting happen? Answer these questions below in Spanish.

____

____

____

Paso 2 Based on your responses above, write a descriptive paragraph to summarize these details. Since your description will be in the past, you will need to pay attention to your use of the preterite and the imperfect. Refer to your text to review the use of these verb forms.

Nombre ______________________ Fecha ______________________

Paso 3 Revise your first draft, making sure your ideas are organized and that your verb forms are accurate; then write your final draft below.

___

___

___

___

___

___

___

___

___

ATAJO 4.0

Functions: Writing about past events; Writing about theme, plot, or scene
Vocabulary: Family members; Religious holidays; Time expressions
Grammar: Verbs: Preterite & Imperfect

Autoprueba

WB8-18 | Una celebración especial Para saber cómo lo pasaron en la fiesta que hizo Ana anoche, completa la siguiente descripción con una palabra apropiada de la lista. **¡OJO!** Vas a tener que conjugar algunos de los verbos.

anfitriona	entremeses	pasarlo
brindis	felicidades	pastel
celebrar	gritar	recordar
cumplir	invitados	regalos
disfraz	llorar	reunirse
disfrazarse	máscara	velas

Ayer Silvia **1.** ______________ treinta años y Ana le hizo una fiesta divertida. Había mucha cerveza, vino y sodas. También Ana preparó varios **2.** ______________ y todos comieron un montón. Todos los **3.** ______________ tuvieron que **4.** ______________ de su personaje histórico favorito. Ana se puso una **5.** ______________ de María Antonieta *(Marie Antoinette)* y su esposo, Jorge, se puso un **6.** ______________ de Simón Bolívar.

A las once de la noche, a la misma hora en que nació Silvia, todos **7.** ______________ para **8.** ______________ el momento. Hicieron un **9.** ______________ y todos **10.** ______________, **11.** «¡______________!». Luego, empezaron a comer el **12.** ______________ de cumpleaños. Esta vez no tenía **13.** ______________ porque Silvia no quería **14.** ______________ cuántos años cumplía. A la medianoche Silvia abrió sus **15.** ______________. Su novio, Raúl, le dio un anillo de diamantes y Silvia empezó a **16.** ______________.

La fiesta acabó a las tres de la mañana. Todos **17.** ______________ muy bien y antes de salir todos le dieron las gracias a la **18.** ______________, que había preparado *(had prepared)* una fiesta tan buena. ¡La celebración fue un éxito total!

Nombre ______________________ Fecha ______________________

WB 8-19 | En la playa y en el campo Escribe la letra de cada actividad descrita *(described)*.

_____ **1.** nadar debajo del agua con un tubo
_____ **2.** nadar debajo del agua con un tanque
_____ **3.** jugar en el agua con una tabla
_____ **4.** navegar en bote de vela en el mar
_____ **5.** descansar tranquilamente en la playa
_____ **6.** cocinar carne al aire libre
_____ **7.** dormir debajo de las estrellas
_____ **8.** navegar por los ríos en un bote

a. bucear
b. acampar
c. tomar el sol
d. correr las olas
e. pasear en canoa
f. hacer esnórquel
g. hacer una parrillada
h. pasear en velero

WB 8-20 | Preguntas Un amigo te hace preguntas por Internet. Completa sus preguntas con la palabra interrogativa apropiada.

1. Soy de la ciudad de Guatemala. ¿______________________ eres tú?
2. Ahora estoy en la universidad. ¿______________________ estás tú ahora mismo?
3. A mí me encanta la música de Pink Floyd. ¿______________________ es tu música favorita?
4. Paso mucho tiempo en la selva con mis amigos. ¿______________________ vas tú para divertirte?
5. Salimos a bailar mucho. ¿______________________ haces tú para divertirte en tu ciudad?
6. Tomo tres clases este semestre. ¿______________________ clases tomas tú?
7. Estudio relaciones internacionales. ¿______________________ estudias tú?

WB 8-21 | Un viaje inolvidable Lee la siguiente narración sobre un viaje memorable de Guillermo. Después, escribe la forma apropiada del pretérito o del imperfecto de cada verbo entre paréntesis.

Cuando yo **1.** ______________________ (ser) más joven, **2.** ______________________ (hacer) una vez un viaje a Belice. **3.** ______________________ (Ir) con toda mi familia. Mi hermanito **4.** ______________________ (tener) tres años y yo **5.** ______________________ (tener) catorce. Después de pensarlo mucho, mis padres **6.** ______________________ (decidir) hacer el viaje a Belice porque quedaba tan cerca de donde nosotros **7.** ______________________ (vivir) en Guatemala en esos años.

Recuerdo todo de ese viaje. El lugar **8.** ______________________ (ser) tan limpio y bonito y en las playas **9.** ______________________ (haber) muchos pájaros y otros animales bonitos. Yo sí **10.** ______________________ (poder) nadar, pero mi hermanito todavía no **11.** ______________________ (saber) nadar. Un día yo **12.** ______________________ (ir) a nadar sin él y él **13.** ______________________ (empezar) a llorar. ¡Pobre Juan! En realidad, pobre de mí, porque ese día mientras yo **14.** ______________________ (nadar) en el mar un pez grande me **15.** ______________________ (morder) *(to bite)*. En un instante yo

16. ______________________ (sentir) un dolor tremendo y **17.** ______________________

(gritar): «¡Mamá, ayúdame!». Mi mamá **18.** ______________________ (meterse) al agua y

me **19.** ______________________ (salvar) la vida. Después de salir del agua yo

20. ______________________ (tener) que ir al hospital. Al final no

21. ______________________ (ser) nada serio, pero de todas formas toda la situación me

22. ______________________ (asustar) mucho.

WB 8-22 | Significados especiales Recuerda que ciertos verbos tienen un significado especial en el pretérito o el imperfecto. Completa las siguientes oraciones con el pretérito o imperfecto según *(according to)* el significado de la oración.

1. Anoche nosotros ______________________ (tener) que asistir a una reunión muy aburrida. No salimos hasta las 10:00 de la noche.
2. El año pasado Elisa ______________________ (saber) que Esteban tenía una hermana. No lo ______________________ (saber) antes.
3. Anita quería llevarme a una celebración familiar pero yo no ______________________ (querer) ir. Me quedé en casa.
4. La semana pasada Dolores trató de sacar dinero del banco pero no ______________________ (poder). El cajero automático estaba descompuesto *(broken)* y el banco estaba cerrado.
5. Cuando yo era más joven, ______________________ (tener) que estudiar mucho.

WB 8-23 | ¿Algo quiere? Completa las oraciones con una palabra apropiada de la lista.

algo algún algunas algunos nada ni... ni
ninguna nunca también tampoco

VENDEDOR: ¿Quiere **1.** ______________________, señor?

CLIENTE: Sí, quiero **2.** ______________________ tomates, por favor.

VENDEDOR: Bien. ¿Quiere **3.** ______________________ manzanas **4.** ______________________? Están muy frescas.

CLIENTE: No, no quiero **5.** ______________________ porque no como fruta.

VENDEDOR: ¿Necesita **6.** ______________________ huevos frescos, señor?

CLIENTE: No, **7.** ______________________ como huevos.

VENDEDOR: ¿Verdad? Mi esposa no come **8.** ______________________ frutas **9.** ______________________ huevos. ¡Qué coincidencia! ¿Necesita pan hoy?

CLIENTE: No gracias, no necesito **10.** ______________________ más.

VENDEDOR: Muy bien... catorce quetzales, por favor.

Nombre ______________________ Fecha ______________________

9 De viaje por el Caribe: Cuba, Puerto Rico y la República Dominicana

VOCABULARIO 1 Viajar en avión

WB 9-1 | Rompecabezas Usa las pistas *(clues)* para solucionar este rompecabezas sobre los viajes. Escribe la palabra más apropiada, según la pista.

1. Un grupo de maletas: __ __ __ __ p __ __ __
2. Donde guardas la ropa para un viaje: __ __ __ __ __ a
3. Un viaje directo de Miami a Puerto Rico es un vuelo sin: e __ c __ __ __
4. El momento en que el avión sale del aeropuerto: s __ __ __ __ a
5. Para saber cuándo sale un vuelo tienes que consultar un: __ __ r __ __ __ o
6. Para comprar un boleto de avión, vas a una: __ __ __ n __ __ __ de viajes.
7. Un boleto de San Francisco a San Juan y de San Juan a San Francisco es un boleto de: __ d __ y __ __ __ l __ __
8. Donde esperas el avión justo antes del vuelo: __ __ e __ __ __
9. La persona que te trae bebidas y comida durante el vuelo: __ s __ __ __ __ __ t __
10. El documento necesario para pasar por la aduana: __ __ __ __ p __ __ __ __
11. Las personas que viajan en un avión: __ __ __ __ __ __ __ __ s

WB 9-2 | Un viaje gratis Quieres viajar en tus vacaciones y ahora consultas con el agente de viajes. ¿Qué preguntas te hace? Para saberlo, rellena los espacios en blanco con la palabra apropiada de la lista. **¡OJO!** En algunos casos tienes que conjugar el verbo.

abordar aduana avión boleto control de seguridad facturar
llegada pasaporte perdón ventanilla viajar

1. ¿Adónde quieres ______________________?
2. ¿Deseas un ______________________ de ida y vuelta o solamente de ida?
3. ¿Prefieres ir en ______________________ o por tren?
4. Por lo general, ¿ ______________________ las maletas cuando vas en avión?
5. ¿Tienes un ______________________ para pasar la aduana sin problemas?

WB 9-3 | Un viaje a Puerto Rico Quieres ir a Puerto Rico este verano y decides pedirle ayuda a tu amigo Ricardo. Es de San Juan y te dice todo lo que hace para planear sus viajes a Puerto Rico. Para saber lo que dice, rellena los espacios en blanco con la palabra apropiada de la lista. **¡OJO!** En algunos casos tienes que conjugar el verbo.

abordar	bajarse	hacer las maletas	recoger
aeropuerto	boletos	horario	ventanilla
agencia de viajes	equipaje de mano	inmigración	viaje
agente	escala	pasaporte	
asiento	facturar las maletas	pasillo	

Cuando hago mis planes para viajar a Puerto Rico, siempre voy a la **1.** ____________________, donde compro los **2.** ____________________. Lola, mi **3.** ____________________, es excelente. Siempre sabe encontrar los mejores precios. Yo le digo las fechas de mi **4.** ____________________ y después ella consulta el **5.** ____________________ de los vuelos. Aunque vivimos más cerca de San Diego, siempre salgo del **6.** ____________________ de Los Ángeles porque los precios son mucho más baratos. El único problema es que de ningún sitio tienen vuelos directos. Todos hacen una **7.** ____________________ en Chicago o en Miami. Lola siempre me consigue un **8.** ____________________ específico en el avión. A mí me gusta ver el paisaje desde el avión y por eso siempre me siento en la **9.** ____________________. Pero a mi novia le gusta caminar por el avión muchas veces durante el vuelo. Por eso ella siempre se sienta en el **10.** ____________________. Ahora, tú sabes que yo fumo como una chimenea, pero ya no podemos fumar en los aviones. Está bien. Yo, lo que hago, es fumar tres o cuatro cigarrillos antes de **11.** ____________________ el avión. Antes del viaje siempre estoy muy ocupado con los preparativos. Siempre hago una lista de todo lo que tengo que empacar *(pack)*. Así *(So)*, cuando **12.** ____________________ no me olvido de nada esencial. Nunca llevo **13.** ____________________ porque nunca hay suficiente espacio en el avión. Cuando llego al aeropuerto siempre tengo que **14.** ____________________, pero no es gran cosa. Voy cómodo en el avión, y al llegar a Puerto Rico, **15.** ____________________ del avión, **16.** ____________________ el equipaje y ¡listo! Bueno, creo que lo vas a pasar súper bien en Puerto Rico. Recuerda que no necesitas un **17.** ____________________ y que no tienes que pasar por la **18.** ____________________ porque Puerto Rico es parte de los Estados Unidos. Y, obviamente, ¡no olvides llevar el traje de baño!

Nombre ______________________ Fecha ______________________

ESTRUCTURA Y USO 1 Simplifying expressions (I): Indirect object pronouns

WB 9-4 | ¿Locos de amor? Pablo e Inés están en su luna de miel y hablan de los recuerdos *(souvenirs)* que van a comprar. Para saber qué compró Pablo para Inés, completa su conversación con el pronombre de objeto indirecto apropiado. Luego contesta la pregunta que está al final del diálogo.

PABLO: Inés, mi amor, ¿a mi mamá ya **1.** ______________ mandamos una tarjeta postal?

INÉS: Pues, yo no **2.** ______________ mandé nada, cielo. Y ahora no queda tiempo. A tus padres **3.** ______________ compramos un recuerdo; no necesitan una tarjeta postal.

PABLO: Tienes razón, mi amor. Pero me siento mal porque ellos ya **4.** ______________ mandaron dos cartas a nosotros, ¡y ellos no están de vacaciones!

INÉS: Pero tus padres son así. ¡No te preocupes *(Don't worry)*! No van a estar enojados. Ahora, a tu hermana, ¿qué **5.** ______________ compraste ayer en San Juan?

PABLO: Nada, mi amor, porque no sabía que quería algo de San Juan.

INÉS: Pues, Pablito, a ti **6.** ______________ pidió una estatua de Lladró, que son muy caras donde vive ella. ¿No lo recuerdas, cielo?

PABLO: No, no recuerdo nada. Creo que estoy demasiado enamorado de ti como para pensar en otras personas.

INÉS: Ah, ¡qué mono eres! Pues, ayer cuando estabas de compras, ¿a mí **7.** ______________ compraste algo?

PABLO: Claro que sí. ¡A ti **8.** ______________ compré mil años más conmigo!

INÉS: ¡Qué romántico! Pero, Pablo, entonces, ¿a quién **9.** ______________ vas a regalar este equipo de buceo que tienes escondido *(hidden)* en el armario?

PABLO: Eh, eh, pues, mi amor, sabes cuánto me gusta bucear . . . y el año pasado yo **10.** ______________ pedí un equipo de buceo y tú nunca **11.** ______________ regalaste el equipo que quería . . . y pues el precio era muy bueno. . . .

INÉS: ¡Pablo! Creo que tienes que volver a San Juan, mi amor.

¿Qué recuerdo le regaló Pablo a Inés? **12.** ______________

WB 9-5 | ¿Qué hiciste? Tu amiga, Teresa Enrollada, siempre tiene problemas difíciles. Cuando ella te cuenta un problema, tú le preguntas cómo va a solucionar su problema. Escribe tus preguntas usando un pronombre de objeto indirecto. Sigue el modelo.

Modelo La profesora está enojada y quiere hablar conmigo. (¿hablar?)
¿Le vas a hablar?
o: *¿Vas a hablarle?*

1. Mis amigos quieren copiar mi tarea. (¿enseñar / tarea?)

____

2. Mi ex novio necesita 300 dólares. (¿dar / dinero?)

____

3. Tengo que hacerte una pregunta importante. (¿hacer / pregunta?)

____

4. Mi nuevo amigo del Internet quería una foto de mí. (¿ofrecer / foto?)

____

5. Este amigo del Internet quiere mandarnos una foto a nosotros dos. (¿mandar / foto?)

____

WB 9-6 | Planes Julio y sus compañeros de casa van de viaje a la República Dominicana y a Haití. Ahora están hablando de lo que cada persona hace para planear el viaje. Forma oraciones completas con los elementos que siguen, incorporando pronombres de objeto indirecto.

1. Carlos / comprar / una maleta / a Anita

____

2. Julio / prometer / hacer las reservaciones / a sus compañeros

____

3. Alicia y Mabel / mandar / un correo electrónico / a su primo en Santo Domingo

____

4. el señor Martínez / ir a recomendar / un hotel / a nosotros

____

5. yo / ir a explicar / los planes / a ti

____

ESTRUCTURA Y USO 2 Simplifying expressions (II): Double object pronouns

WB 9-7 | ¡Feliz cumpleaños! Carmen le cuenta a una amiga sobre la fiesta de cumpleaños de Olga que tuvo lugar *(took place)* anoche. Completa su historia con un pronombre de objeto directo o un pronombre de objeto indirecto. **¡OJO!** Vas a usar solo uno en cada caso y no los dos juntos.

Ayer fue el cumpleaños de Olga y ella **1.** _______ pasó muy bien. Todos sus amigos **2.** _______ dieron muchos regalos. **3.** _______ compraron en diferentes tiendas especializadas del Viejo San Juan. Por ejemplo, Paco **4.** _______ compró una blusa de seda. A Olga le gustó mucho la blusa y ella **5.** _______ dio un beso a Paco. Mateo, el novio de Olga, también **6.** _______ dio un regalo especial. A nosotros Mateo **7.** _______ dijo que iba a ser algo increíble, y realmente fue increíble. Después de que Olga abrió todos sus regalos, Mateo miró a Olga y **8.** _______ dijo: «Olga, **9.** _______ quiero mucho, y tú **10.** _______ sabes. Y también creo que tú **11.** _______ quieres a mí, ¿verdad? Pues, **12.** _______ compré este regalo, **13.** ¡ábre_______ ahora mismo!». Cuando Olga **14.** _______ abrió, empezó a gritar. Era un anillo de diamantes. De repente ella **15.** _______ miró a nosotros y **16.** _______ dijo: «¡Voy a casarme con Mateo!».

Nombre ______________________ Fecha ______________________

WB 9-8 | Regalos para todos Ernesto le pregunta a Fernando sobre los regalos que dio y recibió en el Día de los Reyes Magos. Selecciona la mejor respuesta a las preguntas de Ernesto, según los dibujos. Sigue el modelo.

Modelo ¿Quién te dio las maletas?
__X__ Tú me las diste.
______ Uds. se las dieron.
______ Nos las dieron Uds.

1. 2. 3. 4.

1. ¿A quién le regalaste el libro?
   ______ Me lo regaló mi abuela.
   ______ Me la regaló mi abuela.
   ______ Se lo regalé a mi abuela.
2. ¿A quién le regalaste los discos compactos?
   ______ Se las regalé a mis hermanas.
   ______ Se los regalé a mis hermanas.
   ______ Me las regaló mis hermanas.
3. ¿Quién les compró las bicicletas a ti y a tu hermano?
   ______ Nos las compraron nuestros padres.
   ______ Se las compramos a nuestros padres.
   ______ Nos los compraron nuestros padres.
4. ¿A quién le mandaste dinero?
   ______ Se los mandé a mis sobrinos.
   ______ Nos los mandaron mis sobrinos.
   ______ Se lo mandé a mis sobrinos.

WB 9-9 | ¡Qué buen servicio! La familia Suárez está pasando una semana de vacaciones en el hotel Meliá de San Juan, Puerto Rico. Completa las siguientes conversaciones entre un empleado *(employee)* del hotel y el señor Suárez. Forma oraciones usando los pronombres de objeto directo e indirecto. Sigue el modelo.

Modelo SR. SUÁREZ: Señor, ¿me puede cambiar el cuarto?
EMPLEADO: Sí, *se lo cambio.*

1. SR. SUÁREZ: Señor, ¿nos puede traer una plancha?
   EMPLEADO: Sí, ______________________________.
2. SR. SUÁREZ: Señor, ¿a mis hijos les puede enseñar la piscina?
   EMPLEADO: Sí, ______________________________.
3. SR. SUÁREZ: Señor, ¿me puede explicar cómo funciona el televisor?
   EMPLEADO: Sí, ______________________________.
4. SR. SUÁREZ: Señor, ¿a mi esposa le puede servir el almuerzo?
   EMPLEADO: Sí, ______________________________.

WB 9-10 | ¡Házmelo! Alfonso se enferma el último día de sus vacaciones y Javier le tiene que hacer varias cosas. Para saber qué le pide Alfonso a Javier, usa los elementos que están abajo para formar mandatos y usar los pronombres de objeto directo e indirecto. **¡OJO!** Cuando usas los dos pronombres con el mandato, tienes que usar un acento escrito sobre la vocal acentuada. Sigue el modelo.

Modelo Tengo sed y necesito un vaso de agua. (traer / el vaso de agua / a mí)
Tráemelo, por favor.

1. A mi novia todavía no le compré su regalo. (comprar / el regalo / a mi novia)
   ____
2. Tengo que preparar mis maletas, pero no puedo. (preparar / las maletas / a mí)
   ____
3. Tengo que mandarles la tarjeta postal a mis padres, pero no puedo. (mandar / la tarjeta postal / a ellos)
   ____
4. Quiero comer fruta. (servir / fruta / a mí)
   ____
5. Necesito una aspirina. (dar / la aspirina / a mí)
   ____
6. Necesitamos reconfirmar los vuelos. (reconfirmar / los vuelos / a nosotros)
   ____

Nombre ______________________ Fecha ______________________

VOCABULARIO 2 El hotel

WB 9-11 | Hoteles El hotel El Lagarto y el hotel Sol y Luna son dos hoteles muy diferentes de San Juan, Puerto Rico. Mira los dibujos y decide si las siguientes oraciones son ciertas o falsas.

	cierto	falso
1. El hotel El Lagarto no tiene ascensor.	☐	☐
2. Los cuartos del hotel El Lagarto tienen baños privados.	☐	☐
3. El hotel El Lagarto no tiene aire acondicionado.	☐	☐
4. Los cuartos del hotel El Lagarto son muy cómodos.	☐	☐
5. El hotel Sol y Luna es un hotel de cuatro estrellas.	☐	☐
6. Los cuartos del hotel Sol y Luna no están muy limpios.	☐	☐
7. Los cuartos del hotel Sol y Luna tienen camas dobles.	☐	☐

WB 9-12 | ¿Un hotel de cuatro estrellas? El señor Vargas quiere quedarse en un hotel de cuatro estrellas cuando va a la República Dominicana. Para saber si encuentra uno, completa su conversación con la recepcionista del hotel Las Brisas con una palabra apropiada de la lista. Luego contesta la pregunta que está al final del diálogo.

aire acondicionado	cama doble	cuarto	llave
ascensor	camas sencillas	cuatro estrellas	quedarse
baño privado	cómodos	limpio	quejarse

SEÑOR VARGAS: Buenos días. Quiero un **1.** ______________ para dos personas, por favor.

RECEPCIONISTA: ¿Con una **2.** ______________ o con dos **3.** ______________, señor?

SEÑOR VARGAS: Una doble, por favor, con un **4.** ________________________.

RECEPCIONISTA: Bien. Tengo un cuarto en el sexto piso: número 606. ¿Está bien, señor?

SEÑOR VARGAS: Pues, el hotel tiene **5.** ________________________, ¿verdad?

RECEPCIONISTA: No, señor. Lo siento. Ese es el encanto del hotel. A nuestros clientes les ofrecemos un descanso de la edad moderna.

SEÑOR VARGAS: Pues, hace mucho calor allí. ¿Tiene **6.** ________________________ el cuarto?

RECEPCIONISTA: No, señor, pero cada cuarto tiene abanico *(handheld fan)*. ¡No se preocupe, señor! Nuestros cuartos son muy **7.** ________________________. ¿Cuántas noches quiere **8.** ________________________?

SEÑOR VARGAS: Tres noches, pero no sé si puedo aguantar *(put up with)* el calor y las escaleras.

RECEPCIONISTA: No va a haber ningún problema, señor. A Ud. nuestro pequeño paraíso le va a gustar mucho. Este no es un hotel de **9.** ________________________, pero todo está muy **10.** ________________________ y Ud. no va a **11.** ________________________ de nada.

SEÑOR VARGAS: Pues, no sé. ¿Puedo ver el cuarto antes de decidir?

RECEPCIONISTA: Sí, señor. Aquí tiene la **12.** ________________________.

¿Es el hotel Las Brisas un hotel de cuatro estrellas? **13.** ________________________

ESTRUCTURA Y USO 3 Giving directions: Prepositions of location, adverbs, and relevant expressions

WB 9-13 | Modos de transporte ¿Cuáles son los siguientes modos de transporte? Ordena las letras para revelar las palabras.

1. icaicletb: ________________________
2. rbaoc: ________________________
3. xita: ________________________
4. cheoc: ________________________
5. tremo: ________________________
6. úbotasu: ________________________

Nombre ______________________ Fecha ______________________

WB 9-14 | En la ciudad Lee la siguiente descripción de la ciudad y selecciona la preposición más apropiada, según el mapa.

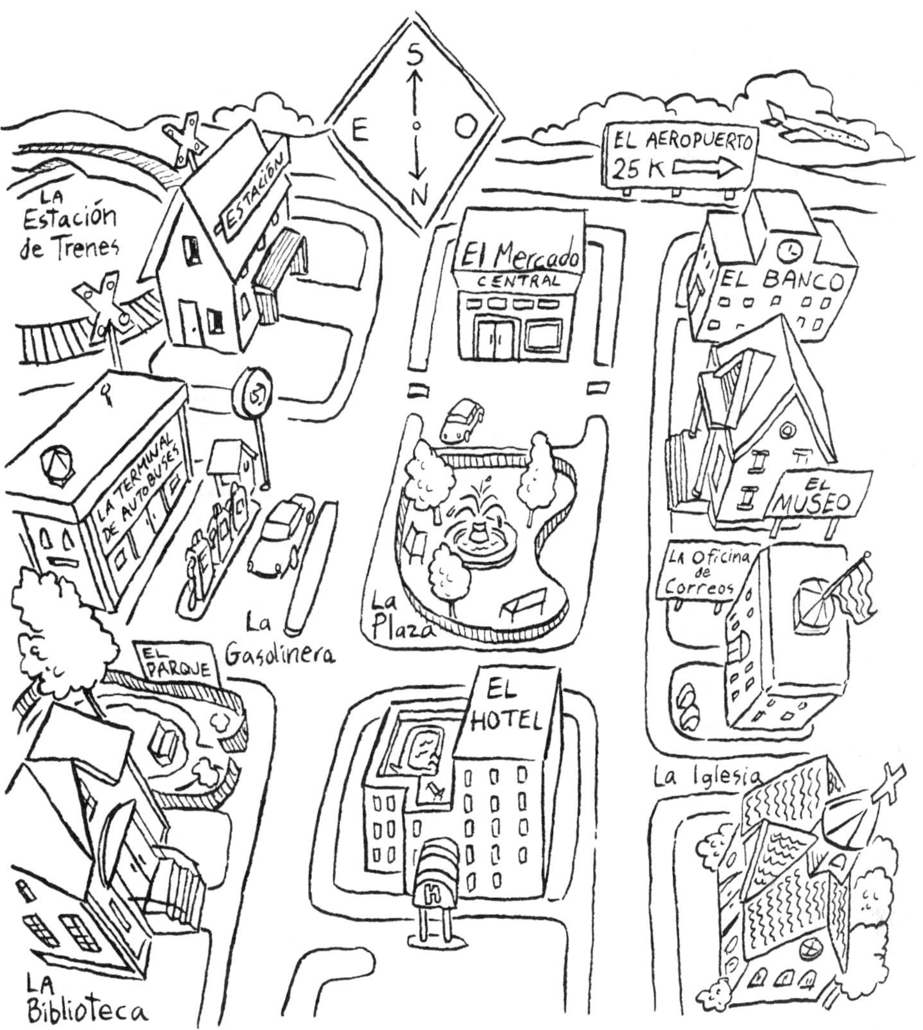

La plaza está en el centro de la ciudad. Hay un parque que está **1.** (lejos de / detrás de / cerca de) la biblioteca. Hay un museo **2.** (entre el / a lado del / a la derecha del) banco y la oficina de correos. **3.** (Lejos del / Entre / Al lado del) parque está la gasolinera. La gasolinera está **4.** (a la derecha de / delante de / lejos de) la terminal de autobuses. **5.** (Enfrente de / Lejos de / Al lado de) la terminal está la estación de trenes, que está **6.** (a la izquierda del / a la derecha del / lejos del) mercado central. **7.** (A la derecha del / En frente del / Detrás del) hotel hay una iglesia. La iglesia está **8.** (lejos de / entre / cerca de) la oficina de correos. El aeropuerto está **9.** (cerca de / lejos de / enfrente de) la cuidad.

WB 9-15 | ¿Cómo llego? La señora López está en el hotel de la ciudad que aparece en el mapa de la actividad **WB 9-14.** Quiere saber cómo llegar a varias partes de la ciudad y pide direcciones en la recepción. ¿Cómo le contestan en la recepción? Mira otra vez el plano de la ciudad y completa las siguientes conversaciones con las palabras apropiadas de la lista. **¡OJO!** Puedes usar la misma palabra más de una vez y no tienes que usar todas las palabras.

A

a la derecha	doble
a la izquierda	en avión
a pie	hacia
cuadras	perdón
cruce	siga

SEÑORA LÓPEZ: **1.** ________________, señora, ¿cómo llego a la estación de trenes?

RECEPCIONISTA: Es muy fácil, señora. Usted puede ir **2.** ________________. Salga *(Leave)* del hotel y **3.** ________________ a la derecha.
4. ________________ la calle y **5.** ________________ derecho
6. ________________ el sur dos **7.** ________________.
La estación está **8.** ________________.

B

a pie	izquierda
cuadras	lejos
derecha	pararse
doble	perdón
en autobús	siga
hacia	un taxi

SEÑORA LÓPEZ: Y dígame, por favor, ¿cómo llego al aeropuerto?

RECEPCIONISTA: Pues, el aeropuerto queda un poco **1.** ________________ de la ciudad, pero usted tiene varias opciones. Puede ir **2.** ________________, pero es más fácil llamar **3.** ________________. Salga del hotel y
4. ________________ a la **5.** ________________.
6. ________________ derecho tres **7.** ________________ y
8. ________________ a la **9.** ________________. De allí el aeropuerto queda a unos 25 kilómetros **10.** ________________ el oeste.

Nombre ______________________ Fecha ______________________

ESTRUCTURA Y USO 4 Telling someone to do something: Formal commands and negative *tú* commands

WB 9-16 | Mandatos Escribe la forma apropiada del mandato según las indicaciones. Sigue el modelo.

Modelo tú, negativo / hablar: *no hables*
usted, positivo / comer: *coma*

1. usted, positivo / viajar: ______________________
2. ustedes, negativo / fumar: ______________________
3. tú, negativo / llegar: ______________________
4. usted, positivo / bañarse: ______________________
5. ustedes, negativo / abrir: ______________________
6. tú, negativo / ir: ______________________
7. usted, positivo / bajarse: ______________________
8. tú, negativo / pedir: ______________________
9. ustedes, positivo / salir: ______________________
10. tú, negativo / dormirse: ______________________

WB 9-17 | En el Viejo San Juan Es la primera semana que Gloria está en San Juan y no conoce la ciudad. Les pide indicaciones a muchas personas que encuentra. Completa las siguientes conversaciones usando los mandatos formales de los verbos indicados.

En la calle

GLORIA: Perdón, señor. ¿Sabe Ud. si hay un mercado por aquí?

SEÑOR ORTEGA: Sí, señora. **1.** ______________ (Seguir) Ud. derecho hasta la esquina. Luego, **2.** ______________ (doblar) a la derecha en la calle Norzagaray y **3.** ______________ (pasar) dos cuadras más hasta la calle Tanca. Allí está el mercado.

GLORIA: Gracias, señor.

SEÑOR ORTEGA: De nada, señora.

En el mercado

EMPLEADO: Señora, **4.** ______________ (decirme) qué quiere Ud.

GLORIA: **5.** ______________ (Darme) medio kilo de esas manzanas, por favor. Y, ¿están frescos los mangos?

EMPLEADO: Sí, **6.** ______________ (mirar) Ud. Están súper frescos.

GLORIA: Muy bien. Y, ¿dónde puedo encontrar la sección de carnes?

EMPLEADO: Lo siento, señora. Aquí no vendemos carnes. **7.** ______________ (Ir) a la carnicería. Queda muy cerca de aquí.

GLORIA: Bien. Entonces, eso es todo. Gracias.

EMPLEADO: De nada. **8.** ______________________ (Tener) Ud. un buen día. ¡Y **9.** ______________________ (volver) pronto!

GLORIA: Gracias. ¡Adiós!

WB 9-18 | ¡Despiértense! Ernesto y sus amigos querían pasar las vacaciones de primavera en un club deportivo en Puerto Rico, pero su agente de viajes se equivocó y los alojó *(lodged them)* en un balneario para gente que quiere bajar de peso *(lose weight)*. A las 6:00 de la mañana del primer día, el director del club viene a despertarlos. ¿Qué les manda? Forma mandatos informales y plurales con los siguientes elementos. **¡OJO!** Los pronombres van conectados al final de los mandatos afirmativos y van delante de los mandatos negativos.

Modelo A todos: levantarse
¡Levántense todos!

A Ernesto: no dormirse otra vez
¡No te duermas otra vez!

1. A todos: vestirse rápidamente

____

2. A Ernesto: no ducharse

____

3. A todos: ponerse los zapatos de tenis

____

4. A todos: echarse a correr 10 millas

____

5. A Ernesto: no pararse para descansar

____

6. A todos: subir la escalera

____

7. A todos: quitarse los zapatos y meterse en la piscina

____

Nombre ______________________ Fecha ______________________

VIAJEMOS POR CUBA, PUERTO RICO Y LA REPÚBLICA DOMINICANA

En estos segmentos del video, vas a aprender un poco sobre Cuba, Puerto Rico y la República Dominicana.

WB 9-19 | Cognados En estos segmentos del video vas a escuchar muchos cognados que pueden facilitar tu comprensión del video. Algunos de estos cognados aparecen aquí. Antes de ver el video, trata de pronunciar cada palabra o frase y luego trata de emparejar *(match)* los cognados con su definición en inglés.

1. ______ máscaras	**a.** marble
2. ______ quioscos	**b.** military
3. ______ militar	**c.** masks
4. ______ socialista	**d.** convents
5. ______ Antillas	**e.** socialist
6. ______ conventos	**f.** Antilles
7. ______ mármol	**g.** statue
8. ______ estatua	**h.** kiosks
9. ______ bautizó (bautizar)	**i.** baptized

WB 9-20 | Cognados en contexto Mira los segmentos del video otra vez y trata de rellenar los espacios en blanco con el cognado apropiado de la actividad **WB 9-19.**

del segmento sobre Cuba:

1. La República ______________________ de Cuba, situada en el Mar Caribe, es la isla más grande de las ______________________ Mayores.

2. En la Habana Vieja están todos los grandes monumentos antiguos, las fortalezas, los ______________________ e iglesias, los palacios, las callejuelas, los balcones.

del segmento sobre Puerto Rico:

3. Este es el Fuerte de San Felipe del Morro, una edificación ______________________ de seis niveles, estructura clave en el fortalecimiento del Imperio Español en el Nuevo Mundo.

4. Estas ______________________ hechas de papel maché representan la influencia africana en la cultura puertorriqueña.

del segmento sobre la República Dominicana:

5. Cristóbal Colón ______________________ la isla La Española.

WB 9-21 | Comprensión Después de ver los segmentos otra vez, selecciona la mejor respuesta a las siguientes preguntas.

1. ¿Dónde está situada la República de Cuba?
   a. En el Océano Atlántico
   b. En el Mar Caribe
   c. Al lado de Puerto Rico
2. ¿Qué es el monumento a José Martí?
   a. Una estatua de mármol ubicado *(located)* en el punto más alto de La Habana
   b. La fortificación construida por los españoles
   c. Una estatua ubicada en el Malecón
3. ¿Cuál es otro nombre para la isla de Puerto Rico?
   a. Bacalaíto
   b. El Malecón
   c. La Ciudad Amurallada
4. ¿Qué es Ponce?
   a. Un monumento histórico del Viejo San Juan
   b. La plaza principal de La Habana
   c. La segunda ciudad más grande de Puerto Rico
5. ¿Cuál es el deporte más practicado y popular en la República Dominicana?
   a. La natación
   b. El béisbol
   c. El tenis
6. ¿Cuál es otro nombre para la República Dominicana?
   a. Madre de Todas las Tierras
   b. Faro a Colón
   c. Malecón

Nombre ______________________ Fecha ______________________

¡A ESCRIBIR!

Strategy: Using commands to give directions

If you're traveling in a Spanish-speaking country or city, chances are you might need to ask for directions. In addition, you might even have to give directions! The most important element of explaining to someone how to get from one place to another is accuracy. If you explain your directions clearly and concisely, people will be able to follow them easily.

Here are six basic requirements for giving directions to a place:

1. Choose the easiest route.
2. Be very clear in your directions.
3. Give the directions in chronological order.
4. Use linking expressions such as **Primero...**, **Luego...**, **Después de eso...**, **Entonces...**, **Usted debe...**, **Después...**, and **Finalmente....**
5. Identify clearly visible landmarks such as:

la avenida *avenue*	**el cruce de caminos** *intersection*
el bulevar *boulevard*	**el edificio** *building*
la calle *street*	**el letrero** *sign*
el camino *road*	**el puente** *bridge*
la colina *hill*	**el semáforo** *traffic light*

6. When possible, include a sketch of the route.

Modelo *Para llegar a mi casa del aeropuerto, siga estas indicaciones. Primero, siga la calle del aeropuerto hasta la salida. Doble a la derecha y siga por el bulevar Glenwood dos kilómetros hasta el primer semáforo, donde hay un cruce de caminos. Entonces, doble a la izquierda y siga por el camino Parkers Mill dos kilómetros (pasando debajo de un puente) hasta la calle Lane Allen. En esa calle, doble a la derecha y siga otros dos kilómetros hasta el segundo semáforo. Después, doble a la izquierda en el camino Beacon Hill y siga derecho medio kilómetro hasta el camino Normandy. Doble a la izquierda y vaya a la cuarta casa a la derecha. Allí vivo yo, y ¡allí tiene su casa!*

Task: Giving directions from the airport to a place in town

The Álvarez family is coming from Puerto Rico to visit your city for the first time. They want to know what they should do while there, where they should stay, and of course, where they should go for fun. Write a letter to señor Álvarez describing your city and giving directions for how to get to your favorite place in the city from the closest airport.

Paso 1 Using the strategy above, write out the directions from the airport to your favorite part of the city.

____

____

____

____

Paso 2 Using the directions you wrote above, write out a first draft of the letter and include information about where the Álvarez family should stay and what they should do in your favorite part of the city.

Paso 3 After revising your first draft, write out your second draft below.

____

____

____

____

____

____

____

____

____

____

____

____

____

____

ATAJO 4.0

Functions: Asking for and giving directions; Linking ideas; Expressing distance; Expressing location

Vocabulary: City; Directions and distance; Means of transportation; Metric systems and measurements

Grammar: Verbs: imperative: **usted(es), ser** and **estar, tener,** and **haber**

Nombre ______________________ Fecha ______________________

Autoprueba

WB 9-22 | Viajes Empareja la descripción de la columna de la izquierda con las palabras de la columna de la derecha.

________	**1.** maletas y mochilas	**a.** la aduana
________	**2.** las horas de salida y llegada	**b.** el horario
________	**3.** las personas que viajan	**c.** el equipaje
________	**4.** donde hacen la inspección de las maletas	**d.** los pasajeros
________	**5.** donde los turistas presentan los pasaportes	**e.** el pasaporte
________	**6.** donde los turistas compran sus boletos de viaje	**f.** la inmigración
________	**7.** el documento oficial para entrar en otro país	**g.** la agencia de viajes

WB 9-23 | En el hotel El Sr. Morales tiene que pasar tres noches en un hotel en San Juan y el gerente le cuenta algunos detalles del hotel. Completa su descripción usando palabras de la lista.

aire acondicionado ascensor cómodo cuartos cuatro estrellas
dobles limpios privado recepción sencillas sucios

Este es un hotel de lujo, es decir, de **1.** ______________. En este hotel todos los **2.** ______________ siempre están **3.** ______________ y nunca están **4.** ______________. Según su preferencia, tenemos habitaciones con camas **5.** ______________ o **6.** ______________. Todas tienen baño **7.** ______________. Como esta zona es tropical y normalmente hace mucho calor, todas las habitaciones también tienen **8.** ______________. La mejor habitación está en el octavo piso, pero no se preocupe, tenemos **9.** ______________. Si durante su visita necesita cualquier cosa, por favor llame a la **10.** ______________. Le pueden traer todo lo que Ud. necesite. Creo que Ud. va a estar muy **11.** ______________ en este hotel.

WB 9-24 | ¿Dónde está todo? Mira el mapa. Estás en la avenida Constitución. Completa las oraciones con las preposiciones apropiadas de la lista. No repitas ninguna palabra.

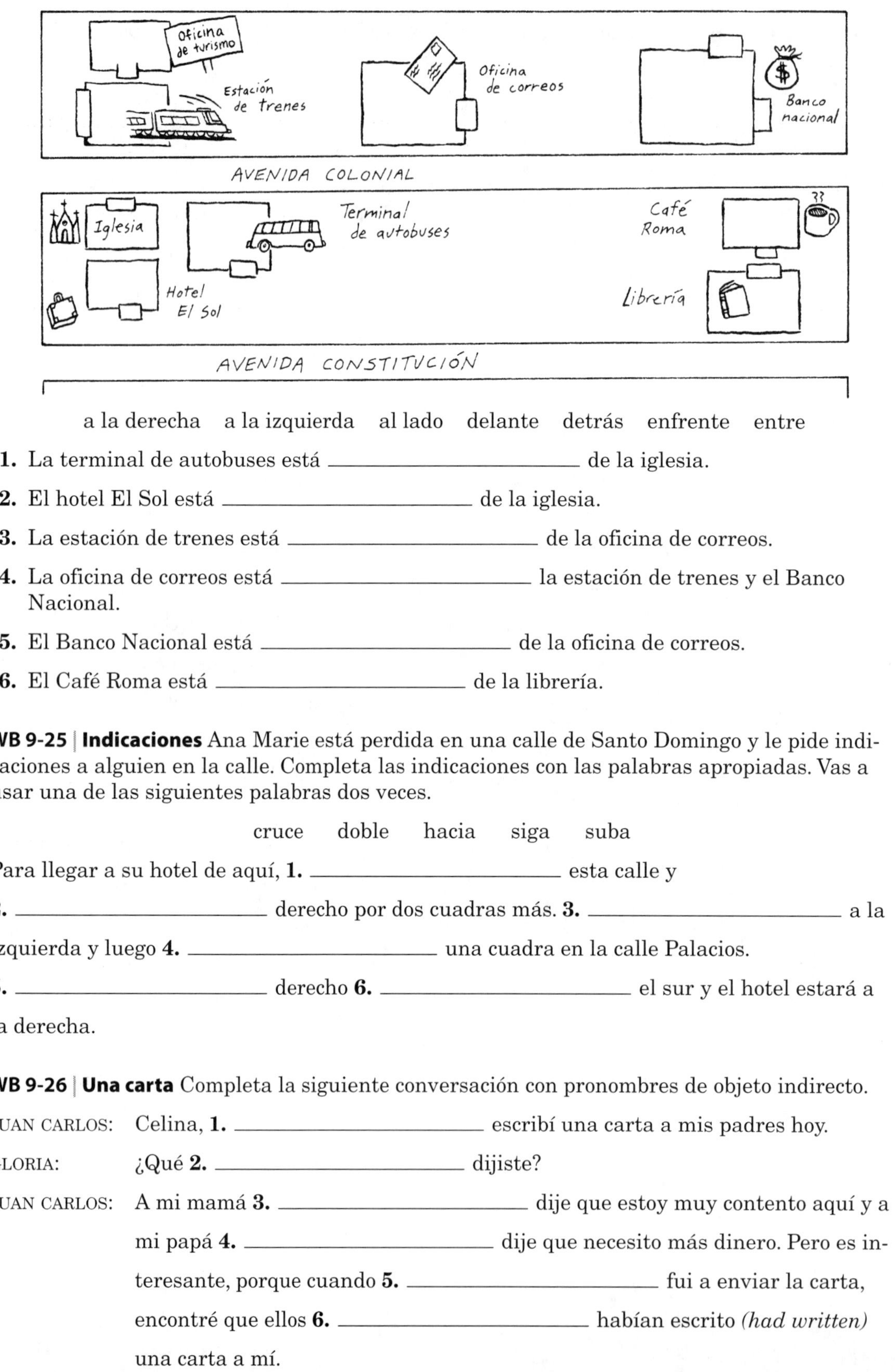

a la derecha   a la izquierda   al lado   delante   detrás   enfrente   entre

1. La terminal de autobuses está ______________ de la iglesia.
2. El hotel El Sol está ______________ de la iglesia.
3. La estación de trenes está ______________ de la oficina de correos.
4. La oficina de correos está ______________ la estación de trenes y el Banco Nacional.
5. El Banco Nacional está ______________ de la oficina de correos.
6. El Café Roma está ______________ de la librería.

WB 9-25 | Indicaciones Ana Marie está perdida en una calle de Santo Domingo y le pide indicaciones a alguien en la calle. Completa las indicaciones con las palabras apropiadas. Vas a usar una de las siguientes palabras dos veces.

cruce   doble   hacia   siga   suba

Para llegar a su hotel de aquí, **1.** ______________ esta calle y **2.** ______________ derecho por dos cuadras más. **3.** ______________ a la izquierda y luego **4.** ______________ una cuadra en la calle Palacios. **5.** ______________ derecho **6.** ______________ el sur y el hotel estará a la derecha.

WB 9-26 | Una carta Completa la siguiente conversación con pronombres de objeto indirecto.

JUAN CARLOS: Celina, **1.** ______________ escribí una carta a mis padres hoy.

GLORIA: ¿Qué **2.** ______________ dijiste?

JUAN CARLOS: A mi mamá **3.** ______________ dije que estoy muy contento aquí y a mi papá **4.** ______________ dije que necesito más dinero. Pero es interesante, porque cuando **5.** ______________ fui a enviar la carta, encontré que ellos **6.** ______________ habían escrito *(had written)* una carta a mí.

Nombre ______________________ Fecha ______________________

GLORIA: ¡Qué coincidencia! ¿Qué **7.** ______________ decían a ti?

JUAN CARLOS: Pues, **8.** ______________ decían que estaban bien y que no **9.** ______________ iban a enviar más dinero. Al final, decidí no mandar **10.** ______________ la carta.

WB 9-27 | Elena, la buena Elena siempre les hace favores a sus amigos. Escribe sus respuestas a las preguntas de sus amigos usando el pronombre de objeto directo e indirecto.

1. Elena, ¿me puedes prestar *(loan)* tu chaqueta azul?

   ____

2. Elena, ¿nos preparas una cena especial?

   ____

3. Elena, ¿nos puedes escribir el ensayo?

   ____

4. Elena, ¿te podemos pasar nuestra tarea?

   ____

5. Elena, ¿le puedes comprar un regalo a Rosa?

   ____

WB 9-28 | ¿Dónde está el banco? Olga sale del mercado y le pide ayuda al dueño. Completa su conversación con un mandato formal de los verbos que están entre paréntesis. **¡OJO!** En algunos casos tienes que usar un pronombre.

OLGA: **1.** ______________ (Perdonar), señor. Por favor, **2.** ______________ (darme) tres tomates más.

DUEÑO: Cómo no, señora. **3.** ______________ (Tomar) Ud. estos. Están muy frescos y dulces.

OLGA: Gracias. **4.** ______________ (Decirme) una cosa, señor. ¿Sabe Ud. si hay un banco cerca de aquí?

DUEÑO: Pues, sí. **5.** ______________ (Salir) del mercado y **6.** ______________ (ir) dos cuadras todo derecho. El banco está a la izquierda.

OLGA: ¡Muchas gracias! **7.** ______________ (Tener) Ud. un buen día.

DUEÑO: Ud. también señora. **8.** ______________ (Volver) pronto. Nos vemos.

Nombre ______________________ Fecha ______________________

10 Las relaciones sentimentales: Honduras y Nicaragua

VOCABULARIO 1 Las relaciones sentimentales

WB 10-1 | Palabras revueltas Pon en orden las letras de las siguientes palabras sobre relaciones sentimentales.

1. samitda: ___ ___ ___ ___ ___ ___ ___
2. tica: ___ ___ ___ ___
3. cirasepaón: ___ ___ ___ ___ ___ ___ ___ ___ ___ ___
4. sader la noma: ___ ___ ___ ___ ___ ___ ___ ___ ___ ___
5. roma: ___ ___ ___ ___
6. promimcoso: ___ ___ ___ ___ ___ ___ ___ ___ ___ ___

WB 10-2 | ¿Qué palabra es? Lee las pistas *(clues)* y escribe las palabras de relaciones sentimentales que se describen.

1. Otro nombre para el amor que demuestran los novios

   ___ ___ ___ ___ ___ ___

2. El viaje que hacen los novios después de casarse

   ___ ___ ___ ___   ___ ___   ___ ___ ___ ___

3. El opuesto al matrimonio

   ___ ___ ___ ___ ___ ___ ___ ___

4. Lo que hacen los novios que no se llevan bien

   ___ ___ ___ ___ ___ ___ ___ ___ ___

5. Decoración utilizada en la ceremonia

   ___ ___ ___ ___

6. Lo que lleva la novia durante la ceremonia

   ___ ___ ___ ___

7. La fase de la relación amorosa justo antes del matrimonio

   ___ ___ ___ ___ ___ ___ ___ ___

8. Nombre para la ceremonia que inicia el matrimonio

   ___ ___ ___ ___

WB 10-3 | La boda de Juan Antonio y María Teresa Carmen está explicándole a su amiga Nuria algo sobre la boda de su hermano Juan Antonio. Para saber cómo fue, completa su descripción con una palabra o frase apropiada de la siguiente lista.

amor	boda	casarse	novia	novios	quería
ramo	de flores	recién casados	rompió	salió	se besaron

Juan Antonio **1.** ______________ con su **2.** ______________ María Teresa por tres años. Ellos están muy contentos ahora, pero no siempre ha sido así. Hace un año María Teresa **3.** ______________ con Juan Antonio porque encontró a otro hombre. Pero después de varios meses, María Teresa se dio cuenta de que **4.** ______________ mucho a mi hermano y ellos se reunieron y decidieron **5.** ______________.

Ellos hicieron muchos planes para el día de la **6.** ______________ y ese día fue fantástico. María Teresa se vistió de blanco y llevó un **7.** ______________ que consistía de rosas rojas, símbolo del **8.** ______________. Mi hermano llevaba un traje elegante y estaba muy guapo. Cuando el ministro les dijo a los **9.** ______________: «ustedes son marido *(husband)* y mujer», ellos **10.** ______________ y salieron de la iglesia. Después, todas fuimos a una recepción en honor de los **11.** ______________. Estoy muy contenta de que todo salió bien con ellos a pesar de sus dificultades.

ESTRUCTURA Y USO 1 Describing recent actions, events, and conditions: The present perfect tense

WB 10-4 | ¡Lo he perdido! Marta ha perdido algo en la universidad. Para saber lo que es, completa la siguiente conversación con formas apropiadas del verbo **haber.**

MARTA: Hola, soy Marta.

CATALINA: Hola, soy Catalina. ¿Qué te **1.** ______________ pasado?

MARTA: **2.** ______________ perdido mi bolsa con mi pasaporte. ¿La **3.** ______________ visto tú por aquí?

CATALINA: Pues, no. Lo siento. No **4.** ______________ visto ninguna bolsa. ¿De dónde eres?

MARTA: Soy de Managua. Mi hermana y yo **5.** ______________ venido a la universidad para estudiar la informática.

CATALINA: ¡Qué bueno! Uds. son nicaragüenses. ¿**6.** ______________ llamado Uds. a la policía?

MARTA: No, nosotras no lo **7.** ______________ hecho todavía. Lo vamos a hacer ahora mismo.

CATALINA: Bien. ¡Buena suerte!

Nombre ______________________ Fecha ______________________

WB 10-5 | Formas verbales Indica la forma correcta del presente perfecto de los siguientes verbos. **¡OJO!** El presente perfecto requiere una forma del verbo **haber** y el participio pasado. Sigue el modelo.

Modelo yo, cantar: *he cantado*

1. yo, hablar: ______________________
2. tú, comer: ______________________
3. él, dormir: ______________________
4. ella, ir: ______________________
5. nosotros, abrir: ______________________
6. vosotros, decir: ______________________
7. ellos, hacer: ______________________
8. ustedes, volver: ______________________
9. yo, escribir: ______________________
10. tú, ver: ______________________

WB 10-6 | Los últimos detalles Linda y su mamá están hablando de la preparación para la boda de Linda. Completa su conversación con la forma correcta del verbo indicado en el presente perfecto. **¡OJO!** Recuerda que varios de los verbos tienen participios irregulares.

LINDA: Bueno, mamá, ¿qué más tenemos que hacer?

MAMÁ: **1.** ¿______________________ (comprar) las invitaciones?

LINDA: Sí, y ya les **2.** ______________________ (mandar) invitaciones a todos los invitados.

MAMÁ: **3.** ¿ ______________________ (pagar) el vestido de boda?

LINDA: Ahhh... Se me olvidó. Y tampoco **4.** ______________________ (hablar) con el sastre *(tailor)* sobre las alteraciones. Y mamá, ¿sabes si papá ya **5.** ______________________ (reservar) su smoking *(tuxedo)*?

MAMÁ: Sí, Linda. ¡No te preocupes! Tu papá ya lo **6.** ______________________ (hacer). ¿No **7.** ______________________ (ver) el recibo?

LINDA: No, mamá. Papá todavía no me lo **8.** ______________________ (traer). Se lo voy a pedir. Bueno, mamá, ¿algo más?

MAMÁ: No, Linda, creo que nosotras **9.** ______________________ (recordar) todo. Ay, a lo mejor queda un detalle. Tu novio, ¿**10.** ______________________ (decir) que quiere casarse contigo?

LINDA: ¡Mamá!

WB 10-7 | ¡Casados ya! Hace dos meses que Miguel y Ana están casados y ahora Ana le escribe una carta a sus abuelos para decirles cómo les va. ¿Qué les ha pasado hasta ahora? Forma oraciones con los siguientes elementos, usando el presente perfecto.

Modelo nosotros / pasarlo bien
Nosotros lo hemos pasado bien.

Queridos abuelos,

1. nosotros / volver / de la luna de miel

   ____

2. la vida de casados / ser / perfecto

   ____

3. cada día / Miguel / decir / que me quiere mucho

   ____

4. nuestros amigos / escribirnos / muchas cartas

   ____

5. nosotros / abrir / una cuenta bancaria

   ____

6. Y, ¿saben qué? / ¡el conejo / morir!

   ____

Con mucho cariño,

Ana y Miguel

ESTRUCTURA Y USO 2 Qualifying actions: Adverbs and adverbial expressions of time and sequencing of events

WB 10-8 | Adverbios Forma adverbios de los siguientes adjetivos. Sigue el modelo.

Modelo frecuente: *frecuentemente*

1. inmediato ____________
2. nervioso ____________
3. regular ____________
4. tranquilo ____________
5. constante ____________
6. rápido ____________

Nombre ______________________ Fecha ______________________

WB 10-9 | Don Juan Berta acaba de conocer a Esteban, el "don Juan" de su residencia universitaria. Ahora le está haciendo preguntas a Cristina sobre cómo es este don Juan. ¿Cómo contesta Cristina? Escribe la respuesta de Cristina, convirtiendo el adjetivo en adverbio.

Modelo ¿Cómo les habla Esteban a las chicas? / paciente
Habla a las chicas pacientemente.

1. ¿Cómo conquista a las chicas Esteban? / fácil
____
2. ¿Cuándo llama a las chicas? / frecuente
____
3. ¿Cómo besa a las chicas? / apasionado
____
4. ¿Cómo corta con las chicas? / rápido
____

WB 10-10 | Las vacaciones de Adolfo Adolfo le escribió un correo electrónico a su *pen pal* sobre sus vacaciones. Termina la carta, rellenando los espacios en blanco con los adverbios apropiados de la siguiente lista.

a veces cada nunca siempre solamente

1. ______________ año voy de vacaciones a las lindas playas de Nicaragua. Cuando era joven, **2.** ______________ iba con mi familia, pero ahora que soy mayor, voy con mi novia. De hecho, prefiero viajar solo con ella; **3.** ______________ invito a nadie más. Normalmente paso dos meses, pero este año **4.** ______________ voy a poder pasar dos semanas. ¡Pero voy a aprovechar el tiempo! **5.** ______________ voy a explorar la selva y después voy a bañarme en el mar y comer fruta fresca.

6. ______________ me gusta pasar tiempo en Managua con algunos de mis amigos, pero este año, con tan poco tiempo, creo que voy a quedarme cerca de la playa y la selva. ¡Sé que lo voy a pasar súper bien!

VOCABULARIO 2 La recepción

WB 10-11 | La recepción ¿Cuáles de las siguientes actividades son parte de una recepción de una boda tradicional en los Estados Unidos? Indica estas actividades con una X.

1. ______ Los novios van de pesca inmediatamente después de la ceremonia.
2. ______ Los invitados felicitan a los novios.
3. ______ La celebración toma lugar en un lugar especial.
4. ______ Los novios se ponen patines y pasean por el salón.
5. ______ La novia les tira su vestido a las chicas solteras.
6. ______ Todos los invitados se visten de gala.
7. ______ El novio pasa la aspiradora.

8. ______ La pareja baila con la música de la orquesta.

9. ______ La pareja entra en el salón y todos los invitados aplauden.

10. ______ Los padres de la novia planchan la ropa.

WB 10-12 | Así se hace Maribel le está contando a su amiga Ángela cómo son las recepciones en su país. Para saber cómo son, completa la descripción con la palabra apropiada de la siguiente lista. **¡OJO!** Tienes que conjugar los verbos en el presente del indicativo.

agarrar aplaudir asistir banquete felicitar orquesta terminar

Después de la ceremonia todos los invitados **1.** ______________ a una fiesta elegante para celebrar el matrimonio. Todo empieza con un brindis para los novios. Después, los invitados toman su champán *(champagne)* y **2.** ______________ a los recién casados.
Generalmente, el **3.** ______________ comienza a las nueve de la noche. Hay todo tipo de comida rica; mientras comen los invitados, la **4.** ______________ toca música moderna y tradicional.
Después de la cena, todos se divierten mucho bailando y charlando hasta muy tarde. Al final, la novia tira su ramo de flores y una chica lo **5.** ______________. Eso significa que ella va a casarse pronto. La fiesta **6.** ______________ cuando los novios se van. Todos **7.** ______________ y los recién casados salen para su luna de miel.

ESTRUCTURA Y USO 3 Talking about future events: Future tense

WB 10-13 | Predicciones Andrés piensa en cómo será su futuro y el futuro de las siguientes personas. Escribe lo que piensa Andrés usando el futuro.

Modelo Yo . . . tomar una clase / trabajar para una organización política el año que viene
Yo tomaré una clase y trabajaré para una organización política el año que viene.

1. Yo . . . ir a Nicaragua para encontrar a Marina / estudiar filosofía con Marina / enamorarme de Marina / olvidarme de mi novia en Honduras

____

____

2. Marina . . . conocerme mejor / asistir a una clase de política contemporánea / querer cambiar de especialidad / decirme que me quiere

____

____

3. El novio de Marina . . . saber que Marina ya no lo quiere / escribirle muchas cartas de amor / hacer muchos esfuerzos para no perderla / tener que encontrar a una nueva novia

____

____

4. Marina y yo . . . irnos de Nicaragua / volver a Honduras / casarnos / tener cuatro hijos

____

____

WB 10-14 | ¿Qué pensará Marina? Marina también está pensando en Andrés y escribe varias de sus predicciones para el futuro. Para saber lo que escribe, completa los párrafos usando el futuro de los verbos apropiados de cada lista.

A

ahorrar tener venir volver

Un día yo **1.** ____________ a Nicaragua. Esta vez mi ex novio Eduardo no **2.** ____________ conmigo. Creo que (yo) **3.** ____________ más dinero que ahora porque mi nuevo novio Andrés y yo lo **4.** ____________ cada semana.

B

divertirse escribir querer visitar

Antes de irme para Managua, yo les **1.** ____________ a mis otros amigos nicaragüenses para decirles que yo los **2.** ____________. Estoy segura de que ellos **3.** ____________ verme y que nosotros **4.** ____________ mucho.

C

haber hacer poder saber ser tomar

Yo **1.** ____________ el viaje en la primavera. En esa temporada **2.** ____________ menos turistas que ahora y todo **3.** ____________ más tranquilo y barato. Yo **4.** ____________ más sobre la política de Nicaragua porque **5.** ____________ más clases. Así **6.** ____________ tener más en común con Andrés.

WB 10-15 | Te haces Walter Mercado Tú te has convertido en el famoso psíquico latino, Walter Mercado, y ahora estás haciendo muchas predicciones para todo el mundo. Escribe tus predicciones.

1. El(La) novio(a) de mi mejor amigo(a) le ____________ (decir) que quiere salir conmigo.
2. Yo ____________ (hacer) un viaje por las Américas.
3. El dueño del lugar donde vivo me ____________ (cancelar) el contrato.
4. Mis padres ____________ (ganar) la lotería.
5. Mis amigos y yo ____________ (mudarnos) a Honduras para vivir.

WB 10-16 | Consulta con el oráculo Carolina decidió preguntarle al oráculo sobre varias de sus predicciones para el futuro. Escribe sus preguntas. **¡OJO!** Recuerda que en las preguntas el sujeto va después del verbo. Sigue el modelo.

Modelo Borat ser presidente de Kazajistán
¿Será Borat presidente de Kazajistán?

1. Hillary Clinton estar al lado de los conservadores
¿____?
2. El Presidente Obama aprender hablar español como nativo
¿____?
3. Las hijas Obama casar con los príncipes *(princes)* Harry y William
¿____?
4. Varios países del mundo aprobar las leyes para permitir el matrimonio entre parejas homosexuales
¿____?
5. Todos los países del mundo llevarse bien
¿____?

ESTRUCTURA Y USO 4 Expressing conjecture or probability: The conditional

WB 10-17 | Si pudiera... Lidia Rodríguez está hablando con su amigo Pedro sobre cómo sería si ella estuviera encargada *(were in charge)* de todas las decisiones importantes de la universidad. Para saber lo que dice, forma oraciones en el condicional usando los elementos dados. Sigue el modelo.

Modelo los estudiantes / no pagar / ninguna matrícula *(tuition)*
Los estudiantes no pagarían ninguna matrícula.

1. los estudiantes / poder / obtener becas *(scholarships)* más fácilmente
____
2. nosotros / no tener que / asistir a clases por la mañana
____
3. haber / fiestas / continuamente
____
4. los profesores / no darles / notas a los estudiantes
____
5. todos los estudiantes / querer / asistir a esta universidad
____

Nombre ______________________ Fecha ______________________

WB 10-18 | Paqui la periodista Paqui es reportera para la sección social de un periódico hispano. Hoy les pide opiniones a varios novios sobre qué harían para tener una boda perfecta. Ayúdale a elaborar la lista de preguntas, rellenando los espacios en blanco con una forma del **condicional** de los verbos indicados.

1. ¿______________ (Tener) Uds. una boda grande o pequeña?
2. ¿Les ______________ (decir) Uds. a los invitados que no quieren regalos extravagantes?
3. ¿ ______________ (Querer) Uds. quedarse hasta el final de la recepción?
4. ¿Les ______________ (gustar) escribir sus propios votos?
5. ¿ ______________ (Saber) los invitados adónde ______________ (tomar) Uds. la luna de miel?

WB 10-19 | Imagínate Patricia soñó *(dreamt)* que el presidente de la compañía Google le dio a ella un puesto en su nueva división en Nicaragua. Es un trabajo garantizado por cinco años con un salario de trescientos mil dólares al año. Se despertó y ahora piensa en cómo sería su vida si su sueño fuera *(were)* realidad. Escribe oraciones con el condicional.

1. Toda mi familia / estar / muy contenta

   ____

2. Yo / mudarse / a Santiago de Chile

   ____

3. Mi familia y yo / le donar / mucho dinero a la gente pobre de Latinoamérica

   ____

4. Mi novio y yo / casarse / en una ceremonia en una playa privada de Chile

   ____

5. Nosotros / no querer volver / a los Estados Unidos

   ____

VIAJEMOS POR HONDURAS Y NICARAGUA

En estos segmentos del video, vas a aprender un poco sobre Nicaragua y Honduras.

WB 10-20 | Cognados En estos segmentos del video vas a escuchar muchos cognados que pueden facilitar tu comprensión del video. Algunos de estos cognados aparecen aquí. Antes de ver los segmentos, trata de pronunciar cada palabra o frase y luego trata de emparejar los cognados con su definición en inglés.

1. ______ inactivo	a. resuscitated (resurrected)
2. ______ reserva natural	b. panoramic
3. ______ silueta	c. hieroglyphics
4. ______ rotondas	d. rotundas
5. ______ resucitado	e. natural reserve
6. ______ panorámica	f. silhouette
7. ______ jeroglíficos	g. inactive

WB 10-21 | Cognados en contexto Mira el video y trata de rellenar los espacios en blanco con el cognado apropiado de la actividad **WB 10-20.**

del segmento sobre Nicaragua:

1. En Managua está la famosa ________________ de Sandino, que es el monumento al líder de la revolución y héroe nacional Augusto César Sandino.
2. La ciudad fue reconstruida después del terremoto de 1974, y hoy vemos ejemplos de su desarrollo urbano, con construcciones como ________________.

del segmento sobre Honduras:

3. Desde el parque Picacho se pueden ver el estadio de fútbol Francisco Morazán y una extensa vista ________________ del centro de la ciudad.
4. La herencia indígena de Honduras tiene su mayor representación en la Escalinata de los ________________, en las ruinas mayas de Copán.

WB 10-22 | Comprensión Después de ver el video otra vez, selecciona la mejor respuesta a las siguientes preguntas.

1. ________________ ¿Cuál de los siguientes volcanes nicaragüenses está inactivo?
   - **a.** Momotombo
   - **b.** Masaya
   - **c.** Mombacho
2. ________________ ¿Quién fue Rubén Darío?
   - **a.** el fundador de Managua
   - **b.** el héroe nacional de Nicaragua
   - **c.** un poeta inmortal del modernismo
3. ________________ ¿Cuál es otro nombre para el país de Nicaragua?
   - **a.** Copán
   - **b.** Junto al agua
   - **c.** El lago bonito
4. ________________ ¿De qué siglo *(century)* es la Basílica de Suyapa en Tegucigalpa?
   - **a.** dieciséis
   - **b.** diecisiete
   - **c.** dieciocho
5. ________________ ¿Cuál es otro nombre para los hondureños?
   - **a.** los orgullosos
   - **b.** los indígenas
   - **c.** los catrachos

Nombre ______________________ Fecha ______________________

¡A ESCRIBIR!

Strategy: Writing a descriptive paragraph

Descriptive paragraphs occur in many contexts. They are often found in works of fiction, such as novels and short stories, but they also appear in newspaper articles, advertising materials, educational publications, and personal letters. A descriptive paragraph contains sentences that describe people, places, things, and/or events.
In this chapter we focus on describing events. To express how often events take place or how often you or others do something, you can use adverbs of frequency such as the following:

a veces	*sometimes*
cada año / todos los años	*each / every year*
dos veces a la semana	*twice a week*
muchas veces	*often*
nunca	*never*
raras veces	*rarely, infrequently*
siempre	*always*
todos los días	*every day*
una vez al mes	*once a month*

You can also modify these expressions to express a wide variety of time frames: **dos veces al mes, tres veces a la semana, cada mes,** and so on.

ATAJO 4.0

Functions: Expressing time relationships; Linking ideas; Talking about habitual actions

Vocabulary: Family members; Leisure; Time expressions

Grammar: Adverbs; Adverb types

Task: Writing a descriptive paragraph

Now you will apply the strategy to describe the activities you do with your "fantasy family."

Paso 1 Begin by assuming that all your dreams have come true. Make a list of all the activities you and your family do now that life is perfect.

____

____

Paso 2 Now think about how frequently you do these activities. Next to each activity, write a phrase describing the frequency. Remember to use the adverbs you learned in your text.

Paso 3 Now write a well-developed paragraph to describe these activities, with whom you do them, and with what frequency. Revise the paragraph and write the second draft below.

____

____

____

____

____

Autoprueba

WB 10-23 | El amor y los novios David y Nidia hablan de su relación. Para saber lo que dicen, completa su conversación con la palabra apropiada de la siguiente lista. **¡OJO!** Si seleccionas un verbo, tienes que conjugarlo. No repitas ninguna palabra.

amor cariño casados enamorados enamorarse llevarse matrimonio noviazgo

DAVID: Mi amor, ¿no es cierto que nuestro **1.** ______________ comenzó el día que nos conocimos?

NIDIA: Sí, cariño, fue **2.** ______________ a primera vista, ¿verdad?

DAVID: Claro, porque **3.** ______________ en un instante.

NIDIA: Tan grande era nuestro **4.** ______________ desde el principio.

DAVID: Ay, cómo recuerdo nuestra primera cita. Me invitaste al cine y luego fuimos a un café.

NIDIA: Sí, ¡y **5.** ______________ tan bien juntos! Estábamos **6.** ______________. ¡Ay!

DAVID: Y al poco tiempo te hice una propuesta de **7.** ______________.

NIDIA: Y cinco años después, ¡todavía estamos **8.** ______________!

WB 10-24 | La boda Mónica le está contando a su amiga cómo son las bodas norteamericanas típicamente. Completa su descripción usando palabras y frases de la siguiente lista. **¡OJO!** Si seleccionas un verbo, es posible que tengas que conjugarlo.

agarrar	aplaudir	banquete	besarse
brindis	casarse	divorciarse	felicitar
luna de miel	novios	orquesta	ramo de flores
recepción	recién casados	separarse	tener lugar

Muchas veces los **1.** ______________ deciden **2.** ______________ en una iglesia. Cuando **3.** ______________ delante del altar, ya están casados. Después de esa ceremonia, los **4.** ______________ salen de la iglesia y todos **5.** ______________. Luego todos salen para la **6.** ______________. A veces estas fiestas **7.** ______________ en un restaurante o en un parque bonito. Allí es típico tener un **8.** ______________ elegante, pero antes de comer alguien les hace un **9.** ______________ a la pareja. Todos los invitados **10.** ______________ a los novios y entonces empiezan a comer. Después de comer, la **11.** ______________ empieza a tocar y todos salen a bailar. Más tarde, la novia tira el **12.** ______________ y una chica lo trata de **13.** ______________. Finalmente, los novios salen para la **14.** ______________ y los otros continúan la fiesta. Con suerte, los novios no **15.** ______________, pero típicamente, el 50 por ciento de los novios **16.** ______________ después de siete años de matrimonio.

Nombre ____________________ Fecha ____________________

WB 10-25 | ¿Qué han hecho? Leonel acaba de volver de un viaje de negocios y quiere saber qué han hecho los diferentes miembros de su familia durante la última semana. ¿Cómo contestan? Forma oraciones completas con los siguiente elementos, usando el presente perfecto.

1. Pablo / leer / tres libros

   ____

2. Teresa y Ángela / ver / una película nueva

   ____

3. mamá y yo / escribir / cartas a la familia

   ____

4. yo / divertirse / con mis amigos

   ____

5. tú / volver / de un viaje largo

   ____

WB 10-26 | Miguel lo hace así ¿Cómo hace Miguel las cosas? Cambia el adjetivo a adverbio y escribe una oración completa para describir cómo hace Miguel las siguiente cosas.

1. leer el periódico / detenido *(careful)*

   ____

2. hablar con las chicas / nervioso

   ____

3. comer / rápido

   ____

4. sacar buenas notas / fácil

   ____

5. ir a fiestas / frecuente

   ____

WB 10-27 | La rutina Arcelia describe su rutina diaria. Completa su descripción con el adverbio apropiado de la siguiente lista.

a veces muchas veces nunca siempre solamente todos los días una vez

1. ________________ me despierto a las 6:00 de la mañana porque tengo muchísimas cosas que hacer en un día típico. **2.** ________________ tengo ganas de volver a dormirme, pero no puedo, así que me levanto en seguida. **3.** ________________ los sábados y domingos puedo levantarme tarde, ya que son mis días de descanso. Cuando me levanto, me preparo rápidamente y en seguida me voy corriendo a la universidad.

4. ________________ voy a un café para tomar un cafecito, pero normalmente no tengo tiempo porque mi primera clase empieza a las 7:30.

5. ________________ pensé que tenía tiempo para el café, pero no lo tenía. Llegué tarde a la clase y el profesor me regañó enfrente de todos. ¡Qué vergüenza!

Después de la clase como el desayuno. **6.** ________________ pierdo el desayuno con mis amigos porque es casi la única oportunidad que tengo para descansar durante todo el día. Después de desayunar voy a mis otras clases y, finalmente, a trabajar. Vuelvo a la casa a las 9:30 de la noche y **7.** ________________ estoy cansada.

WB 10-28 | ¿Cómo lo hago? La novia de Jorge está fuera del país y Jorge quiere mandarle un correo electrónico, pero no sabe hacerlo. Para ayudarlo, escribe las instrucciones para mandar un correo electrónico, usando los adverbios de secuencia que aprendiste en tu libro de texto: **primero, luego, después, entonces** y **finalmente.**

______ Te compras software para el e-mail.

______ Te sacas una cuenta electrónica de Internet.

______ Le pides a tu novia su dirección electrónica.

______ Le envías el mensaje.

______ Puedes escribir el mensaje que quieres mandar.

1. ____
2. ____
3. ____
4. ____
5. ____

Nombre ______________________ Fecha ______________________

WB 10-29 | El primer día Lorena Magaña empieza su primer día como planeadora de bodas *(wedding planner).* Su secretaria le ha dejado el siguiente mensaje para hablar del horario del primer día. Completa el mensaje, rellenando los espacios en blanco con la forma apropiada del futuro de los verbos que están entre paréntesis.

Hola, Lorena:

Hoy tú **1.** ______________ (tener) muchas cosas que hacer. Tu primera reunión **2.** ______________ (comenzar) a las diez y **3.** ______________ (ser) en la oficina de la iglesia. Los novios **4.** ______________ (venir) a buscarte a las nueve y media para acompañarte al hotel. Ellos no **5.** ______________ (saber) que el gerente del hotel **6.** ______________ (querer) saber todas decisiones para la recepción, pero no importa. Tú se lo **7.** ______________ (decir) cuando los acompañes al hotel.

A la una **8.** ______________ (haber) otra reunión con los músicos. Esta no **9.** ______________ (durar) mucho tiempo.

A las tres de la tarde yo te **10.** ______________ (ver) aquí en la oficina. Tenemos que hablar de tu propia boda y creo que **11.** ______________ (poder) hacerlo a esa hora. ¡No te preocupes! Para ti yo **12.** ______________ (hacer) todos los planes, pero solo necesito saber de ti algunos detalles importantes.

Bueno, sé que **13.** ______________ (ser) una planeadora excelente y que en tu primer día te **14.** ______________ (ir) súper bien.

Suerte,

Ana María

WB 10-30 | Puros sueños David y Magali acaban de comprar dos boletos para la lotería. Ahora están conversando sobre sus planes para el dinero que piensan que van a ganar. Completa su conversación usando el condicional de los verbos indicados.

DAVID: ¿Qué **1.** ______________ (hacer) tú con tanto dinero, Magali?

MAGALI: Yo **2.** ______________ (viajar) a todos los países del mundo.

DAVID: Me **3.** ______________ (gustar) acompañarte. **4.** ¿ ______________ (poder) ir yo?

MAGALI: ¡Cómo no! Nosotros **5.** ______________ (salir) inmediatamente después de ganar.

DAVID: ¡Qué bueno! ¿Adónde **6.** ______________ (ir) nosotros primero?

MAGALI: Pues mira, esto lo he pensado bastante. Primero **7.** ______________ (tomar) un avión desde acá hasta Tegucigalpa. **8.** ______________ (pasar) unas semanas viajando por Honduras y, ya que también **9.** ______________ (querer) pasar unas semanas en Nicaragua, después **10.** ______________ (volar) a Buenos Aires.

DAVID: Y después de eso, nosotros **11.** ______________ (tener) que ir a Europa, ¿no?

MAGALI: ¡Claro que sí! ¡Espero que ganemos!

Nombre ______________________ Fecha ______________________

11 El mundo del trabajo: Chile

VOCABULARIO 1 Profesiones y oficios

WB 11-1 | Sopa de palabras Pon en orden las letras de los siguientes nombres de profesiones.

1. dabaogo ______________
2. rloepuequ ______________
3. narquebo ______________
4. ótagarfof ______________
5. enioringe ______________
6. urisaqita ______________
7. ostepridia ______________
8. dorcanot ______________

WB 11-2 | ¿Qué profesión es? Lee las siguientes descripciones y escribe el nombre de la profesión que describe.

1. Traduce textos de un idioma a otro: ______________
2. Protege a los ciudadanos de una ciudad: ______________
3. Puede arreglar el lavabo: ______________
4. Diseña casas y edificios: ______________
5. Escribe programas para computadoras: ______________
6. Médico que cuida los dientes: ______________
7. Supervisor en el lugar de trabajo: ______________
8. Prepara comida en un restaurante ______________

ESTRUCTURA Y USO 1 Making statements about motives, intentions, and periods of time: *Por* vs. *para*

To hear more about **por** and **para,** visit Heinle iRadio at www.cengage.com/spanish/viajes.

WB 11-3 | ¿Por o para? Lee las siguientes oraciones con las preposiciones **por** y **para.** Luego pon la letra de la razón por la que se usa **por** o **para** al lado de la oración.

a. in order to / for the purpose of
b. during
c. through
d. employment
e. opinion
f. on behalf of
g. duration of time
h. cost
i. destination
j. specific time
k. member of a group

______ **1.** Alicia tiene que estudiar para el examen.

______ **2.** Claudio gana $40,00 por hora.

______ **3.** Antonio sale para el trabajo a las 6:00.

______ **4.** Antonio trabaja para Telefónica.

______ **5.** Para Carmela, ser dentista es muy agradable.

______ **6.** Julia iba a trabajar por su amiga ayer.

______ **7.** Juan Carlos trabajó por 30 años.

______ **8.** Compró el CD para Julieta.

______ **9.** Para ser extranjera, Teresita habla español muy bien.

______ **10.** Nidia necesita el artículo para el martes que viene.

WB 11-4 | Entrevista Ernesto es el jefe de una compañía y va a entrevistar a un candidato. Ayúdale con las preguntas. Rellena los espacios en blanco con **por** o **para.**

1. ¿____________ cuántos años ha trabajado Ud.?
2. ¿____________ qué compañías ha trabajado?
3. ____________ Ud., ¿cuál es el mejor lugar en el mundo hispano ____________ trabajar y vivir?
4. ¿Cree Ud. que es difícil ____________ un norteamericano vivir y trabajar en un país extranjero?
5. ¿Cuánto dinero piensa Ud. ganar ____________ hora?
6. ¿____________ cuándo piensas comenzar el nuevo trabajo?

WB 11-5 | ¿Puedes ir? Tita y Sara hacen planes para ir de compras, pero Sara tiene que trabajar. Completa su conversación con la forma apropiada de **por** o **para.**

SARA: ¿Aló?

TITA: Hola, Sara, habla Tita. Oye, ¿quieres ir de compras hoy **1.** ____________ la tarde?

SARA: Sí, me encantaría, pero hoy tengo que trabajar **2.** ____________ Amanda. Está enferma hoy y no puede trabajar.

TITA: ¡Otra vez! Esta es la tercera vez este mes. **3.** ____________ ser una chica tan joven, está enferma muchísimo.

SARA: Ya lo sé. **4.** ____________ mí ya es demasiado, pero ¿qué puedo hacer? Es mi hermanita.

TITA: Bueno, **5.** ¿____________ cuántas horas tienes que trabajar hoy?

SARA: Solo dos o tres. **6.** ¿____________ qué no pasas **7.** ____________ mi casa a las siete de la tarde?

TITA: A las siete va a haber mucho tráfico así que voy a salir **8.** ____________ tu casa a las seis. ¿Sabes qué? ¿Va a estar allí Mónica?

SARA: No lo sé. ¿Qué quieres con Mónica?

Nombre ______________________ Fecha ______________________

TITA: Pues, mi hermano, Carlos, le compró algo **9.** ____________ su cumpleaños, pero le da mucha vergüenza dárselo. Entonces, se lo voy a llevar yo.

SARA: ¡Ay, **10.** ____________ Dios! ¡Esa Mónica tiene a todos los chicos pero locos de verdad!

VOCABULARIO 2 La oficina, el trabajo y la búsqueda de un puesto

WB 11-6 | Una de estas cosas no es como las otras Selecciona la palabra que no va con las otras de su lista.

	a.	b.	c.	d.
1. ________	**a.** fax	**b.** fotocopiadora	**c.** sueldo	**d.** computadora
2. ________	**a.** solicitud	**b.** impresora	**c.** candidato	**d.** currículum
3. ________	**a.** jubilarse	**b.** puesto	**c.** entrevista	**d.** beneficios
4. ________	**a.** reunión	**b.** empresa	**c.** sala de conferencias	**d.** llenar
5. ________	**a.** contratar	**b.** correo electrónico	**c.** solicitar	**d.** entrevista

WB 11-7 | ¡Un buen trabajo! Carolina Corral le escribe una carta a su hermana Tita para decirle un poco sobre lo que está haciendo su hijo, Jorge. Completa la carta rellenando los espacios en blanco con una palabra apropiada de la siguiente lista. **¡OJO!** Tienes que conjugar algunos de los verbos en el pretérito.

beneficios	candidato	contratar	correo electrónico
currículum	empresa	entrevista	jubilarse
llamar	llenar	pedir un aumento	puesto
reunirse	solicitud	sueldo	tiempo completo

Hola Tita,

Espero que estés bien (*you are well*) en todo. Aquí te cuento que mi querido Jorgito acaba de graduarse de la universidad y ahora busca trabajo con una **1.** ____________ internacional. La semana pasada encontró un **2.** ____________ con AT&T en el campo de telecomunicaciones.

Ya que las telecomunicaciones son su especialidad, Jorge va a ser un buen **3.** ____________ para el trabajo. Jorge **4.** ____________ a la compañía por teléfono y pidió una **5.** ____________.

Se la mandaron inmediatamente y en seguida (*right away*) él la **6.** ____________ y se la mandó de vuelta. Y, ¡ahora quieren hacerle una **7.** ____________!

Es un trabajo de **8.** ____________, es decir, cinco días a la semana desde las 8:00 de la mañana hasta las 6:00 de la tarde. Tal vez va a ser difícil, pero la compañía ofrece muy buenos **9.** ____________. Le van a pagar los seguros médicos privados y el **10.** ____________ es relativamente alto para un principiante (*beginner*): ¡ofrecen 20.000 pesos al año! Jorge dice que después de su primer año, si todo va bien, él puede **11.** ____________. También dice que la persona que antes hacía este trabajo acaba de **12.** ______________ y él, al final de su carrera de 20 años con la compañía, ganaba 60.000 pesos al año. Jorge va a tener que viajar mucho, pero cuando sea (*whenever*) puedo mandarle algún **13.** ______________ para estar en contacto con él.

Jorge quiere prepararse bien, así que hoy va a **14.** ______________ con su consejero y él le va a ayudar a pulir (*polish*) su **15.** ______________. Jorge está súper preocupado porque quiere este trabajo, pero yo sé que AT&T lo va a **16.** ______________. Claro, es mi hijo, así que ¡es perfecto!

Un abrazo fuerte y un besito,

Carolina

ESTRUCTURA Y USO 2 Expressing subjectivity and uncertainty: The subjunctive mood

To hear more about the **subjunctive mood,** visit Heinle iRadio at www.cengage.com/spanish/viajes.

WB 11-8 | El diario ¿Qué encontró Andrés en el diario de Laura cuando lo leyó? Para saberlo, lee los siguientes pensamientos de Laura. Nota que cada oración usa el subjuntivo. Escribe el verbo que está en el subjuntivo y escoge la letra de la razón por qué se usa en cada caso. Sigue el modelo. Al final, indica lo que descubre Tomás.

Modelo Quiero que Tomás limpie la casa más.
limpie / a (volition)

a. volition **b.** negation **c.** doubt **d.** emotion

1. Dudo que la novia de Tomás lo quiera. ______

2. Siento que la novia de Tomás tenga otra novio. ______

3. Estoy muy contenta de que Tomás trabaje conmigo. ______

4. No hay otra mujer que conozca mejor a Tomás que yo. ______

5. Estoy muy triste que Tomás no sepa cómo es su novia. ______

6. El siquiatra recomienda que yo hable con Tomás sobre mis sentimientos. ______

7. Es imposible que yo le diga a Tomás cómo me siento. Tengo demasiado miedo. ______

8. ______ ¿Qué descubre Tomás al leer el diario de Laura?

a. que Laura va a jubilarse

b. que Laura va a divorciarse de su esposo

c. que a Laura no le gusta su trabajo

d. que Laura está enamorada de Tomás

Nombre ______________________ Fecha ______________________

WB 11-9 | Los consejos Después de descubrir el secreto de Laura, Tomás le pide consejos a su jefe. ¿Qué consejos le da? Selecciona el consejo más lógico en cada caso. Sigue el modelo.

Modelo _a_ a. Recomiendo que ya no hables con Laura en el trabajo.
b. Es necesario que consultes con el médico.

1. _______ **a.** Es necesario que consultes con la jefe de Laura.
b. Estoy contento que quieras ser arquitecto.

2. _______ **a.** Dudo que la fotocopiadora no funcione.
b. La compañía no permite que sus empleados tengan relaciones amorosas.

3. _______ **a.** Es probable que Laura cambie de trabajo.
b. No creo que debas comprarle flores.

4. _______ **a.** Recomiendo que dejes de leer su diario.
b. No es cierto que la nueva candidata sea más bonita que Laura.

WB 11-10 | Situaciones Tus amigos te piden ayuda con varias situaciones. Lee cada situación y escoge el consejo más lógico en cada caso.

1. _______ Un amigo quiere estudiar en Chile el próximo año. El problema es que no ha ahorrado suficiente dinero y necesita 1.000 dólares más. ¿Qué sugieres que haga?
a. Recomiendo que te levantes más temprano.
b. Insito en que pidas un préstamo.
c. Prohíbo que pagues sus facturas por los siguientes tres meses.

2. _______ Una amiga tuya acaba de cortar con su novio. Dice que piensa en él todo el día y no sabe qué hacer. ¿Qué recomendación le das?
a. Prefiero que le ofrezcas dinero para que sea tu novio.
b. Deseo que solicites un nuevo puesto de trabajo.
c. Recomiendo que busques otro novio.

3. _______ Dos amigos tuyos necesitan un lugar donde vivir porque acaban de echarlos *(kick them out)* de su propio apartamento y ahora quieren vivir contigo. ¿Qué recomendación les das?
a. Prefiero que comiencen a buscar apartamentos baratos.
b. Deseo que saquen dinero del cajero automático.
c. No quiero que se diviertan.

WB 11-11 | ¡Tantos consejos! Hoy Ramón va a dejar su trabajo y todos sus amigos quieren darle consejos. ¿Qué le dicen? Para saberlo, rellena los espacios en blanco con la forma apropiada del verbo en el presente del subjuntivo.

1. Antonia recomienda que Ramón le _______________ (escribir) una carta a su jefe.
2. Tomás quiere que Ramón _______________ (hablar) directamente con su jefe.
3. María Dolores prefiere que Ramón no _______________ (venir) al trabajo hoy.
4. Carmen quiere que Ramón le _______________ (dar) una semana más al jefe antes de dejar el puesto.
5. José insiste en que Ramón no _______________ (dejar) el puesto y que simplemente _______________ (pedir) un aumento.

WB 11-12 | Marimandona Gloria es la jefa de una compañía y siempre les dice a sus empleados que hagan algo. Luz Consuelo le está contando a un amigo qué les dice su jefa. Forma oraciones completas con los elementos dados. **¡OJO!** Tienes que usar el presente del subjuntivo en la frase subordinada. Sigue el modelo.

Modelo Gloria / querer / Juan Carlos y Antonio / traerle café / todas las mañanas
Gloria quiere que Juan Carlos y Antonio le traigan café todas las mañanas.

1. Gloria / insistir en / todos los empleados / trabajar / 10 horas al día

____

2. Gloria / no permitir / Magaly y yo / usar / el correo electrónico

____

3. Gloria / prohibir / nosotros / hacerle / preguntas

____

4. Gloria / no querer / yo / divertirme / durante las horas de trabajo

____

5. Gloria / mandar / Alejandro / servirle / el almuerzo / todos los días

____

WB 11-13 | Tertulia Estás en el café donde Cecilia, Felipe y otros amigos se reúnen todos los días. Cada uno expresa sus deseos y tú los escuchas. ¿Qué dicen? Rellena los espacios en blanco con la forma correcta de los verbos indicados. Tienes que decidir entre el presente del indicativo y el presente del subjuntivo.

1. Yo ______________ (insistir) en que la policía ______________ (ser) más justa.
2. Javier ______________ (desear) que el presidente ______________ (saber) más de las necesidades de la gente.
3. Felipe ______________ (desear) que ______________ (haber) más trabajos para todos.
4. Cecilia ______________ (recomendar) que tú no ______________ (dormirse) mientras hablamos.
5. Nosotros ______________ (esperar) que tú ______________ (ir) de vacaciones más a menudo.
6. Felipe y Cecilia ______________ (preferir) que todos ______________ (estar) felices por toda la vida.
7. Ellos ______________ (querer) que no ______________ (tener) que trabajar tanto.

Nombre ______________________ Fecha ______________________

WB 11-14 | ¡Qué horror! Tere tiene que cuidar a su primo, un niño travieso *(rascal)*. Decide mandarle un correo electrónico a su mamá para decirle lo que está haciendo su hijo. Rellena los espacios en blanco con la forma apropiada del verbo que está entre paréntesis. Tienes que decidir si necesitas usar el infinitivo o el presente del subjuntivo. **¡OJO!** Solo es necesario usar el subjuntivo cuando hay un cambio de sujeto.

Hola Lupe,

Te cuento que ahora quiero **1.** ______________ (matar) a tu hijo. Manuel insiste en no **2.** ______________ (acostarse) y no sé qué hacer. Deseo que Manuel **3.** ______________ (dejar) de jugar con sus juguetes porque ya es demasiado tarde, pero prefiere que nosotros **4.** ______________ (jugar) más. De hecho, insiste en que nosotros **5.** ______________ (seguir) jugando. No deseo **6.** ______________ (ser) antipática, pero te juro que ¡este niño me tiene loca! Espero que tú **7.** ______________ (poder) ayudarme. Me interesa saber qué recomiendas que yo **8.** ______________ (hacer) con este niño travieso. Por favor, ¡contéstame pronto!

Tere

VIAJEMOS POR CHILE

En este video, vas a aprender un poco sobre Chile.

WB 11-15 | Geografía Mira el mapa y responde a las siguientes preguntas sobre Chile.

1. ¿Qué letra corresponde al país de Chile? ______________
2. ¿Cuáles son los tres países vecinos de Chile? ______________

   ____

   ____

WB 11-16 | Cognados En el video vas a escuchar muchos cognados que pueden facilitar tu comprensión del video. Algunos de estos cognados aparecen aquí. Antes de ver el segmento, trata de pronunciar cada palabra o frase y luego trata de emparejar los cognados con su definición en inglés.

1. ______ centro financiero	**a.** teleferic (tram)
2. ______ patriota	**b.** constructions (buildings)
3. ______ exhiben (exhibir)	**c.** financial center
4. ______ construcciones	**d.** exhibit
5. ______ teleférico	**e.** patriot

WB 11-17 | Cognados en contexto Mira el video otra vez y trata de rellenar los espacios en blanco con el cognado apropiado de la actividad **WB 11-16.**

1. Santiago reúne barrios tradicionales, ______________ antiguas y modernos edificios vanguardistas.
2. La Plaza de Armas es un lugar agradable para pasear y admirar los cuadros *(paintings)* que ______________ los artistas.
3. Otro gran atractivo es el ______________.

WB 11-18 | Comprensión Después de ver el video otra vez, decide si las siguientes oraciones son **ciertas** o **falsas.**

	cierto	falso
1. Santiago es la capital de Chile.	☐	☐
2. La avenida principal de Santiago se llama Mapocho.	☐	☐
3. La ciudad de Santiago tiene un metro.	☐	☐
4. Los edificios de Santiago reflejan sus muchas influencias indígenas.	☐	☐
5. El presidente de Chile vive en un palacio muy elegante.	☐	☐
6. En la Plaza de Armas hay un monumento a Simón Bolívar.	☐	☐
7. Para la gente joven el Palacio de la Moneda es un destino muy popular.	☐	☐

Nombre ____________________ Fecha ____________________

¡A ESCRIBIR!

Strategy: Writing from an idea map

An idea map is a tool for organizing your ideas before you begin developing them in a composition. In this section you are going to use an idea map to write a paragraph about the personal qualities that make you an ideal employee. Using an idea map will help you organize your thoughts about this topic before you write about it.

Writing task: Writing about what makes you an ideal employee

Paso 1 Spend 10 minutes thinking about the personal qualities that make you a good employee. Write each of these qualities down on a piece of paper. Do not worry about grammar or spelling at this point. Just get your ideas on paper.

Paso 2 Try to categorize the ideas you have just written. For example, did you mention information about your character? About your professional experience? About your academic history? These categories can help you to organize your paragraph.

Paso 3 For each of your qualities, draw a line to a space on the paper where you can write an example that demonstrates this quality. For example, if you mentioned that you have studied in one of the best universities in the country, write the name of the university in the space. These examples will help form the content of your paragraph.

Paso 4 Look at the map you have drawn and write a sentence that summarizes all the information you have included. This will be the topic sentence of your paragraph. An example: **Tanto mi experiencia profesional como mi preparación académica me hacen el (la) empleado(a) ideal.**

Paso 5 Write your paragraph following the organization of your map.

Paso 6 After writing a first draft, review the grammar and spelling and then write a second draft on the next page.

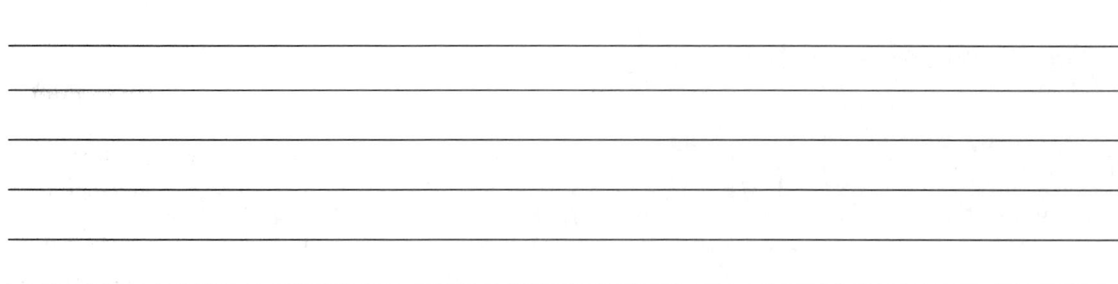

ATAJO 4.0

Functions: Expressing hopes and aspirations; Expressing intention
Vocabulary: Professions, trades, working conditions
Grammar: Verbs: present; Verbs: subjunctive

Nombre ______________________ Fecha ______________________

Autoprueba

WB 11-19 | ¿Qué debe hacer? Ernesto está un poco confundido sobre su futura carrera. Quiere hacerlo todo. Ahora está describiendo lo que le gusta hacer. Para cada una de sus descripciones, escribe el nombre de la profesión que describe.

1. Me gusta dibujar y diseñar edificios.

   ____

2. Me gusta cortar pelo.

   ____

3. Me encantan los números.

   ____

4. Quiero escribir artículos interesantes.

   ____

5. Me interesa escribir programas de software.

   ____

6. Quiero enseñar en una escuela.

   ____

7. Me encantan las lenguas.

   ____

8. Quiero proteger a la gente.

   ____

9. Me interesa analizar los problemas de la gente.

   ____

10. Me fascinan los dientes.

   ____

WB 11-20 | Solicitando trabajo Juan Antonio trabaja para un servicio de empleos. Hoy le está explicando a Ana María los pasos que tiene que seguir para conseguir un buen puesto. Para saber lo que dice, rellena los espacios en blanco con la palabra apropiada de la lista.

beneficios	computadora	contratar	currículum
despedir	empleados	entrevista	fotocopias
impresora	imprimir	jubilarte	llamar
proyectos	solicitar	solicitud	sueldo
tiempo completo	tiempo parcial		

Si vas a **1.** ______________ un puesto, lo primero que tienes que hacer es actualizar *(to update)* tu **2.** ______________. Tienes que escribirlo en la **3.** ______________ e **4.** ______________ el documento en un papel muy fino. Recomiendo una **5.** ______________ láser. Después, tienes que hacer muchas **6.** ______________, porque lo vas a mandar a muchas compañías.

Si encuentras un trabajo que te interese, tienes que pedir una **7.** ______________ de la compañía. Creo que debes **8.** ________________ por teléfono para pedirla. Así vas a tener tu primera oportunidad de impresionar a los empleados de la compañía. Si les caes bien, pueden ofrecerte una **9.** ________________ inmediatamente.

Si te invitan a la compañía, vístete bien. Lleva un traje azul o negro. Ese día te van a explicar mejor el puesto y los **10.** ________________ que vas a tener que llevar a cabo.

También te van a describir los **11.** ________________ que les ofrecen a los **12.** ________________. Ese no es el momento de hablar del **13.** ________________. Si la compañía decide que te quiere **14.** ________________, te lo van a decir y entonces puedes hablar de dinero.

Antes de aceptar el trabajo, tienes que establecer si es un puesto de **15.** ________________ o de **16.** ________________. También vas a querer hablar más de los beneficios. Vas a querer saber cuál es la edad para **17.** ________________, y vas a querer saber qué seguros ofrecen si te tienen que **18.** ________________.

WB 11-21 | De vacaciones Marta ha estado de vacaciones y ahora ha vuelto a su oficina. Completa su conversación con Elena. Rellena los espacios en blanco con las preposiciones **por** o **para.**

MARTA: ¿Sabes qué, Elena? La semana pasada estuve en un crucero y pasamos **1.** ________________ el canal de Panamá. ¡Fue fantástico! Regresé anoche **2.** ________________ la tarde.

ELENA: ¡Que bueno, Marta! **3.** ¿________________ cuánto tiempo estuviste en el crucero?

MARTA: Fue un crucero de catorce días. No te diste cuenta de que yo no estaba aquí.

ELENA: Ay, Marta, lo siento, pero no. Tuve que preparar un informe **4.** ________________ el jefe y él lo quería **5.** ________________ hoy. No noté nada porque estaba trabajando como loca.

MARTA: Ay, sí, Héctor, el jefe horrible. **6.** ________________ ser padre de dos hijos tan simpáticos, es un hombre demasiado antipático. Pues, dime, ¿terminaste?

ELENA: Sí, casi. Solo hace falta sacar una fotocopia, pero la máquina está descompuesta. ¿No hay otra **7.** ________________ aquí?

MARTA: Sí, en la oficina de Juan. Pero antes de irte, compré este regalito **8.** ________________ ti. Si no te gusta, selecciona otro. Compré un montón de cosas en el Caribe **9.** ________________ muy poco dinero.

ELENA: Bueno, gracias. Pues, ahora, ¿qué vas a hacer?

MARTA: Me siento un poco cansada todavía. Creo que voy **10.** ________________ la casa para descansar. No le digas nada a Héctor.

ELENA: No, no le digo nada. ¡Adiós!

MARTA: Chao.

Nombre ______________________ Fecha ______________________

WB 11-22 | El amor y los negocios Mientras trabajas en la computadora de un colega de trabajo, encuentras el siguiente correo electrónico que alguien le escribió a un hombre que trabaja en la compañía rival. Selecciona los verbos apropiados de la lista para acabar el correo. Conjuga los verbos en el presente del subjuntivo.

divertirse enamorarse escribir ir llamar mandar mirar pensar perder tener

Querido amor:

Gracias por tu mensaje. También he pensado mucho en ti. Quiero que me **1.** ______________ más correos electrónicos y que me **2.** ______________ por teléfono a veces. Espero que **3.** ______________ un buen día hoy, y que no te **4.** ______________ ninguna otra mujer. También prefiero que tú no **5.** ______________ en otras mujeres. ¡Sabes que soy muy celosa! Sabes que te quiero mucho y espero con todo el corazón que tú **6.** ______________ de mí. Sé que tu jefe no quiere que sus empleados **7.** ______________ mucho tiempo con los correos electrónicos, pero te pido que me **8.** ______________ por lo menos uno al día y así voy a saber que estás pensando en mí. Quiero invitarte a salir el viernes que viene. Quiero que nosotros **9.** ______________ al nuevo restaurante caribeño y que **10.** ______________ mucho.

Espero verte muy pronto.

Con todo mi cariño,

Paula

WB 11-23 | Entre amigos Completa la siguiente conversación entre dos colegas del trabajo. Rellena los espacios en blanco con una forma apropiada del verbo indicado. Tienes que decidir entre el infinitivo y el presente de subjuntivo.

LUIS: Tengo ganas de descansar un poco, Jorge. Quiero **1.** ______________ (salir) a tomar algo. ¿Quieres **2.** ______________ (venir) conmigo al Coyote Pub?

JORGE: No, prefiero que nosotros **3.** ______________ (seguir) trabajando un poco más. Solo nos queda una hora más.

LUIS: Tienes razón, pero quiero que nosotros **4.** ______________ (trabajar) rápidamente para así terminar temprano.

JORGE: Bueno, pero después de terminar no quiero **5.** ______________ (ir) al Coyote. Mi esposa insiste en que yo siempre **6.** ______________ (volver) a casa después del trabajo. Así que prefiero que tú me **7.** ______________ (acompañar) a mi casa para tomar algo. ¿Qué te parece?

LUIS: Pues, está bien. Entonces te acompaño.

Nombre ______________________ Fecha ______________________

12 El medio ambiente y las políticas ambientales: Costa Rica y Panamá

VOCABULARIO 1 La geografía rural y urbana

WB 12-1 | Palabras revueltas Usa las pistas y pon las letras en orden para revelar las palabras de geografía rural y urbana.

1. Lugar donde usas tu carro: acaterrer ______________________.
2. La subes y bajas: licona ______________________.
3. Un ritmo rápido de la vida: dolarecea ______________________.
4. Mucha población en una zona pequeña: andes ______________________.

WB 12-2 | ¿Una vida tranquila? Completa los perfiles *(profiles)* de las siguientes personas, rellenando los espacios en blanco con las palabras apropiadas de la lista.

agricultor arroyo basura bellos bosque colinas cultiva

finca metrópolis rascacielos ruido tierra transporte público

1. Juan Carlos es ______________________. Trabaja en el campo cultivando la ______________________.
2. María Teresa vive cerca de Chicago. No tiene que batallar el tráfico porque usa el sistema de ______________________, pero sí tiene que aguantar *(put up with)* el ______________________ y la ______________________, es decir, los problemas típicos de la vida en la ______________________.
3. Manuel Antonio y Ana Lisa viven en una ______________________ donde tienen muchos animales. Desde la ventana de la casa pueden ver toda la naturaleza del lugar. Al lado de la casa pasa un ______________________ donde se bañan en los días calurosos *(warm)*. Los fines de semana, ellos andan en bicicleta y andan por las ______________________ altas donde se cultiva café.
4. Francisco Javier es accionista y vive en un apartamento en un ______________________ de la ciudad de Nueva York. El edificio está al lado de un parque que tiene árboles muy ______________________. El apartamento tiene un balcón donde él ______________________ flores.

WB 12-3 | Geografía Lee las pistas y escribe la palabra de geografía que describe.

1. La causa de mucho ruido urbano: el ______________________
2. Cuerpo de agua parecido a un río: el ______________________
3. Demasiada gente concentrada en una metrópolis: la ______________________

4. Lo que ya no se usa y se tira: la ______________________

5. Echar agua a las plantas: ______________________

6. La Amazonia es una ______________________

7. Sin problemas o complicaciones: ______________________

8. Autobuses, metros y trenes son formas de ______________________ público.

9. Lugar donde se producen varios productos: una ______________________

10. Lugar donde se cultivan plantas: una ______________________

11. Edificios altísimos: los ______________________

12. La persona que cultiva la tierra: el ______________________

13. La persona que trabaja en el campo: el ______________________

14. Destinación popular para una luna de miel: la ______________________

ESTRUCTURA Y USO 1

Expressing emotion and opinions: Subjunctive following verbs of emotion, impersonal expressions, and *ojalá*

To hear more about **the subjunctive**, visit Heinle iRadio at www.cengage.com/spanish/viajes.

WB 12-4 | Emociones ¿Qué opinan los estudiantes de la clase de la profesora Ramírez sobre el medio ambiente y el futuro? Selecciona la forma apropiada del verbo que está entre paréntesis.

1. Espero que los agricultores (cultivan / cultiven) más hierbas naturales.

   ____

2. Es importante que todos (conservan / conserven) los recursos naturales.

   ____

3. Me preocupa que nosotros no (tratamos / tratemos) bien la tierra.

   ____

4. Es ridículo que (hay / haya) tanta basura en las calles.

   ____

WB 12-5 | Consejería Trabajas para un consejero y hoy te pide que le ayudes con los consejos que les va a dar a sus clientes. Selecciona el consejo más lógico para cada caso.

1. ______ Carlos quiere visitar un lugar bello y tranquilo.
   a. Es necesario que vaya al bosque de Monteverde.
   b. Es mejor que visite la metrópolis.

2. ______ Alicia busca una alternativa al coche porque no le gusta el tráfico.
   a. Es importante que deje de trabajar.
   b. Es lógico que tome el transporte público.

3. _____ A Adolfo y Érika les preocupa que no llevan una vida tranquila.
a. Es posible que tengan miedo de cultivar plantas.
b. Es necesario que no trabajen tanto.

4. _____ A Silvia le molesta que sus vecinos tiren tanta basura a la calles.
a. Es importante que se queje del problema con sus vecinos.
b. Es ridículo que le moleste la basura.

WB 12-6 | La primera visita a Costa Rica ¿Qué piensan Luis y Ana de Costa Rica después de su primer día en el país? Completa su conversación con la forma apropiada del presente del subjuntivo del verbo que está entre paréntesis.

ANA: ¡Es increíble este país! ¿No te parece, Luis?

LUIS: Sí, Ana. ¡Qué bueno que nosotros **1.** ______________ (estar) aquí y no en Atlanta!

ANA: Me alegro de que el lugar **2.** ______________ (ser) tan bonito y tranquilo.

LUIS: Tranquilo, sí. Es increíble que acá en San José, la capital, no **3.** ______________ (haber) mucho tráfico ni mucho ruido.

ANA: Es cierto. Me sorprende a mí que en un lugar tan grande, la ciudad no **4.** ______________ (tener) muchos problemas de sobrepoblación, como la contaminación, el tráfico, la basura, etcétera.

LUIS: De acuerdo. Es muy interesante eso porque vivimos en una ciudad más pequeña pero nos quejamos siempre de que la gente no **5.** ______________ (respetar) el medio ambiente. Es una lástima que todo el mundo no **6.** ______________ (poder) ser como Costa Rica.

ANA: Bueno, Luis, es imposible que todo el mundo **7.** ______________ (ajustarse) *(to adjust itself)* al modelo de Costa Rica. Pero de todas formas, sería *(it would be)* una situación ideal.

LUIS: Pues, sí. Oye, mañana es necesario que nosotros **8.** ______________ (hacer) el tour por el bosque nuboso Monteverde. ¿Está bien?

ANA: Sí, pero ¿por qué es necesario hacerlo mañana?

LUIS: Pues, mañana es viernes, y si no lo hacemos mañana es posible que el sábado no **9.** ______________ (ir) a poder hacerlo porque va a haber mucha gente.

ANA: Tienes razón, pero entonces es importante que tú **10.** ______________ (llamar) ahora para hacer la reserva.

LUIS: Bueno, la voy a hacer ahora mismo.

WB 12-7 | Una reunión de Greenpeace Estás en una reunión de Greenpeace y todos los miembros están expresando sus opiniones sobre varios temas importantes. Para saber lo que dicen, forma oraciones con los elementos dados. Recuerda que solamente los verbos en la frase subordinada van a estar en el presente del subjuntivo.

Modelo Yo / sentir / algunas de nuestras actividades / ser / radicales
Yo siento que algunas de nuestras actividades sean radicales.

1. Nosotros / tener miedo de / nuestros esfuerzos / no tener éxito / en este caso

   ____

2. Javier / esperar / nuestro grupo / conservar / el medio ambiente

   ____

3. Ojalá / el gobierno / nos apoyar

   ____

4. Es una lástima / las grandes compañías / no hacer / más inversiones «verdes»

   ____

5. Es ridículo / la gente / tener miedo / de nosotros

   ____

6. Nosotros / sentir / mucha gente / no entender / los objetivos de Greenpeace

   ____

VOCABULARIO 2 La conservación y la explotación

WB 12-8 | Problemas y soluciones Identifica cuáles son problemas ambientales y cuáles son soluciones. Pon las letras con su categoría correcta.

Problemas ambientales: ______________________________

Soluciones: ______________________________

a. la destrucción de la capa de ozono
b. explotar la energía solar
c. el desperdicio
d. la contaminación del aire
e. reciclar productos de plástico, metal, vidrio *(glass)* y papel
f. la reforestación
g. desarrollar métodos alternativos de transporte público
h. la destrucción de los bosques
i. la escasez de recursos naturales
j. acabar con la contaminación de las grandes fábricas

Nombre ______________________ Fecha ______________________

WB 12-9 | Una clase de ecología Jorge acaba de tomar una clase de ecología y dice que la clase le ha cambiado la vida. ¿Cómo ha cambiado Jorge? Completa el siguiente párrafo con la palabra apropiadas de la lista para saberlo.

capa de ozono conservar contaminación energía solar escasez medio ambiente naturaleza proteger reciclar recursos naturales resolver transporte público

Antes de tomar la clase de ecología yo nunca pensaba en la **1.** ______________.
Nunca me preocupaban los problemas del **2.** ______________, como la **3.** ______________ de petróleo o la destrucción de la **4.** ______________.
Sin embargo, en la clase aprendí que cada persona tiene que **5.** ______________ nuestros **6.** ______________ y que tenemos que **7.** ______________ el aire y la tierra. Ahora sé que tengo que hacer mi parte para **8.** ______________ nuestros problemas ambientales. Voy a **9.** ______________ todos los productos de plástico y de papel que uso en mi casa para evitar el desperdicio. También, voy a tratar de usar **10.** ______________ para calentar mi piscina. Finalmente, siempre que sea posible, voy a tomar el autobús o cualquier otra forma de **11.** ______________ para así no contribuir a la **12.** ______________ del aire. Sé que yo solo no puedo cambiar el mundo, pero en la clase aprendí que puedo hacer mi parte para cambiarlo.

ESTRUCTURA Y USO 2

Expressing doubts or uncertainty; hypothesizing and anticipated actions: The subjunctive with verbs or expressions of doubt and uncertainty; adjective clauses, and time clauses

To hear more about **the subjunctive,** visit Heinle iRadio at www.cengage.com/spanish/viajes.

WB 12-10 | ¿Qué hacemos ahora? Luis y Ana todavía están en Costa Rica y están planeando cómo quieren pasar los próximos días de vacaciones. Para saber lo que dicen, completa su conversación con la forma apropiada de los verbos que están entre paréntesis. **¡OJO!** Tienes que decidir si el verbo debe estar en el presente del indicativo subjuntivo.

LUIS: Ana, mañana creo que nosotros **1.** ______________ (deber) ir al Parque Nacional Volcán Poás. Tomás y María también van mañana. ¿Qué te parece?

ANA: Bueno, no pienso que ellos **2.** ______________ (ir) mañana. Me dijeron que iban a otro lugar. Pienso que **3.** ______________ (ser) mejor ir a Puntarenas mañana. Allí es donde está el Parque Nacional Palo Verde.

LUIS: No creo que **4.** ______________ (estar) allí el Palo Verde. En Puntarenas pienso que **5.** ______________ (poder) visitar las playas y tal vez el parque de Manuel Antonio.

ANA: Ay, Manuel Antonio. Sí, lo quiero ver. No creo que **6.** ______________ (quedar) muy lejos del hotel La Mariposa, ¿verdad?

LUIS: Es cierto que La Mariposa **7.** ______________ (estar) al lado del parque. Pero, bueno... ¿Qué hacemos, entonces?

ANA: Mañana es lunes y es dudoso que **8.** ______________ (haber) mucha gente en cualquier lugar, así que todo depende de ti.

LUIS: Como no estamos seguros que Tomás y María **9.** ______________ (visitar) el Volcán Poás mañana, ¿por qué no los llamamos y así averiguamos? Si van mañana, los podemos acompañar.

ANA: Pienso que **10.** ______________ (ser) una buena idea.

WB 12-11 | ¡Qué preciosidad! Luis y Ana decidieron ir al Parque Nacional Manuel Antonio y ahora están comentando el viaje y el lugar. Para saber lo que dicen, completa su conversación con la forma correcta de los verbos que están entre paréntesis. **¡OJO!** Tienes que decidir si los verbos deben estar en el presente del indicativo o del subjuntivo.

LUIS: No creo que el viaje a Quepos **1.** ______________ (pasar) rápidamente.

ANA: Yo creo que nosotros **2.** ______________ (tardar) demasiado tiempo en llegar.

LUIS: María y Tomás piensan que los titís *(squirrel monkeys)* **3.** ______________ (venir) a jugar en la playa de Manuel Antonio.

ANA: Yo dudo que los titís **4.** ______________ (venir) a jugar en la playa.

LUIS: Yo creo que **5.** ______________ (haber) más de 600 tipos de aves en el parque de Manuel Antonio.

ANA: No es cierto que **6.** ______________ (haber) tantas aves en ese lugar.

LUIS: No estoy seguro que el parque **7.** ______________ (estar) abierto toda la noche.

ANA: Es imposible que el parque **8.** ______________ (cerrar) temprano.

WB 12-12 | Más planes Ahora Ana y Luis están planeando un viaje al Volcán Poás. Para saber lo que dicen, completa su conversación con la frase más lógica y gramatical. **¡OJO!** Antes de empezar, repasa el uso del subjuntivo en las frases adjetivales en tu libro de texto.

1. Tenemos que buscar el autobús ______________.
   a. que va a Poás
   b. que dure por lo menos tres horas
   c. que sea muy barato

2. Queremos un autobús ______________.
   a. que es muy barato
   b. que dure por lo menos tres horas
   c. que pueda hacer el viaje de San José a Poás

3. Es mejor alquilar un coche ______________.
   a. que dura cuatro horas
   b. que pueda hacer el viaje de San José a Poás
   c. que es muy barato

4. Tomás tiene un coche ______________.
   a. que dure por lo menos tres horas
   b. que vaya directamente a Poás
   c. que puede hacer el viaje de San José a Poás

Nombre ______________________________ Fecha ______________________________

5. Podemos tomar ese servicio de taxi ____________.
   a. que es muy barato
   b. que dure por lo menos tres horas
   c. que vaya directamente a Poás

6. En el hotel no conocen ningún servicio de taxi ____________.
   a. que es muy barato
   b. que sea muy barato
   c. que puede hacer el viaje de San José a Poás

7. Necesitamos buscar un tour del parque ____________.
   a. que dure por lo menos tres horas
   b. que vaya directamente a Poás
   c. que dura cuatro horas

WB 12-13 | Lo que quieran ¿Cómo es la vida de Andrea y sus amigos, y cómo quieren que sea? Para saberlo, forma oraciones con los elementos dados. **¡OJO!** Tienes que decidir si los verbos deben estar en el indicativo o el subjuntivo. Sigue el modelo.

Modelo Andrea / querer vivir / en una ciudad / no tener contaminación
Andrea quiere vivir en una ciudad que no tenga contaminación.

1. Carmen / tener / una casa / estar en la ciudad

____

2. Carmen y Andrea / buscar / compañeros de casa / ser simpáticos

____

3. Alberto / tener / un coche / usar / poca gasolina

____

4. Ramón / necesitar / un trabajo / pagar / mucho dinero

____

WB 12-14 | ¿Vamos o no vamos? Ana y Julia están conversando sobre si van o no van a ir al cine con Antonio y Tomás. Completa su conversación seleccionando la conjunción más lógica en cada caso.

ANA: Julia, Antonio nos invitó al cine, pero no sé si quiero ir. ¿Quieres ir?

JULIA: Bueno, Ana, voy **1.** ____________ (con tal de que / para que / a menos que) vaya también David, el hermano de Antonio. ¿Sabes que me gusta mucho? Si él no va, yo no voy.

ANA: Julia, ¡no seas tan difícil! **2.** ____________ (Cuando / Aunque / Después de que) no vaya David, te vas a divertir mucho con Antonio y conmigo. También nos va a acompañar Tomás.

JULIA: ¿Tomás? Ay, no, por favor. Ese tipo me molesta demasiado. No voy, entonces. **3.** ____________ (Para que / Cuando / Hasta que) veas a Antonio y Tomás, diles que estoy muy enferma y por eso no podía acompañarte. A propósito *(By the way)*, ¿qué película van a ver?

ANA: No te lo voy a decir **4.** ______________ (tan pronto como / cuando / a menos que) nos acompañes. Si no vas, ¿qué te importa qué película vemos?

JULIA: Ay, chica, **5.** ______________ (antes de que / en caso de que / después de que) te enojes conmigo, te voy a decir que sí los voy a acompañar... **6.** ¡______________ (para que / tan pronto como / hasta que) invites a David! ¡Por favor!

ANA: Julia, David no puede ir al cine esta tarde; tiene que trabajar. Pero, mira, **7.** ______________ (sin que / en caso de que / después de que) salgamos del cine, vamos a visitar a David en su lugar de trabajo. ¿Qué te parece?

JULIA: Me parece muy bien. Pero no voy a salir de la casa **8.** ______________ (sin que / para que / aunque) me digas el título de la película que vamos a ver. ¡Espero que sea la nueva película sobre el medio ambiente!

ANA: Sí, Julia, es la nueva sobre el medio ambiente.

WB 12-15 | La telenovela del momento Varios estudiantes están hablando de la nueva telenovela, «La ciudad y el campo». Para saber lo que dicen, forma oraciones completas usando los elementos dados. **¡OJO!** Tienes que poner el verbo de la cláusula subordinada en el subjuntivo.

Modelo Gerardo ir a casarse con Juanita / aunque / a Juanita no le gustar vivir en la metrópolis.
Gerardo va a casarse con Juanita aunque a Juanita no le guste vivir en la metrópolis.

1. Javier / no ir a volver a Panamá / hasta que / la policía encontrar al asesino

   ____

2. Elena / tomar tratamientos médicos / para que / ella y Omar poder tener un bebé

   ____

3. Manuel / ir a tomar el transporte público / solo cuando / alguien le robar el carro

   ____

4. Alberto y Claudia / ir a mudarse / a menos que / los vecinos dejar de hacer ruido

   ____

5. Santi / ir a estar mejor / tan pronto como / casarse con la campesina de su sueños

   ____

Nombre ______________________ Fecha ______________________

WB 12-16 | Los hábitos de Jorge Para saber cuán *(how)* peculiar es Jorge, selecciona la frase que mejor termine cada oración. Luego, explica tu selección, indicando si la oración implica:

a. una acción habitual

b. algo que va a ocurrir en el futuro

c. algo que es cierto

d. algo que es incierto.

Sigue los modelos.

Modelos Jorge empieza a ver la tele tan pronto como [llegue a casa / llega a casa].
llega a casa *Explicación:* *a. acción habitual*

Aunque su madre [le diga / le dice] que no vea tanta televisión, sigue haciéndolo.
le dice *Explicación:* *c. algo cierto*

1. Jorge ve las telenovelas cuando [no pasen programas sobre el medio ambiente / no pasan programas sobre el medio ambiente].

______________ Explicación: ______________

2. Jorge piensa comprar otra finca después de que [le paguen en el trabajo / le pagan en el trabajo].

______________ Explicación: ______________

3. Jorge siempre trabaja en el campo por los menos cinco horas al día aunque [tenga mucha tarea / tiene mucha tarea].

______________ Explicación: ______________

4. Jorge nunca sale de la casa hasta que [vea la nieve en la pantalla / ve la nieve en la pantalla].

______________ Explicación: ______________

5. Jorge piensa estudiar ecología tan pronto como [termine sus estudios actuales / termina sus estudios actuales].

______________ Explicación: ______________

WB 12-17 | ¿Qué hacemos esta noche? Daniel quiere hacer algo divertido esta noche y le manda el siguiente correo electrónico a su amigo Carlos. Para saber lo que dice, rellena los espacios en blanco con la forma apropiada del verbo. Usa el presente del indicativo o el presente del subjuntivo, según sea necesario.

Hola Carlos:

Esta noche no sé qué vamos a hacer. La verdad es que no me importa mucho exactamente qué hacemos, con tal de que nosotros **1.** ______________ (hacer) algo divertido. Hoy es el cumpleaños de Amalia y su novio le va a hacer una fiesta. Aunque **2.** ______________ (ser) una fiesta de cumpleaños, creo que lo van a pasar bien allí. Otra opción es ir al cine del centro para ver una película. Me gusta ese cine porque tan pronto como **3.** ______________ (salir) las películas nuevas, las pasan allí, y no cobran demasiado. Prefiero ver una película de intriga a menos que tú **4.** ______________ (querer) ver algo diferente.

Mira, Carlos, cuando tú **5.** ____________ (recibir) este mensaje, llámame y podemos decidir qué hacemos. En caso de que yo no **6.** ____________ (estar) en casa, llámame a casa de Elvia. Ella va a ayudarme con mi tarea de matemáticas. No te preocupes, ¡no voy a salir con Elvia esta noche! De hecho *(In fact)*, no voy a hacer planes para esta noche hasta que tú me **7.** ____________ (llamar).

VIAJEMOS POR COSTA RICA Y PANAMÁ

En estos segmentos del video, vas a aprender un poco sobre Costa Rica y Panamá.

WB 12-18 | Geografía Mira el mapa e identifica los países de Costa Rica y Panamá.

1. __________ Escribe la letra del mapa que corresponde a Costa Rica.
2. __________ Escribe la letra del mapa que corresponde a Panamá.

WB 12-19 | Cognados En los segmentos del video vas a escuchar muchos cognados que pueden facilitar tu comprensión del video. Algunos de estos cognados aparecen aquí. Antes de ver los segmentos, trata de pronunciar cada palabra o frase y luego trata de emparejar *(match)* los cognados con su definición en inglés.

1. ____ precolombino	**a.** abundance
2. ____ privilegiado	**b.** pre-Columbian
3. ____ himno nacional	**c.** national anthem
4. ____ interoceánico	**d.** privileged
5. ____ abundancia	**e.** banking center
6. ____ centros bancarios	**f.** interoceanic

WB 12-20 | Cognados en contexto Mira los segmentos del video otra vez y trata de rellenar los espacios en blanco con el cognado apropiado de la actividad **WB 12-19.**

del segmento sobre Costa Rica

1. El Museo Nacional está localizado en un antiguo fuerte. Allí se puede apreciar arte ______________ y de la época colonial de Costa Rica.
2. Los ticos son gente de naturaleza amable y tranquila, que viven y disfrutan la paz de un país ______________.

Nombre ______________________ Fecha ______________________

del segmento sobre Panamá

3. Su capital es la ciudad de Panamá. Allí se encuentra el Canal de Panamá; canal ______________ entre las costas del Océano Atlántico y el Océano Pacífico.

4. La Ciudad de Panamá es uno de los ______________ más fuertes del mundo y el centro financiero y de seguros más poderoso de toda Latinoamérica.

WB 12-21 | Comprensión Después de ver el video otra vez, indica si las siguientes oraciones son **ciertas** o **falsas.**

	cierto	falso
1. Costa Rica contiene aproximadamente 50% de la biodiversidad del planeta.	☐	☐
2. San José de Costa Rica tiene una copia pequeña de la famosa Ópera de París.	☐	☐
3. Los "ticos" son las personas que viven en la Ciudad de Panamá.	☐	☐
4. La palabra Panamá significa "abundancia de peces".	☐	☐
5. La mayoría de la población de Panamá es de origen europea.	☐	☐
6. El Puente de las Américas pasa sobre el Canal de Panamá.	☐	☐

¡A ESCRIBIR!

Strategy: Making your writing persuasive

Writers often try to convince readers to understand or adopt particular points of view.

Persuasive writing is used by writers of editorials, by political figures, and often by professionals, such as attorneys, medical personnel, educators, and reviewers or critics. In this section, you will write an essay in which you try to convince your reader of your point of view regarding a particular environmental issue. The following words and phrases will allow you to connect your ideas in this type of composition.

To express opinions . . .

creo que *I believe*
pienso que *I think*
en mi opinión *in my opinion*

To support opinions . . .

primero *first*
una razón *one reason*
por ejemplo *for example*

To show contrast . . .

pero *but*
aunque *although*
por otro lado *on the other hand*

To summarize . . .

por eso *therefore*
finalmente *finally*
en conclusión *in conclusion*

ATAJO 4.0

Functions: Persuading; Expressing an opinion; Agreeing and disagreeing; Comparing and contrsting

Vocabulary: Animals; Automobile; Geography; Means of transportation

Grammar: Verbs: present; Verbs: subjunctive

Task: Writing a persuasive essay

Paso 1 Form your opinion about one of the following topics (one that you didn't select in your textbook).

- El problema global más grande
- La mejor manera de resolver los problemas del mundo
- Si es justo mantener los animales en los zoológicos
- Si el gobierno debe permitir la manipulación genética

Paso 2 On a separate sheet of paper write a sentence that demonstrates your opinion about the topic you selected. Then write two to three reasons that support your opinion. Finally, write your essay. Remember that the essay must include:

- Introductory statement of your opinion
- Reasons in favor of your opinion, along with specific examples where possible
- Conclusion—a summary of your opinion

Paso 3 After writing the first draft, revise the content and check the grammar. Try to incorporate several of the expressions you learned in this chapter to express your opinion. If you use these phrases, decide whether they require the indicative or the subjunctive. When you are finished, write your final draft here.

Nombre ______________________ Fecha ______________________

Autoprueba

WB 12-22 | La geografía rural y urbana Completa los espacios en blanco con las palabras apropiadas de cada lista.

acelerada medio ambiente basura bella contaminación metrópolis
público recogen ruido sobrepoblación tráfico transporte

A

La ciudad de Nueva York es una de las **1.** ______________ más conocidas en todo el mundo. Como en cualquier otra ciudad grande, el ritmo de la vida es muy **2.** ______________ en Nueva York y allí es común encontrar problemas asociados con la **3.** ______________. Estos problemas incluyen el **4.** ______________, el **5.** ______________ y la **6.** ______________ del aire. Sin embargo, la ciudad tiene un sistema de **7.** ______________ que facilita el movimiento de gente y también protege el **8.** ______________. Para ser una ciudad tan grande, no está demasiado sucia. La gente no arroja mucha **9.** ______________ a las calles y hay muchas personas que la **10.** ______________ cuando alguien lo hace. A pesar de ser grande, es una ciudad **11.** ______________.

arroyos campesinos colinas cultivar regar tranquila

B

A diferencia de la vida urbana, la vida rural es bastante **1.** ______________, pero es todavía bastante dura. Los **2.** ______________ trabajan desde muy temprano de la mañana. Sus trabajos incluyen **3.** ______________ la tierra, **4.** ______________ las plantas y atender a los animales. Sin embargo, las zonas rurales pueden ser muy pintorescas. Las **5.** ______________ y los **6.** ______________ ayudan a crear un ambiente bastante agradable para trabajar, vivir y jugar.

capa de ozono desarrollar desperdicio destrucción energía solar escasez
explotar petróleo reciclar recursos naturales reforestar resolver

C

Tanto en las zonas urbanas como en las zonas rurales hay problemas ecológicos que hay que **1.** ______________ para proteger el medio ambiente. Si no hacemos algo rápidamente, vamos a acabarnos todos los **2.** ______________, como el **3.** ______________. Algunas soluciones son **4.** ______________ los bosques, preservar la **5.** ______________ y **6.** ______________ programas para limpiar el aire. También es importante **7.** ______________ otras formas de energía, como la **8.** ______________. Cada individuo puede hacer su parte para evitar el **9.** ______________ y la **10.** ______________ de la naturaleza. Por ejemplo, todos pueden **11.** ______________ las botellas, latas *(cans)* y papeles que usan en la casa. Si todos hacen su parte, no vamos a tener que hablar de la **12.** ______________ de los recursos importantes.

WB 12-23 | Un secreto Completa la siguiente conversación usando apropiadamente el infinitivo o el subjuntivo de los verbos que están entre paréntesis.

JORGE: Me alegro de que nosotros **1.** ______________ (estar) en Costa Rica otra vez. Me gusta **2.** ______________ (poder) explorar las selvas y ver todas las especies de animales.

LUIS: Sí, creo que es bueno **3.** ______________ (venir) a Costa Rica cada año, pero siento que Moni y Alicia no **4.** ______________ (estar) aquí con nosotros.

JORGE: ¿Cómo? ¡Es ridículo que tú **5.** ______________ (decir) eso! Es mejor que las novias no nos **6.** ______________ (acompañar) en estos viajes.

LUIS: ¡Jorge! Me sorprende que **7.** ______________ (pensar) así. Creo que es una lástima que Moni y Alicia no **8.** ______________ (ir) a poder disfrutar de la belleza de Costa Rica.

JORGE: Bueno, Luis, cálmate. Quiero mucho a mi novia. Pero también creo que es importante que los hombres **9.** ______________ (tener) su tiempo libre, ¿no? Y otra cosa: ojalá que esta conversación **10.** ______________ (ser) secreto nuestro, ¿eh?

WB 12-24 | Hablando del viaje Carmen y Tere están hablando del viaje que van a tomar a Costa Rica. Para saber lo que dicen, forma oraciones usando los siguientes elementos. Tienes que determinar si los verbos deben estar conjugados o en el presente de indicativo o en el presente de subjuntivo.

1. TERE: yo / creer / estas vacaciones / ser / excelentes

CARMEN: sí, pero yo / dudar / David / querer venir / este año

TERE: ____

CARMEN: ____

2. TERE: Gabriela / no estar segura / el hotel / ser / bueno

CARMEN: yo / estar segura / todos los hoteles / ir a ser / muy buenos

TERE: ____

CARMEN: ____

3. TERE: en San José nosotros / tener que buscar / un restaurante / servir / gallo pinto *(a Costa Rican dish of rice, beans, and cilantro)*

CARMEN: yo / conocer / un buen hotel / servir / gallo pinto

TERE: ____

CARMEN: ____

4. TERE: yo / querer visitar / una reserva biológica / tener muchas especies exóticas

CARMEN: Manuel Antonio / ser una reserva preciosa / tener todo tipo de animales exóticos

TERE: ____

CARMEN: ____

WB 12-25 | Consejos para la cita Esta noche Paulo tiene cita con la mujer de sus sueños, Silvia. Su amigo Carlos trata de darle consejos para que todo salga bien. Para saber lo que dicen, rellena los espacios en blanco con una forma apropiada del verbo. **¡OJO!** Tienes que leer la conversación y entender bien el contexto para decidir si el verbo debe ir en el presente del subjuntivo o el presente del indicativo.

CARLOS: Hola, Paulo, ¿qué me cuentas? ¿Cómo estás?

PAULO: ¡Estoy súper bien! Sabes que Silvia por fin viene a visitarme, bueno, con tal de que **1.** ______________ (limpiar) la casa antes de que ella **2.** ______________ (venir).

CARLOS: ¿Silvia? ¿Te va a visitar a ti? Pero tu casa es un desastre. ¿Qué vas a hacer para que Silvia no **3.** ______________ (asustarse) cuando **4.** ______________ (llegar)?

PAULO: Mira, Carlos, aunque mi casa sí **5.** ______________ (estar) un poco sucia, no es un desastre. La puedo limpiar.

CARLOS: Pues, suponiendo que sí puedas limpiar la casa, ¿qué van a hacer Uds.?

PAULO: No lo sé. Creo que voy a alquilar un video de Jackie Chan. Creo que a Silvia le va a gustar. Pero, en caso de que no le **6.** ______________ (gustar), también voy a alquilar mi película favorita, *Napoleon Dynamite*. Sé que con una de esas no puedo fallar *(miss)*.

CARLOS: ¡Paulo, Paulo! ¿Cuándo **7.** ______________ (ir) a aprender? ¿Cuántas veces te lo tengo que decir? Cuando **8.** ______________ (invitar) a tu casa a una chica como Silvia, tienes que pensar en ella. Tienes que preguntarle a ella qué quiere ver. Esta noche, pregúntale a Silvia qué quiere ver y entonces, cuando ella te **9.** ______________ (decir) el título de la película, Uds. dos pueden ir juntos a la tienda para alquilarla.

PAULO: Entonces, ¿no crees que una película de Jackie Chan le vaya a gustar?

CARLOS: Paulo, aunque le **10.** ______________ (gustar), tienes que esperar hasta que ella **11.** ______________ (decidir) qué es lo que prefiere ver. ¡Qué cabezota *(stubborn person)* eres!

Lab Manual

Nombre ______________________ Fecha ______________________

P ¡Mucho gusto!

VOCABULARIO 1 Saludos y despedidas

CD1, Track 2 **LM P-1 | Saludos y despedidas** You will hear six brief dialogues. After listening to each one, identify the correct speakers and situations by writing the letter of the dialogue in the appropriate space below.

_______ **1.** Two students meeting each other for the first time.

_______ **2.** Two close friends saying good-bye.

_______ **3.** A student addressing her professor.

_______ **4.** Two people of the same age saying hello.

_______ **5.** A patient greeting his doctor.

_______ **6.** A daughter greeting her mother.

CD1, Track 3 **LM P-2 | ¿Qué dices?** For each statement you hear, you will hear two replies. Choose the correct reply/replies by selecting **a** or **b**.

1. a b **2.** a b **3.** a b **4.** a b **5.** a b **6.** a b

CD1, Track 4 **LM P-3 | ¿Tú o Ud.?** Listen to the following greetings. Decide if the speaker is addressing people in a formal or an informal manner by selecting ***tú*** or ***Ud.***

1. tú Ud. **2.** tú Ud. **3.** tú Ud. **4.** tú Ud.

ESTRUCTURA Y USO 1 Talking about yourself and others: Subject pronouns and the present tense of the verb *ser*

CD1, Track 5 **LM P-4 | El verbo *ser*** You will hear sentences containing forms of the verb ***ser***. Decide which subject pronoun corresponds to the sentences. Write the appropriate letter next to each pronoun.

_______ **1.** yo

_______ **2.** tú

_______ **3.** Ud.

_______ **4.** nosotros

_______ **5.** ella

_______ **6.** ellos

CD1, Track 6 **LM P-5 | ¿Cómo son?** Say whether you agree ***(sí)*** or disagree ***(no)*** with the recorded statements. Write ***sí*** or ***no*** accordingly.

1. ______________________

2. ______________________

3. ______________________

4. ______________________

5. ______________________

CD1, Track 7 **LM P-6 | ¿Cómo eres tú?** You will hear a total of six statements. Pick three that identify you and write down their corresponding letters in the blanks provided.

1. ____________ **4.** ____________

2. ____________ **5.** ____________

3. ____________ **6.** ____________

ESTRUCTURA Y USO 2 Identifying quantities: *Hay* and numbers 0–30

CD1, Track 8 **LM P-7 | Identificación** Match the statement you hear with its corresponding illustration. **¡OJO!** Pay close attention to the ***hay*** form.

1. ____________

2. ____________

3. ____________

4. ____________

5. ____________

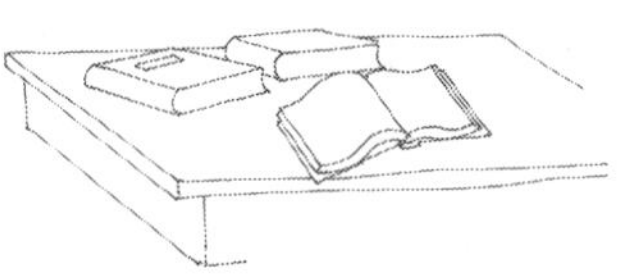

6. ____________

Nombre ______________________ Fecha ______________________

CD1, Track 9 **LM P-8 | Los números** Listen carefully to the following numbers. After repeating them aloud, write them in the spaces below, first as numerals and then spelled out.

1. ________ ______________________
2. ________ ______________________
3. ________ ______________________
4. ________ ______________________
5. ________ ______________________
6. ________ ______________________
7. ________ ______________________
8. ________ ______________________
9. ________ ______________________
10. ________ ______________________

CD1, Track 10 **LM P-9 | Las matemáticas** Listen carefully to the following math problems and write down the numerical responses in the spaces provided.

1. ______________
2. ______________
3. ______________
4. ______________
5. ______________
6. ______________

VOCABULARIO 2 Palabras interrogativas

CD1, Track 11 **LM P-10 | Interrogaciones** Listen carefully to the partial questions and choose the right interrogative word from the list. Identify your choice with the letter of the question that best corresponds to that interrogative word.

______ **1.** Cómo
______ **2.** Cuál
______ **3.** Cuándo
______ **4.** Cuántos
______ **5.** De dónde
______ **6.** Por qué
______ **7.** Qué
______ **8.** Quién
______ **9.** Dónde
______ **10.** Cómo

CD1, Track 12 **LM P-11 | Información personal** Listen to the following statements and select the appropriate interrogative word. Make certain it agrees in gender and in number.

1. Cuánta Cuánto Cuántos Cuántas
2. Quién Quiénes
3. Cuál Cuáles
4. Cuánta Cuánto Cuántos Cuántas
5. Cuál Cuáles
6. Dónde Cuándo

CD1, Track 13 **LM P-12 | ¿Quién eres?** Answer the following questions posed by detective Austin, ***el «Poderoso»***. **¡OJO!** Make sure you spell out the numbers!

1. ______________________________
2. ______________________________
3. ______________________________
4. ______________________________
5. ______________________________
6. ______________________________

Nombre ______________________ Fecha ______________________

En una clase de español
Los Estados Unidos

VOCABULARIO 1 En la clase

CD1, Track 14 **LM 1-1 | La clase de español de la profesora Muñoz** You will hear pairs of sentences based on the following illustration. After repeating each sentence aloud, select the one that best describes the illustration. Indicate your choice by selecting **a** or **b.**

1. a b **2.** a b **3.** a b **4.** a b **5.** a b **6.** a b

CD1, Track 15 **LM 1-2 | ¿Es posible?** Mari is going to tell you who or what can be found either in a classroom or in a backpack. **¡OJO!** She sometimes exaggerates. Listen to what she says and select **a. *Es posible*** or **b. *Es imposible*** according to the statements she makes. Follow the model.

Modelo En la clase: la pizarra
a. Es posible

1.	**a.** Es posible	**b.** Es imposible	**6.**	**a.** Es posible	**b.** Es imposible
2.	**a.** Es posible	**b.** Es imposible	**7.**	**a.** Es posible	**b.** Es imposible
3.	**a.** Es posible	**b.** Es imposible	**8.**	**a.** Es posible	**b.** Es imposible
4.	**a.** Es posible	**b.** Es imposible	**9.**	**a.** Es posible	**b.** Es imposible
5.	**a.** Es posible	**b.** Es imposible	**10.**	**a.** Es posible	**b.** Es imposible

CD1, Track 16 **LM 1-3 | ¿De qué color es?** Listen to the colors of the following objects. Repeat the colors after the speaker and write them in the spaces provided. Then, answer the questions with the appropriate color.

1. El papel es ______________________________.

   Es ______________________________.

2. Los bolígrafos son ______________________________.

   Son ______________________________.

3. La mochila es ______________________________.

   Es ______________________________.

4. La pizarra es ______________________________.

   Es ______________________________.

5. Los escritorios son ______________________________.

   Son ______________________________.

ESTRUCTURA Y USO 1 Talking about people, things, and concepts: Definite and indefinite articles, gender, and how to make nouns plural

CD1, Track 17 **LM 1-4 | ¿Definido o indefinido?** Choose the correct sentence from each set by selecting **a** or **b.** **¡OJO!** Pay close attention to the use of definite and indefinite articles.

1. a b **2.** a b **3.** a b **4.** a b **5.** a b

CD1, Track 18 **LM 1-5 | ¡En plural!** You will hear vocabulary words in the singular form. Write their plural forms including articles in the spaces provided.

1. ______________________ **5.** ______________________

2. ______________________ **6.** ______________________

3. ______________________ **7.** ______________________

4. ______________________ **8.** ______________________

CD1, Track 19 **LM 1-6 | ¿Cuántas? ¿Cuántos?** Answer the following questions in a complete sentence. Follow the model.

Modelo ¿Cuántas computadoras hay en la clase?
Hay una computadora en la clase.

1. ____

2. ____

3. ____

4. ____

5. ____

6. ____

Nombre ______________________ Fecha ______________________

VOCABULARIO 2 Lenguas extranjeras, materias y lugares universitarios

CD1, Track 20 **LM 1-7 | Los estudiantes internacionales de la profesora Muñoz** Listen to a brief description of eight international students in Professor Muñoz's class and complete the following sentences by stating their native language.

1. Felicitas Semprini habla ______________________.
2. Trini Whitmanabaum habla ______________________.
3. Miguel Paz d'Islilla habla ______________________.
4. Marilina Ribelina habla ______________________.
5. Kianu Tomasaki habla ______________________.
6. Stéphane Pagny habla ______________________.
7. Sergei Morosoff habla ______________________.
8. João do Maura habla ______________________.

CD1, Track 21 **LM 1-8 | ¿Qué cursos?** Listen again to **Track 20** and identify what courses each student studies. List their courses in the spaces provided below.

1. Felicitas Semprini estudia ______________________.
2. Trini Whitmanabaum estudia ______________________.
3. Miguel Paz d'Islilla estudia ______________________.
4. Marilina Ribelina estudia ______________________.
5. Kianu Tomasaki estudia ______________________.
6. Stéphane Pagny estudia ______________________.
7. Sergei Morosoff estudia ______________________.
8. João do Maura estudia ______________________.

CD1, Track 22 **LM 1-9 | En mi universidad** Listen to the following university places. Then write the proper name of the corresponding building at your university. Follow the model.

Modelo la clase de español
Hellems Hall 202

1. ______________________
2. ______________________
3. ______________________
4. ______________________
5. ______________________
6. ______________________

ESTRUCTURA Y USO 2 Describing everyday activities: Present tense of regular *-ar* verbs

CD1, Track 23 **LM 1-10 | ¿Qué hacen?** ***(What do they do?)*** Listen to the sentences describing what each of the following people is doing. Then match the letter with the corresponding illustration.

1. ____________________

2. ____________________

3. ____________________

4. ____________________

5. ____________________

6. ____________________

Nombre ______________________ Fecha ______________________

CD1, Track 24 **LM 1-11 | Este semestre** Liliana is very excited about all of the things she and her friends are doing this semester; but who does what? Listen to each of her statements and then choose who the subject of each sentence is. Follow the model:

Modelo Descansas por la noche.
b. tú

1. a. yo	**b.** mis compañeros y yo	**c.** la profesora
2. a. ellas	**b.** usted	**c.** mis amigas y yo
3. a. ustedes	**b.** la profesora	**c.** yo
4. a. mis compañeros	**b.** mi compañera de cuarto	**c.** tú
5. a. los profesores	**b.** yo	**c.** mi amigo

CD1, Track 25 **LM 1-12 | La vida de los estudiantes internacionales** Listen to a student's daily routine and compare it to your own by writing a sentence that describes your life. Follow the model.

Modelo Sergei estudia mucho por la noche.
Estudio durante el día.

1. ______________________
2. ______________________
3. ______________________
4. ______________________
5. ______________________
6. ______________________

CD1, Track 26 **LM 1-13 | Mi rutina semanal *(weekly)*** Fernando participates in many different activities during the week. Listen carefully as he describes his weekly routine. Match each activity with the corresponding day(s) of the week.

1. _______ canta en una banda	**a.** lunes
2. _______ toca la guitarra	**b.** martes
3. _______ dibuja en el parque	**c.** miércoles
4. _______ trabaja en la librería	**d.** jueves
5. _______ enseña música	**e.** viernes
	f. sábado
	g. domingo

ESTRUCTURA Y USO 3 Telling time and talking about the days of the week

CD1, Track 27 **LM 1-14 | ¿Qué hora es?** Match the time you hear with the corresponding times written below.

_______ **1.** 2:15 p.m.

_______ **2.** 8:30 a.m.

_______ **3.** 1:25 p.m.

_______ **4.** 8:45 p.m.

_______ **5.** 12:00 p.m.

_______ **6.** 10:45 p.m.

CD1, Track 28 **LM 1-15 | Los días de la semana** Identify the days of the week you hear and write them in the space provided.

1. ___________________________________

2. ___________________________________

3. ___________________________________

4. ___________________________________

5. ___________________________________

6. ___________________________________

PRONUNCIACIÓN 1 *a, e, i, o,* and *u*

CD1, Track 29 Even though the letters **a, e, i, o, u,** and sometimes **y** are used to represent vowel sounds in both English and Spanish, the pronunciation of the vowel sounds is different. English vowels are generally longer than those in Spanish. In addition, English vowel sounds often merge with other vowels to produce combination sounds. As a general rule, pronounce Spanish vowels with a short, precise sound.

CD1, Track 30 **LM 1-16 | ¡Así suena!** Listen and repeat.

a: **a**rm**a**rio p**a**pel l**á**piz cu**a**derno mochil**a**

H**a**y tres l**á**pices en l**a** mochil**a**.

e: r**e**loj m**e**sa s**e**cr**e**taria **e**scritorio pupitr**e**

En la clas**e** hay un r**e**loj, un **e**scritorio y veint**e** pupitr**e**s.

i: l**i**bro moch**i**la c**i**nta s**i**lla telev**i**sor

En la un**i**vers**i**dad hay s**i**llas, l**i**bros y telev**i**sores.

o: cons**e**jer**o** b**o**lígraf**o** bibli**o**teca pr**o**fes**o**r b**o**rrad**o**r

H**o**y el profes**o**r n**o** necesita el b**o**rrad**o**r.

u: n**u**eve **u**niversidad **U**d. al**u**mnos **ú**nica

Un profesor de la **u**niversidad tiene n**u**eve al**u**mnos.

Nombre ______________________ Fecha ______________________

PRONUNCIACIÓN 2 *h* and *ch*

CD1, Track 31 The letter **h** is the only silent letter in the Spanish alphabet; it is never pronounced: **historia.** **Ch** is pronounced as in the English word *church:* **mochila.**

CD1, Track 32 **LM 1-17 | ¡Así suena!** Listen and repeat.

h: **h**istoria **h**oy **h**ola **h**amburguesa **H**éctor

Hoy **h**ay un examen en la clase de **h**istoria.

ch: mo**ch**ila o**ch**o **ch**ico diecio**ch**o pon**ch**o

El **ch**ico tiene o**ch**o pon**ch**os y mo**ch**ilas. ¡Son mu**ch**os!

¡A VER!

LM 1-18 | Comprensión After watching the **¡A ver!** video segment for Chapter 1, answer **cierto** *(true)* or **falso** *(false)* to the following statements.

	cierto	falso
1. Hay dos chicos y tres chicas en la casa.	☐	☐
2. Todos son estudiantes.	☐	☐
3. Javier es de Argentina.	☐	☐
4. Valeria estudia filología.	☐	☐
5. Los padres de Antonio son de los Estados Unidos.	☐	☐
6. Alejandra es colombiana.	☐	☐
7. Sofía vive en Aragón, España.	☐	☐

LM 1-19 | Las materias Match the name of each student with his or her major.

1. _______ Javier	**a.** administración de empresas
2. _______ Alejandra	**b.** filología
3. _______ Sofía	**c.** danza moderna
4. _______ Valeria	**d.** medicina
5. _______ Antonio	**e.** diseño

Nombre ______________________ Fecha ______________________

En una reunión familiar: México

VOCABULARIO 1 La familia

CD2, Track 2 **LM 2-1 | Los miembros de la familia** Listen to each description and find the family relation to which it refers. Then, write the letter of the correct description next to it.

_______ **1.** mi tío
_______ **2.** mi hermana
_______ **3.** mi abuela
_______ **4.** mi madre
_______ **5.** mis primos
_______ **6.** mi abuelo
_______ **7.** mi tía
_______ **8.** mi padre
_______ **9.** mi hermano

CD2, Track 3 **LM 2-2 | Tu familia** Listen to the following sentences and select the response that best fits your family situation.

1. a b c
2. a b c
3. a b c
4. a b c
5. a b c
6. a b c

CD2, Track 4 **LM 2-3 | No es de la familia.** You will hear a list of family relationships in pairs. Repeat each pair aloud. On the lines provided, write the pairs that do not belong.

1. ______________________
2. ______________________
3. ______________________
4. ______________________
5. ______________________
6. ______________________

ESTRUCTURA Y USO 1 Indicating ownership and possession: Possession with *de(l)* and possessive adjectives

CD2, Track 5 **LM 2-4 | ¿Cómo son?** Juan Carlos is describing some family members. Complete his descriptions with the possessive adjectives that you hear. Follow the model below.

Modelo El padre de Juan Carlos es paciente.
Su padre es paciente.

1. ______________ hermanas son cómicas.
2. ______________ padres son generosos.
3. ______________ hermanos son responsables.
4. ______________ novias son atléticas.
5. ______________ abuelita es artística.
6. ¿Y ______________ abuelita es artística?

CD2, Track 6 **LM 2-5 | ¿Cómo se llaman?** Do you know the names of your classmates, professors, friends, pets, etc.? Answer the questions that you hear by filling in the possessive adjectives as well as the names. Follow the model.

Modelo ¿Cómo se llaman tus abuelos?
Mis abuelos se llaman *Alfonso y Alberto*.

1. ______________ madre se llama ______________.
2. ______________ profesor (o profesora) de español se llama ______________.
3. ______________ amigos se llaman ______________ y ______________.
4. ______________ mascotas se llaman ______________ y ______________.
5. ______________ madre se llama ______________.
6. ______________ compañero (o compañera) de clase se llama ______________.

CD2, Track 7 **LM 2-6 | ¿De quién es?** Listen to the following questions and complete the answers. Follow the model.

Modelo El bebé es del hermano de Jill. ¿De quién es el bebé?
Es *del* hermano de Jill. Es *su* bebé.

1. Es ______________ hermana de María. Es ______________ nieto.
2. Es ______________ padres de Tomás. Es ______________ casa.
3. Son ______________ Lupe y Miguel. Son ______________ parientes.
4. Es ______________ José y Simona. Es ______________ libro.
5. Es ______________ prima de Carolina. Es ______________ fiesta.
6. Son ______________ Julieta. Son ______________ gatos.

ESTRUCTURA Y USO 2 Describing people and things: Common uses of the verb *ser*

CD2, Track 8 **LM 2-7 | ¿Qué son?** You will hear some sentences about family members and their professions. Complete the sentences that you hear by matching the items in the first column with the items in the second column.

1. ________ Nosotras somos — **a.** piloto.
2. ________ Ellos son — **b.** doctor.
3. ________ Tú eres — **c.** hermanos.
4. ________ Mi hermano es — **d.** profesora.
5. ________ Yo soy — **e.** estudiantes.

Nombre ____________________ Fecha ____________________

CD2, Track 9 **LM 2-8 | Identificación** Listen carefully to each statement. Complete each statement with the correct form of the verb ***ser*** that you hear in the recording.

1. Tú ____________________ mi novio.

2. Roma ____________________ nuestra profesora.

3. Uds. ____________________ mis hermanos.

4. Mónica y yo ____________________ buenas amigas.

5. Yo ____________________ estudiante.

CD2, Track 10 **LM 2-9 | Las descripciones** You will hear a description for each of the illustrations below. Match each one by writing the corresponding letter in the space provided.

1. ____________________ **2.** ____________________ **3.** ____________________

4. ____________________ **5.** ____________________ **6.** ____________________

ESTRUCTURA Y USO 3 Describing people and things: Agreement with descriptive adjectives

CD2, Track 11 **LM 2-10 | ¡Así no son!** Below are six drawings representing Ángel's family. You will hear some descriptions that state the opposite of what each drawing represents. Match the drawings with the descriptions that state the opposite of what you see. Follow the model.

Modelo *El tío Lito es delgado.*

1. ____________________

2. ____________________

3. ____________________

4. ____________________

5. ____________________

6. ____________________

Nombre ______________________ Fecha ______________________

CD2, Track 12 **LM 2-11 | ¡Así son!** Now you are going to listen to real descriptions of Ángel's family members. Write down the descriptive adjectives that you hear to complete the sentences. **¡OJO!** There are two adjectives per sentence.

1. Mis cuñados son ______________ y ______________.
2. Sus hijos son ______________ y ______________.
3. Mis tías son ______________ y ______________.
4. Mis hermanos son ______________ y ______________.
5. Mi padre es ______________ y ______________.
6. Mi madre es ______________ y ______________.

CD2, Track 13 **LM 2-12 | ¡Guapos y famosos!** Listen to the descriptions of the following celebrities. Match the descriptions with the celebrities.

1. ________ Oprah Winfrey
2. ________ Jodie Foster
3. ________ Arnold Schwarzenegger
4. ________ Danny DeVito
5. ________ Brad Pitt
6. ________ Nicole Kidman

VOCABULARIO 2 Las nacionalidades

CD2, Track 14 **LM 2-13 | ¿De dónde son?** You will hear the names of ten famous people and their home countries. Complete the sentences by writing each person's nationality in the space provided.

Modelo Penélope Cruz es de España.
Penélope Cruz *es española.*

1. Gérard Depardieu ______________
2. Antonio Banderas ______________
3. Anna Kournikova ______________
4. Gael García Bernal ______________
5. Sting ______________
6. Silvio Berlusconi ______________

CD2, Track 15 **LM 2-14 | ¿Qué lengua(s) hablan?** You will again hear the names of these famous people and their home countries. Complete the sentences by writing the language they most likely speak.

1. Gérard Depardieu habla ______________.
2. Antonio Banderas habla ______________.
3. Anna Kournikova habla ______________.
4. Gael García Bernal habla ______________.
5. Sting habla ______________.
6. Silvio Berlusconi habla ______________.

CD2, Track 16 **LM 2-15 | ¿De qué nacionalidad?** You will hear the names of countries. For each country that you hear, write the nationality of the people who live in these countries.

Modelo Brasil
brasileños

1. ______________________________
2. ______________________________
3. ______________________________
4. ______________________________
5. ______________________________
6. ______________________________

ESTRUCTURA Y USO 4 Describing daily activities at home or at school: Present tense of *-er* and *-ir* verbs

CD2, Track 17 **LM 2-16 | Mi suegra es una viuda alegre** Listen to the story of a "happy widow" and fill in the blanks with the conjugated regular ***-er*** and ***-ir*** verbs you hear.

Mi suegra, Candela Sosa Noés, es una viuda alegre. Candela aún es joven —cincuenta y un años— bastante atractiva y **1.** ____________ mucho dinero. Personalmente, **2.** ____________ que **3.** ____________ la vida loca. Mi esposa y yo siempre **4.** ____________ las cartas que ella **5.** ____________ de diferentes lugares del mundo. Candela es un ídolo para sus nietos, Paqui y Tomasín. Paqui, la mayor, habla constantemente de su moderna abuelita Candela que **6.** ____________ wiski, baila salsa y ¡lleva bikini!

CD2, Track 18 **LM 2-17 | La vida loca de Candela** You will hear a series of activities typical of Candela's life. After repeating each one, rewrite it using the corresponding change of subject. **¡OJO!** Pay special attention to the verb conjugations.

Modelo Candela recibe muchos regalos.
Uds. *reciben muchos regalos.*

1. Nosotros ______________________________.
2. Tus padres ______________________________.
3. Sus amigas ______________________________.
4. Tú ______________________________.
5. Yo también ______________________________.

Nombre ______________________ Fecha ______________________

ESTRUCTURA Y USO 5 Expressing possession, age, and physical states: Common uses of the verb *tener*

CD2, Track 19 **LM 2-18 | ¿Cuántos tienen?** Listen to the following questions and write in the correct answer.

1. ______________________
2. ______________________
3. ______________________
4. ______________________
5. ______________________
6. ______________________

CD2, Track 20 **LM 2-19 | ¿Cómo reaccionas?** Read the following statements. Then listen to a series of idiomatic expressions with **tener** and match them to the logical statement.

1. ____________ La temperatura es de 100°F.
2. ____________ Son las 2:00 de la tarde y no he comido *(I haven't eaten)*.
3. ____________ Miro una película *(film)* de horror.
4. ____________ Estoy en Alaska en diciembre *(December)*.
5. ____________ Es la 1:30 de la mañana y estoy despierto *(awake)*.
6. ____________ Mañana tengo examen de español.

ESTRUCTURA Y USO 6 Counting to 100

CD2, Track 21 **LM 2-20 | Los números** Spell out the numbers as you hear them.

1. ______________________
2. ______________________
3. ______________________
4. ______________________
5. ______________________
6. ______________________

CD2, Track 22 **LM 2-21 | La lotería** You bought a lottery ticket with the numbers below. Listen to the audio to find out which winning numbers you have on your lottery ticket. As you hear the winning numbers called out, write down the numbers that match on your ticket. Did you win the lottery?

Your lottery ticket: 80 58 45 32 61 79

. . . And my matching numbers are . . . ______________________

CD2, Track 23 **LM 2-22 | Las edades** Candela (the "happy widow") tells her friends' ages. Match her friends with their ages.

1. ______	mi amigo Pedro	**a.** 54
2. ______	mi amiga Lupe	**b.** 36
3. ______	mis amigas Sonia y Silvia	**c.** 87
4. ______	mis amigos Julio y Fernando	**d.** 99
5. ______	mi amigo José	**e.** 48
6. ______	mi amiga Ana	**f.** 63

PRONUNCIACIÓN 1 *r* and *rr*

 To learn more about **r** and **rr,** go to Heinle iRadio at www.cengage.com/spanish/viajes.

CD2, Track 24 In Spanish there are two **r** sounds: the single **r** sound and the double **rr** sound. As you may have already noticed from the vocabulary words in this chapter and in previous chapters, the Spanish **r** is pronounced very differently from the English *r*. As a matter of fact, it has no equivalent in English. The single **r** is pronounced by flapping the tongue against the roof of the palate. The single **r** sound occurs when it is in the middle of a word, such as **prima** or **Karina.** When the **r** is placed at the beginning of a word, it has a double **r** sound, such as in the word **rubio** or **rojo.** To pronounce the double **r,** make your tongue vibrate behind the upper front teeth as you exhale. Try pronouncing the English word *thrive*. The vibration of the tongue in the *thr* sound is very close to the Spanish double **r** sound.

CD2, Track 25 **LM 2-23 | ¡Así suena!** Listen and repeat.

Single *r* sound: sob**r**ina; mo**r**ena; gene**r**osa; trabajado**r**es; pe**r**ezosos; libe**r**al.

Double *r* sound: **r**esponsable; **r**eservado; i**rr**esponsable; **r**ecibir; bu**rr**ito; **r**ápido.

The two sounds combined: E**r**es una pe**r**sona inte**r**esante pe**r**o un poco a**rr**ogante y **r**ebelde.

PRONUNCIACIÓN 2 *d*

CD2, Track 26 The Spanish **d** has two sounds. When the letter **d** is placed at the beginning of a word, such as in **Diego,** or after **l** or **n** such as in **Aldo** and **Fernando,** the sound resembles the English *d* as in *dog*. In these instances, the tongue touches the back of the front teeth rather than the gum ridge, as in English. When the **d** occurs between vowels, then the sound resembles the English *th* as in *that,* for example, in **tímido** or **prado.**

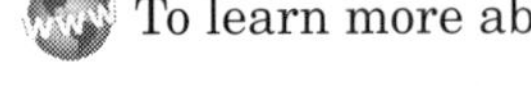 To learn more about **d,** go to Heinle iRadio at www.cengage.com/spanish/viajes.

CD2, Track 27 **LM 2-24 | ¡Así suena!** Listen and repeat.

The sound *d* at the beginning or after *l* and *n*: **d**ominicano; **d**eber; sal**d**o; man**d**o; **d**orado; cal**d**o

The sound *d* in the middle of a word: a**d**orno; gor**d**o; cana**d**iense; esta**d**ouni**d**ense; salva**d**oreño; apelli**d**o

The two sounds combined: **d**a**d**o; **d**e**d**o; **d**u**d**a; **d**on**d**e; **d**uen**d**e; **d**ormi**d**o

Nombre ______________________ Fecha ______________________

¡A VER!

LM 2-25 | Comprensión After watching the **¡A ver!** video segment for Chapter 2, answer **cierto** *(true)* or **falso** *(false)* to the following statements.

	cierto	falso
1. Alejandra tiene una hermana.	☐	☐
2. Alejandra tiene dos perros.	☐	☐
3. Javier tiene un hermano mayor.	☐	☐
4. Javier tiene hermanos que estudian sicología.	☐	☐
5. El padre de Valeria es arquitecto.	☐	☐
6. Valeria tiene dos hermanas.	☐	☐

LM 2-26 | La familia de Alejandra In the video segment, Alejandra describes her family members to Sofía. Watch the scene of the video closely and complete the family descriptions below with the words that are missing.

SOFI: ¿Estas son fotos de tu familia en Colombia?

ALEJANDRA: Sí, mira. Estos son mi **1.** ______________ y mi **2.** ______________.
Y en esta foto estamos mi **3.** ______________ y yo. Y estos son mis
4. ______________: Gitano y Lady.

SOFI: ¡Tu padre es **5.** ______________ y tu madre es blanca, de pelo negro y
6. ______________ como tú! Te pareces mucho a ella.

Nombre ______________________ Fecha ______________________

El tiempo libre: Colombia

VOCABULARIO 1 Los deportes y los pasatiempos

CD2, Track 28 **LM 3-1 | Los deportes, los pasatiempos y el tiempo libre** Do you remember the Incredible Juanjo? He enjoys all sports and leisure-time activities. Listen carefully and select the correct response indicating whether the activity you hear is a sport **(un deporte)** or a leisure-time activity **(un pasatiempo / el tiempo libre)** by putting an **x** under the appropriate heading.

Modelo ver la tele
un pasatiempo / el tiempo libre

	un deporte	un pasatiempo / el tiempo libre
1.		
2.		
3.		
4.		
5.		
6.		

CD2, Track 29 **LM 3-2 | Adivina, adivina** You will hear two or more clues. Select the activity associated with them and write in the letter of the correct response in the space provided.

_____ 1. **a.** la natación

_____ 2. **b.** sacar fotos

_____ 3. **c.** bailar

_____ 4. **d.** tomar el sol

_____ 5. **e.** visitar un museo

_____ 6. **f.** estar conectado en línea

CD2, Track 30 **LM 3-3 | ¿Es posible?** Listen to the following sentences. Indicate whether these activities are possible ***(posible)*** or impossible ***(imposible)*** by writing ***posible*** or ***imposible*** in the space provided.

Modelo tomar el sol con las gafas de sol
posible

1. ______________ 3. ______________ 5. ______________

2. ______________ 4. ______________ 6. ______________

ESTRUCTURA Y USO 1 Expressing likes and dislikes: *Gustar* + infinitive and *gustar* + nouns

CD2, Track 31 **LM 3-4 | ¿Qué les gusta?** Listen to the descriptions based on the six illustrations below. Identify each description with the illustration and write the letter in the appropriate space.

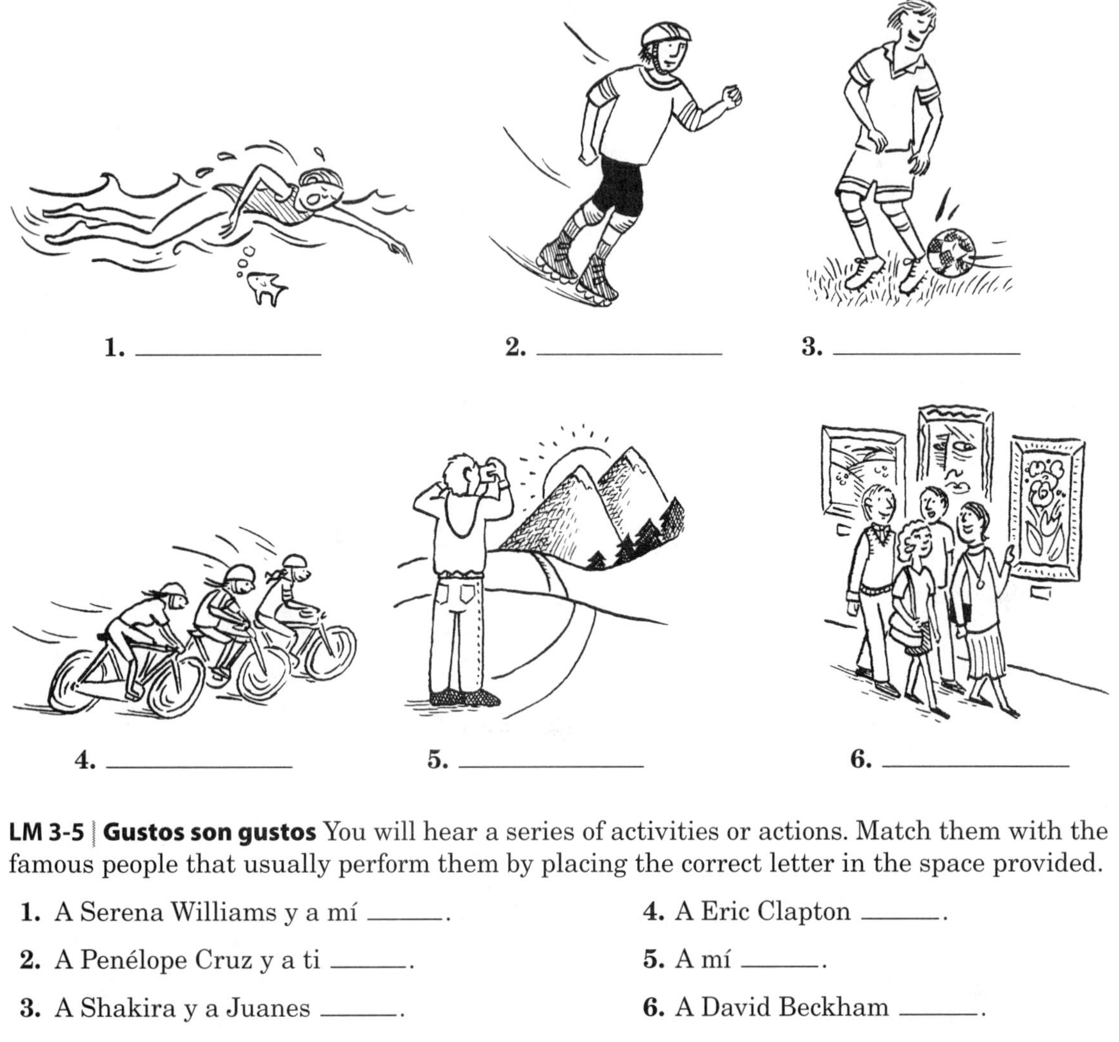

1. ____________ **2.** ____________ **3.** ____________

4. ____________ **5.** ____________ **6.** ____________

CD2, Track 32 **LM 3-5 | Gustos son gustos** You will hear a series of activities or actions. Match them with the famous people that usually perform them by placing the correct letter in the space provided.

1. A Serena Williams y a mí ______.

2. A Penélope Cruz y a ti ______.

3. A Shakira y a Juanes ______.

4. A Eric Clapton ______.

5. A mí ______.

6. A David Beckham ______.

CD2, Track 33 **LM 3-6 | Los gustos de tu familia** Listen to the statements and complete them according to your family's likes and dislikes. Follow the model.

Modelo tu padre / ver películas
A mi padre *le gusta ver películas.*

1. A mí ________________________________.

2. A mis hermanos ________________________________.

3. A mi madre ________________________________.

4. A mi padre ________________________________.

5. A mi tío y a mí ________________________________.

6. A mi novio(a) ________________________________.

Nombre ______________________ Fecha ______________________

VOCABULARIO 2 Los lugares

CD2, Track 34 **LM 3-7 | ¿Dónde vas?** Tell where you go to do the things you hear. Follow the model.

Modelo comprar papel
papelería

1. ______________________
2. ______________________
3. ______________________
4. ______________________
5. ______________________
6. ______________________

CD2, Track 35 **LM 3-8 | Encuentra el lugar** Listen as Pepe, who is new in town, talks about what he likes to do. As he tells you, point him to the place he can go to fulfill his wishes. Match his statement to the correct picture by writing the letter in the appropriate space.

A. 

B. 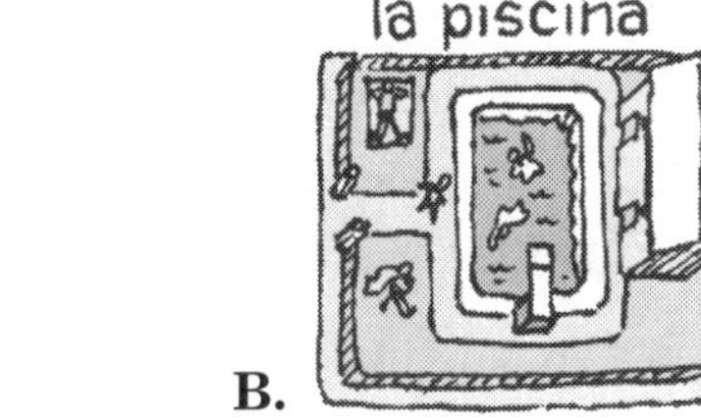

C. 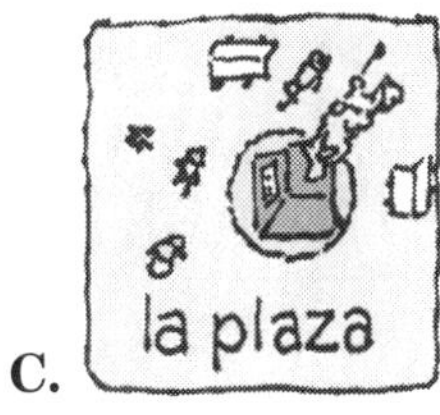

D. 

E. 

F. 

1. ________ 3. ________ 5. ________

2. ________ 4. ________ 6. ________

ESTRUCTURA Y USO 2 Expressing plans with *ir*: *Ir a* + destination and *ir a* + infinitive

CD2, Track 36 **LM 3-9 | Los polos opuestos se atraen** ***(Opposites attract)*** Gabriel and his girlfriend Silvia are soulmates. Although they like doing things together, their favorite activities don't always coincide. Listen to the dialogue and in preparation for Activity **LM 3-10** fill in the blanks with the missing words.

GABRIEL: Hola, cielo. ¿Qué hacemos este fin de semana?

SILVIA: No sé, amor. ¿Qué le parece ____________ **1** ____________ **2**? A Ud. le gusta ____________ **3** ____________ **4** ____________ **5** y a mí me gusta mucho ____________ **6**. Vamos a dar ____________ **7** ____________ **8**.

GABRIEL: Sí, vamos a invitar a los muchachos a ver el ____________ **9** ____________ **10** ____________ **11** y…

SILVIA: ¡No! Esa no es una ____________ **12**.

GABRIEL: De acuerdo, cielo. Si es un día bello y hace sol, vamos a hacer un ____________ **13**, Ud. y yo solitos. Vamos a dar un ____________ **14** ____________ **15** por el campo...

SILVIA: ¡Gabriel! Si hace buen tiempo vamos a ____________ **16** ____________ **17**. A mí me gusta ____________ **18**.

GABRIEL: ¡Qué buena idea! A mí me gusta mucho jugar al ____________ **19**. Si vamos a la playa voy a jugar al ____________ **20**.

SILVIA: ¡Gabriel, Ud. es imposible!

GABRIEL: Pero Silvia…

SILVIA: Ya sé lo que voy a hacer.

GABRIEL: ¿Qué?

SILVIA: Voy a ir a casa de mis padres. Y Ud. va a ver el partido de ____________ **21** con sus amigos.

GABRIEL: Pero Silvia...

SILVIA: ¡Adiós!

CD2, Track 37 **LM 3-10 | ¿Qué van a hacer las almas gemelas?** After listening to the dialogue, what do you think these soulmates will and will *not* do? Follow the model.

Modelo dar una fiesta
Ella va a dar una fiesta.

1. ____________________
2. ____________________
3. ____________________
4. ____________________
5. ____________________
6. ____________________

Nombre ______________________ Fecha ______________________

CD2, Track 38 **LM 3-11 | ¿Quién tiene razón?** How would you reply to your friend's proposition? Write your response in a complete sentence following the model.

Modelo Vamos al museo.
No, yo no voy al museo.
o *Sí, vamos al museo.*

1. ______________________
2. ______________________
3. ______________________
4. ______________________
5. ______________________
6. ______________________

ESTRUCTURA Y USO 3 Describing leisure-time activities: Verbs with irregular *yo* forms

CD2, Track 39 **LM 3-12 | Más actividades** Listen closely to the following activities and their letters. Match each letter to the drawing. Follow the model.

Modelo la familia
ver la televisión

1. tú ______ 2. Laura ______ 3. los novios ______

4. el disc jockey ______ 5. yo  6. mis amigos y yo ______

CD2, Track 40 **LM 3-13 | Lo que la gente hace** Using the drawings in Activity **LM 3-12**, write a complete sentence conjugating the verb. Follow the model.

Modelo la familia
La familia ve la televisión.

1. ______
2. ______
3. ______
4. ______
5. ______
6. ______

CD2, Track 41 **LM 3-14 | ¿Qué haces tú?** You will hear a series of statements by someone who is trying to impersonate you. Indicate whether what's being said is true ***(cierto)*** or false ***(falso)*** by writing ***cierto*** or ***falso*** in the space provided. Write the English translation of what is being said.

1. ______
2. ______
3. ______
4. ______
5. ______
6. ______

ESTRUCTURA Y USO 4 Expressing knowledge and familiarity: *Saber, conocer,* and the personal *a*

CD2, Track 42 **LM 3-15 | ¿Saber o conocer?** Listen to the following statements. Choose the correct one by writing **a** or **b** in the space provided.

1. ______ 4. ______
2. ______ 5. ______
3. ______ 6. ______

CD2, Track 43 **LM 3-16 | ¿Cuál es?** Listen to each sentence carefully and write the infinitive form of the verb used ***(saber*** or ***conocer)*** in the space provided.

1. ______ 4. ______
2. ______ 5. ______
3. ______

CD2, Track 44 **LM 3-17 | ¿Saber o conocer? Esa es la cuestión.** Listen carefully to each set of sentences and select the correct one by writing ***saber*** or ***conocer*** in the space provided.

1. ______ 4. ______
2. ______ 5. ______
3. ______ 6. ______

Nombre ______________________ Fecha ______________________

ESTRUCTURA Y USO 5 Talking about the months, seasons, and the weather

CD2, Track 45 **LM 3-18 | ¿Qué estación es?** Listen to the following months and choose the season to which they belong in the Northern Hemisphere. Follow the model.

Modelo marzo
b. primavera

1. **a.** invierno **b.** primavera **c.** verano **d.** otoño
2. **a.** invierno **b.** primavera **c.** verano **d.** otoño
3. **a.** invierno **b.** primavera **c.** verano **d.** otoño
4. **a.** invierno **b.** primavera **c.** verano **d.** otoño
5. **a.** invierno **b.** primavera **c.** verano **d.** otoño
6. **a.** invierno **b.** primavera **c.** verano **d.** otoño

CD2, Track 46 **LM 3-19 | ¿Qué tiempo hace?** Listen to the questions related to the weather. Choose the most logical expression from the following three: ***hace fresco, hace calor, hace frío.*** Follow the model.

Modelo ¿Qué tiempo hace en Canadá en invierno?
Hace frío.

1. ______________________
2. ______________________
3. ______________________
4. ______________________
5. ______________________
6. ______________________

CD2, Track 47

PRONUNCIACIÓN 1 Diphthongs: *ia, ie, io,* and *iu*

The letter **i** (and also **y**) placed before the vowels **a, e, o,** and **u** sound like the English words *yacht, yet, yoke*, and *you*.

To learn more about **diphthongs,** go to Heinle iRadio at www.cengage.com/spanish/viajes.

CD2, Track 48 **LM 3-20 | ¡Así suena!** Listen and repeat.

ia: famil**ia** estud**ia** Amal**ia** residenc**ia** universitar**ia**

Amal**ia** es estud**ia**nte y vive en la residenc**ia** universitar**ia**, no con su famil**ia**.

ie: f**ie**sta b**ie**n par**ie**ntes t**ie**ne v**ie**ne

¡Qué b**ie**n! Mis par**ie**ntes v**ie**nen a la f**ie**sta.

io: Anton**io** Jul**io** nov**io** felicitac**io**nes qu**io**sco

Anton**io** y Jul**io** compran per**ió**dicos en el qu**io**sco.

iu: v**iu**da c**iu**dad or**iu**nda vent**iu**no d**iu**rna

El día vent**iu**no, la v**iu**da va a venir a la c**iu**dad.

CD2, Track 49

PRONUNCIACIÓN 2 Diphthongs: *ua, ue, ui,* and *uo*

The letter **u** before the vowels **a, e, i/y,** and **o** sound like the English words *quit, quartz*, and *quench.*

 To learn more about **diphthongs,** go to Heinle iRadio at www.cengage.com/spanish/viajes.

 CD2, Track 50

LM 3-21 | ¡Así suena! Listen and repeat.

ua: **cua**dernos Ed**ua**rdo **cua**tro **Gua**dalupe g**ua**pa

Guadalupe es la más g**ua**pa para Ed**ua**rdo.

ue: b**ue**na p**ue**s P**ue**rto Rico Man**ue**l esc**ue**la

P**ue**s, Man**ue**l es un b**ue**n estudiante en P**ue**rto Rico.

ui/y: c**ui**dar r**ui**nas m**uy** c**ui**tas s**ui**cidio

Antonio está en la r**ui**na y sus c**ui**tas le hacen pensar en el s**ui**cidio.

uo: c**uo**ta

La c**uo**ta de la casa es muy alta.

¡A VER!

LM 3-22 | Los deportes The video segment that you are about to watch is divided in three topics or sections: a section about playing sports, another section about visiting "El Viejo *(Old)* San Juan" and a third section about the weather in San Juan. Watch the entire **¡A ver!** video segment for Chapter 3. To complete this activity, pay particular attention to the first section (about sports). After watching this segment, circle the sports that were *not* mentioned in the conversation.

1. **a.** fútbol americano **b.** montar a caballo **c.** alpinismo
2. **a.** buceo **b.** esnórkeling **c.** patinar sobre hielo
3. **a.** hockey sobre hielo **b.** levantar pesas **c.** ciclismo
4. **a.** correr **b.** tenis **c.** yoga
5. **a.** danza **b.** esquiar **c.** vóleibol

LM 3-23 | El tiempo libre y el clima Watch the video segment a second time and pay attention to the last two sections (or topics of conversation). As you did in the previous activity, circle what was *not* mentioned in the conversation.

1. **a.** visitar museos **b.** caminar por toda la ciudad **c.** tomar el trolebús
2. **a.** tomar muchas fotos **b.** ir al mercado **c.** ir a un bar
3. **a.** ir de compras **b.** ir al cine **c.** ir a la playa
4. **a.** ir al centro **b.** ir al Castillo San Felipe del Morro **c.** tomar el sol
5. **a.** la primavera **b.** el verano **c.** el invierno
6. **a.** sol **b.** nieve **c.** lluvia

Nombre ______________________ Fecha ______________________

4 En la casa: España

VOCABULARIO 1 La casa

CD3, Track 2 **LM 4-1 | La casa de Doña Rosa** You will listen to a series of statements describing Doña Rosa's house. Repeat each statement. Look at the drawing and indicate whether the descriptions that you hear are **cierto** *(true)* or **falso** *(false)*.

	cierto	falso
1.	☐	☐
2.	☐	☐
3.	☐	☐
4.	☐	☐
5.	☐	☐
6.	☐	☐
7.	☐	☐

CD3, Track 3 **LM 4-2 | Un robo en el condominio** Take a look at the illustrations before and after the burglary. The police make an inventory of the items that are missing. Listen to the missing items and write them down. Follow the model.

Modelo ¿Qué falta *(What is missing)* en el baño?
En el baño no está *el espejo.*

1. En la sala no están ______________________ y ______________________.
2. En la habitación no están ______________________ y ______________________.
3. En la cocina no está ______________________.
4. En el estudio no están ______________________.

Nombre ______________________ Fecha ______________________

CD3, Track 4 **LM 4-3 | ¿Dónde están?** Listen and indicate in which part of the house you would find each thing. Choose from the list provided. You will use some answers more than once. Follow the model.

Modelo el armario
Está en *la habitación.*

la cocina la habitación la sala el baño

1. Está en ______________________.
2. Está en ______________________.
3. Está en ______________________.
4. Está en ______________________.
5. Está en ______________________.
6. Están en ______________________.

ESTRUCTURA Y USO 1

Describing household chores and other activities: Present tense of stem-changing verbs *(e → ie; o → ue; u → ue; e → i)*

CD3, Track 5 **LM 4-4 | ¿Quién lo hace?** Listen to the sentences and write down who does the actions described in the audio. Choose from the list below. Follow the model.

Modelo Vienen a clase con los exámenes.
los profesores

los profesores los bebés un mal estudiante un buen estudiante una madre nosotros

1. ______________________
2. ______________________
3. ______________________
4. ______________________
5. ______________________
6. ______________________

CD3, Track 6 **LM 4-5 | Diferencias irreconciliables** Listen to a conversation between Pilar and Álvaro, a newlywed couple. Each has different preferences and hobbies. Pay attention to the irregular verbs and complete the sentences with the verbs that you hear.

1. ÁLVARO: ¿Qué ____________ hacer ahora?
2. PILAR: Ahora ____________ leer un libro.
3. ÁLVARO: Yo no ____________ estar en silencio. ¿ ____________ hablar?
4. PILAR: ¿Qué ____________?
5. ÁLVARO: ¡Nada! ¡No ____________ importancia!

CD3, Track 7 **LM 4-6 | ¡Lo normal!** Listen to the questions and the partial answers (verbs are in the infinitive—non-conjugated) about people doing certain things in certain places. Write down complete sentences with the information that you hear. Pay attention to the subjects in each of the questions as you will use them in your answers when you conjugate the verbs. Follow the model.

Modelo ¿Qué hacen los camareros? (servir la comida)
Los camareros sirven la comida.

1. ______________________________
2. ______________________________
3. ______________________________
4. ______________________________
5. ______________________________
6. ______________________________

VOCABULARIO 2 Los quehaceres domésticos

CD3, Track 8 **LM 4-7 | ¡Te toca a ti!** You will hear a list of household chores. Write the chores that each person listed below needs to do.

	Pepita	Ramón	Lola	Jorge
1.				
2.				
3.				
4.				
5.				
6.				
7.				

Nombre ______________________ Fecha ______________________

CD3, Track 9 **LM 4-8 | ¿Quién lo hace?** Listen to the chores and write the name of the person you see performing the chore in the drawing.

Modelo saca la basura
Ana

1. ______________________
2. ______________________
3. ______________________
4. ______________________
5. ______________________
6. ______________________

CD3, Track 10 **LM 4-9 | ¿En qué parte de la casa?** Based on the household chores you hear, write where the people in the drawing from Activity **LM 4-8** do these household chores.

Modelo lava la ropa
en la cocina

1. ______________________
2. ______________________
3. ______________________
4. ______________________
5. ______________________
6. ______________________

ESTRUCTURA Y USO 2 Expressing preferences and giving advice: Affirmative *tú* commands

CD3, Track 11 **LM 4-10 | Los seis consejos de oro** Since Francisco moved out of the house to go to college, his mom has been reminding him constantly of all those things he ought to do. Listen to the sentence and write the verbs that you hear in the imperative mood.

Modelo Escribe muchos correos electrónicos.
Escribe

1. ______________________
2. ______________________
3. ______________________
4. ______________________
5. ______________________
6. ______________________

CD3, Track 12 **LM 4-11 | ¿Qué tengo que hacer?** Listen to what you must do today. Match the commands that you hear with the sentences below. Follow the model.

Modelo Los platos están sucios.
a. [Lava los platos.]

1. Las plantas están secas.
2. No tienes paciencia.
3. La cama no está hecha.
4. No hay nada en la nevera.
5. Llegas tarde a clase.
6. La puerta está abierta.

CD3, Track 13 **LM 4-12 | ¡Repite, por favor!** Luisito is a naughty little boy. When he is told what to do and what not to do around the house, he pretends that he does not hear well. Write the correct commands based on what you hear in the spaces below.

Modelo ¡Tienes que sacar la basura!
¡Saca la basura!

1. ¡____!
2. ¡____!
3. ¡____!
4. ¡____!
5. ¡____!
6. ¡____!

Nombre ______________________ Fecha ______________________

ESTRUCTURA Y USO 3 Talking about location, emotional and physical states, and actions in progress: The verb *estar*

CD3, Track 14 **LM 4-13 | ¿Dónde están? ¿Cómo están?** Listen to the following sentences that will tell you where the people pictured below are located and how they feel physically or emotionally. Match each sentence you hear with an illustration and write how each person feels.

1. ______________________

2. ______________________

3. ______________________

4. ______________________

5. ______________________

6. ______________________

CD3, Track 15 **LM 4-14 | ¿Cómo estás cuando... ?** Indicate how you feel when you are facing certain situations by writing **cierto** *(true)* or **falso** *(false)* based on the statements that you will hear. When the statements are false, correct the statement.

Modelo Cuando no hablas con tu novia estás contento.
Falso. Estoy triste.

1. ______________________________
2. ______________________________
3. ______________________________
4. ______________________________
5. ______________________________
6. ______________________________

CD3, Track 16 **LM 4-15 | Un espión *(Peeping Tom)* en el condominio** Miguel, Francisco's roommate, lives directly across from the Casa de Troya. With his telescope he can watch what the neighbors are doing this instant. Match what he sees with the drawings by placing the appropriate letter in the blank.

1. ______________________________
2. ______________________________
3. ______________________________
4. ______________________________
5. ______________________________

Nombre ______________________ Fecha ______________________

ESTRUCTURA Y USO 4 Counting from 100 and higher: Numbers from 100 to 1,000,000

CD3, Track 17 **LM 4-16 | Los números** Francisco is moving out, and he is selling his furniture. As people ask for the prices for each item, pay close attention to the prices so that you can reproduce them below both numerically and spelled out.

Modelo El espejo cuesta cien euros.
100 *cien*

numeric form	spell out
1. ______________	______________
2. ______________	______________
3. ______________	______________
4. ______________	______________
5. ______________	______________
6. ______________	______________

PRONUNCIACIÓN 1 *s, ce, ci,* and *za, zo, zu*

CD3, Track 18

In most of peninsular Spain (except in Andalucía, in the Canarias, and the Baleares), the letter combination **ci, ce, za, zo,** and **zu** are pronounced like the English sound *th* as in *those.* The pronunciation of the letter **s** is also stronger and is similar to the English *s* as in *snake.*

To learn more about **c, s,** and **z,** go to Heinle iRadio at www.cengage.com/spanish/viajes.

CD3, Track 19 **LM 4-17 | ¡Así suena!** Listen and repeat.

ce: **Ce**cilia, es ne**ce**sario ha**ce**r la **ce**na.

ci: La co**ci**na de la ve**ci**na está en una residen**ci**a de an**ci**anos.

za: Mi **za**pato lo hizo un **za**patero.

ze: **Ze**us es un dios Griego.

zi: La **zi**nnia es una flor muy **zí**ngara.

zo: El **zo**o está en una **zo**na con **zo**rros.

zu: ¡El **zu**mo es **azu**l!

s: La ca**s**a de **S**ilvia e**s** e**s**tupenda y e**s**tá **s**iempre **s**úper limpia.

¡A VER!

LM 4-18 | ¿Qué tienen los cuartos? In the video segment **¡A ver!** from Chapter 4, the actors describe the bedrooms of la Hacienda Vista Alegre where they are staying. Watch and listen to the conversation where they describe the bedrooms. Then, complete the sentences with the correct words—related to the bedrooms—that are missing.

Hay tres **1.** ________________. Hay un cuarto con **2.** ________________ **3.** ________________

cerca del **4.** ________________. ¿Tiene **5.** ________________? No, pero tiene dos camas, un

6. ________________ ________________, un **7.** ________________ y muchas

8. ________________.

LM 4-19 | Muebles y electrodomésticos Watch the video a second time and pay attention to the kitchen's furniture and appliances. Answer **sí** or **no** to the following statements.

1. En la cocina hay una tostadora. sí no
2. En la cocina hay una lavadora. sí no
3. En la cocina hay un horno de microondas. sí no
4. En la cocina hay un cuadro. sí no
5. En la cocina hay una estufa. sí no
6. En la cocina hay un escritorio. sí no

Nombre ______________________ Fecha ______________________

La salud: Bolivia, Ecuador y Perú

VOCABULARIO 1 Las partes del cuerpo

CD3, Track 20 **LM 5-1 | Una lección de anatomía** Listen and repeat as you hear different parts of the body. Label each body part on the drawing.

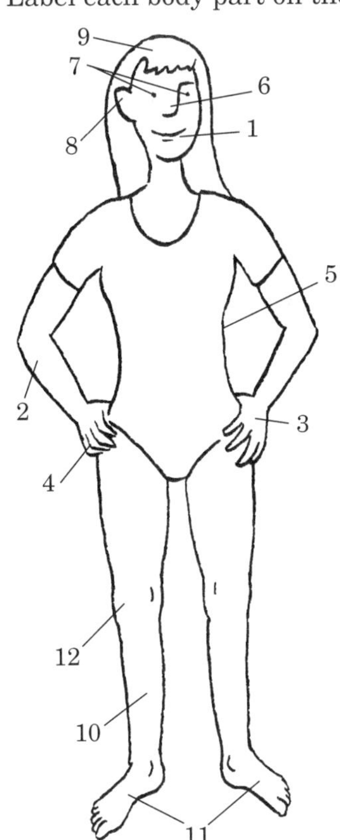

1. ______________________
2. ______________________
3. ______________________
4. ______________________
5. ______________________
6. ______________________
7. ______________________
8. ______________________
9. ______________________
10. ______________________
11. ______________________
12. ______________________

CD3, Track 21 **LM 5-2 | ¿Dónde están?** As you hear the names of different parts of the human body, write them in the columns and blanks provided according to where they would be found on the body.

En la cara	En el pecho	En las piernas
1. ____________	4. ____________	7. ____________
2. ____________	5. ____________	8. ____________
3. ____________	6. ____________	9. ____________

CD3, Track 22 **LM 5-3 | Asociaciones** Listen to each word and write the part of the human body with which you associate it.

1. ______________________
2. ______________________
3. ______________________
4. ______________________
5. ______________________
6. ______________________

ESTRUCTURA Y USO 1 Talking about routine activities: Reflexive pronouns and present tense of reflexive verbs

CD3, Track 23 **LM 5-4 | La rutina diaria de Tomás** You will hear a series of daily activities. Match them with the illustrations below by writing each activity in the blank provided.

1. ______________ 2. ______________ 3. ______________

4. ______________ 5. ______________ 6. ______________

CD3, Track 24 **LM 5-5 | El matrimonio Calviño-Chávez** Listen to the dialogue between Dr. Carlos Dardo Chávez and his wife Doctora Nilda Calviño Guner, a dentist. Then write all the reflexive verbs you hear in the correct column. Follow the model. **¡OJO!** There are 13 verbs.

Modelo Dra. Calviño Guner: Me ducho.
Dra. Calviño Guner: *Se ducha.*

Dra. Calviño Guner	Dr. Dardo Chávez
______________	______________
______________	______________
______________	______________
______________	______________
______________	______________
______________	______________
______________	______________

Nombre ______________________ Fecha ______________________

CD3, Track 25 **LM 5-6 | ¿Cómo se dice?** Listen to the detailed description of what Drs. Dardo Chávez and Calviño Guner do, and then write the appropriate letter in the space provided.

_______ **1.** Se acuestan tarde.

_______ **2.** El Dr. Dardo se afeita.

_______ **3.** Se despiertan muy temprano.

_______ **4.** La Dra. Calviño se pone la ropa después de bañarse.

_______ **5.** El Dr. Dardo no se pinta.

_______ **6.** La Dra. Calviño se peina todos los días.

_______ **7.** No se cuidan.

ESTRUCTURA Y USO 2 Talking about things you have just finished doing: *Acabar de* + infinitive

CD3, Track 26 **LM 5-7 | ¿Qué acaban de hacer?** Listen to the following activities and write down how each individual in question just finished completing them. Follow the model.

Modelo Tomás se levanta de la cama.
Tomás acaba de levantarse.

1. ______________________

2. ______________________

3. ______________________

4. ______________________

5. ______________________

CD3, Track 27 **LM 5-8 | ¿Qué pasa antes?** You will hear a sentence stating an activity about to take place. Indicate which activity most likely was recently completed just before. Follow the model.

Modelo Va a levantarse.
Acaba de despertarse y se va a levantar.

1. ______________________

2. ______________________

3. ______________________

4. ______________________

5. ______________________

6. ______________________

VOCABULARIO 2 La salud

CD3, Track 28 **LM 5-9 | Doctora, ¿qué tengo?** Listen to the patient's symptoms and recommend a treatment. Write the letter for the treatment you consider necessary.

______ **1. a.** Necesita tomar jarabe y descansar.

b. Necesita dejar de hacer ejercicio.

______ **2. a.** Necesita hacer ejercicio y comer bien.

b. Necesita guardar cama, beber muchos líquidos y tomar aspirina.

______ **3. a.** Necesita tomar Pepto Bismol™ y cuidar su dieta.

b. Necesita ir al hospital inmediatamente.

______ **4. a.** Necesita unas medicinas y descanso.

b. Necesita bañarse y acostarse temprano.

CD3, Track 29 **LM 5-10 | ¿Qué le duele?** Fran overdoes it sometimes. Everything hurts! Listen to her and mark what part of her body is in pain.

______ **1.** Le duele la garganta.

______ **2.** Le duele la cabeza.

______ **3.** Le duele el estómago.

______ **4.** Le duele la mano.

______ **5.** Le duelen los ojos.

______ **6.** Le duelen las piernas.

ESTRUCTURA Y USO 3 Describing people, things, and conditions: *Ser* vs. *estar*

CD3, Track 30 **LM 5-11 | ¿Cómo es?** Listen to the description of Dr. Calviño Guner. Pay special attention to the uses of ***ser*** and ***estar***. Write in the missing verbs as you hear them.

1. ______________ la doctora Calviño Guner. **2.** ______________ de Bolivia.

3. ______________ boliviana. **4.** ______________ dentista. **5.** ______________ casada.

6. ______________ baja. Hoy **7.** ______________ el 16 de febrero y **8.** ______________

mi cumpleaños. Esta noche hay una fiesta para mí. La fiesta **9.** ______________ en mi casa.

En este momento **10.** ______________ en mi casa. Mi casa **11.** ______________ en

Monteros. Monteros **12.** ______________ en Bolivia. **13.** ______________ muy contenta.

14. ______________ bailando y comiendo en la fiesta.

Nombre ______________________ Fecha ______________________

CD3, Track 31 **LM 5-12 | Sobre la Dra. Calviño Guner** Based on the description from activity **LM 5-11,** answer the questions using the correct forms of ***ser*** and ***estar.***

1. ______________________
2. ______________________
3. ______________________
4. ______________________
5. ______________________
6. ______________________

ESTRUCTURA Y USO 4 Pointing out people and things: Demonstrative adjectives and pronouns

CD3, Track 32 **LM 5-13 | ¿Qué quieres, *esa, esta o aquella*?** Answer each question by replacing the demonstrative adjective with the demonstrative pronoun. Follow the model.

Modelo ¿Prefieres esas pastillas?
Sí, prefiero esas.

1. ______________________
2. ______________________
3. ______________________
4. ______________________
5. ______________________
6. ______________________

PRONUNCIACIÓN 1 *p* and *t*

CD3, Track 33 The letters **p** and **t,** when placed at the beginning of a word, are pronounced with more strength in English than in Spanish. In English, the sound is stronger like in *Peter* or *Tom.*

In Spanish, however, the sound of these two letters is softer; it is very similar to the *p* in *spill* and to the *t* in *still.*

www To learn more about the letters **p** and **t,** go to Heinle iRadio at www.cengage.com/spanish/viajes.

CD3, Track 34 **LM 5-14 | ¡Así suena!** Listen, repeat, and write what you hear.

1. ______________________
2. ______________________
3. ______________________
4. ______________________

¡A VER!

LM 5-15 | ¿Cierto o falso? After watching the **¡A ver!** video segment for Chapter 5, answer **cierto** *(true)* or **falso** *(false)* to the following statements.

	cierto	falso
1. Los chicos van a una clase de baile folclórico.	☐	☐
2. Alejandra es la instructora.	☐	☐
3. Todos aprenden el paso básico: ritmo del sicá.	☐	☐
4. Alejandra se lastimó el tobillo y le duele la rodilla.	☐	☐
5. Víctor no quiere que baile.	☐	☐
6. Alejandra y Víctor van a salir esa noche.	☐	☐

LM 5-16 | ¿Quiénes son? Read the following statements. Match each one with the right person by writing the correct letter in the space provided.

a. Se lastimó el tobillo y le duele el pie.	_____ **1.** Javier
b. Baila con Alejandra y con Valeria.	_____ **2.** Víctor
c. No quería bailar.	_____ **3.** Alejandra
d. Es el instructor.	_____ **4.** Sofía
e. Él baila muy mal.	_____ **5.** Antonio
f. En el baile folclórico del final del video, el traje típico de esta chica es blanco.	_____ **6.** Valeria

Nombre ______________________ Fecha ______________________

¿Quieres comer conmigo esta noche? Venezuela

VOCABULARIO 1 La comida

CD4, Track 2 **LM 6-1 | ¡Qué hambre tengo!** Place your order according to what you hear. Make sure you match the food/beverage with the illustrations below.

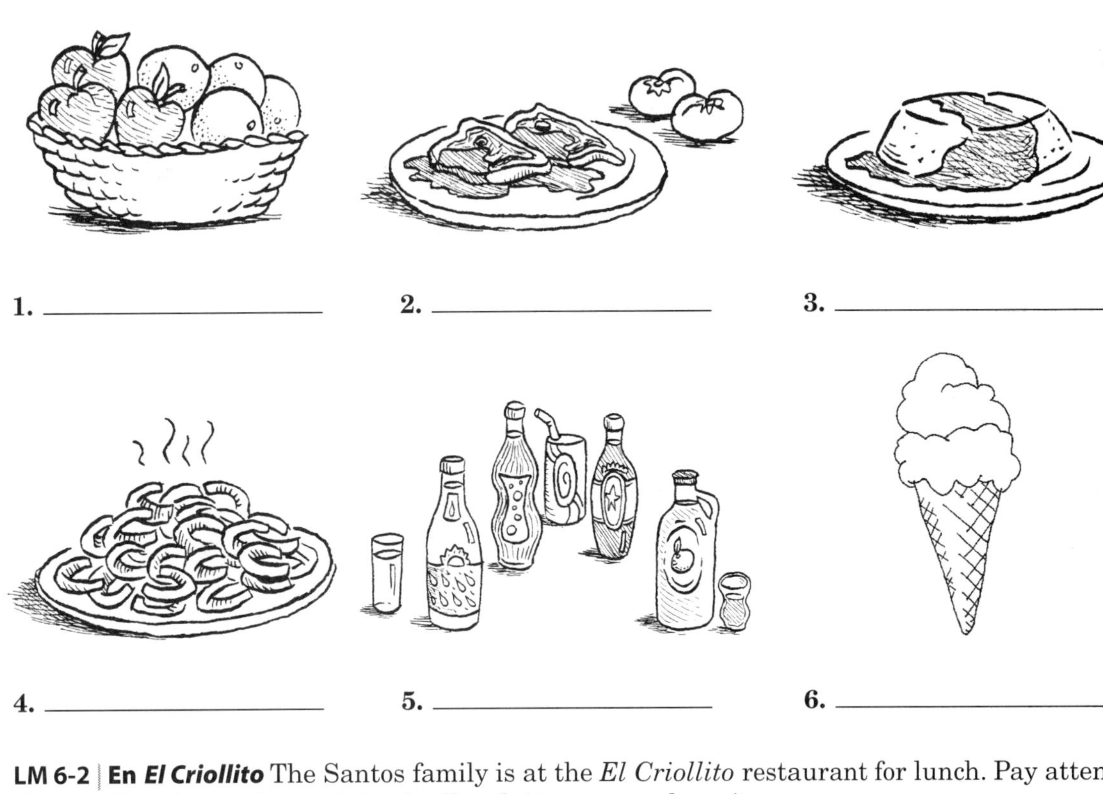

1. ______________ 2. ______________ 3. ______________

4. ______________ 5. ______________ 6. ______________

CD4, Track 3 **LM 6-2 | En *El Criollito*** The Santos family is at the *El Criollito* restaurant for lunch. Pay attention to what they order, and check off each item as you hear it.

_______ una sopa de verduras

_______ las chuletas de cerdo en salsa de tomate

_______ las arepas

_______ el pollo asado

_______ unos refrescos

_______ el flan casero

CD4, Track 4 **LM 6-3 | ¡Buen provecho!** Listen to different food categories and write a food item of your choice that belongs to that category. Do not repeat a food item!

Modelo los entremeses
las arepas

1. ______
2. ______
3. ______
4. ______
5. ______
6. ______

ESTRUCTURA Y USO 1 Making comparisons: Comparatives and superlatives

CD4, Track 5 **LM 6-4 | Comparando alimentos** Listen to the following comparisons regarding food habits. Select the symbols below to indicate if what you hear is a comparison of equality, inequality, or a superlative. Symbols: = **(tan)** – **(menos)** + **(más)** ↑ **(mejor)** ↓ **(peor)**

Modelo Los colombianos beben menos café que los argentinos.
– *(menos)*

1. = – + ↑ ↓
2. = – + ↑ ↓
3. = – + ↑ ↓
4. = – + ↑ ↓
5. = – + ↑ ↓
6. = – + ↑ ↓

CD4, Track 6 **LM 6-5 | ¿Qué serán?** Listen to the following comparative descriptions and select the word that corresponds best with the description that you hear.

1. las chuletas los calamares la langosta
2. la carne de res el pavo el pollo
3. la banana la naranja la manzana
4. el aceite el agua el café
5. el vino el té la leche
6. la cerveza el vino el jugo

CD4, Track 7 **LM 6-6 | Tú, ¿qué crees?** Listen to the following statements about eating habits and indicate if the statements that you hear are **cierto** *(true)* or **falso** *(false)*.

1. cierto falso
2. cierto falso
3. cierto falso

4. cierto falso
5. cierto falso
6. cierto falso

VOCABULARIO 2 El restaurante

CD4, Track 8 **LM 6-7 | Definiciones** Listen to the following definitions and choose the words or expressions that best match the definitions that you hear.

1. ¡Buen provecho!	¡Salud!	¡Cómo no!
2. la propina	la cuenta	las bebidas
3. los postres	el menú	la especialidad de la casa
4. ligero	caliente	fresco
5. ¡Salud!	¡Yo quisiera!	¡No puedo más!
6. Te invito.	Estoy satisfecho.	Estoy a dieta.

CD4, Track 9 **LM 6-8 | En el restaurante** Rosa and Luis are at a restaurant. Listen to the dialogue and fill in the blanks with the words that you hear.

EL CAMARERO: ¡Buenos días! ¿Qué **1.** ______________ comer?

ROSA: Yo **2.** ______________ algo **3.** ______________. Estoy a **4.** ______________. Una sopa de mariscos, por favor.

LUIS: Voy a comer pescado con la ensalada de la casa.

EL CAMARERO: ¿Algo para **5.** ______________?

LUIS: Unas arepas.

EL CAMARERO: Aquí tienen, ¡buen **6.** ______________!

CD4, Track 10 **LM 6-9 | ¿Cómo está?** Listen to Alberto's questions about the food his mother has prepared. Answer his questions using the vocabulary from this section. Do not repeat the same words more than twice, and be logical!

Modelo —Mamá, ¿cómo está el helado?
—¡Está rico!

1. ¡Está ______________________________!

2. ¡Está ______________________________!

3. ¡Están ______________________________!

4. ¡Está ______________________________!

5. ¡Están ______________________________!

6. ¡Está ______________________________!

ESTRUCTURA Y USO 2 Describing past events: Regular verbs and verbs with spelling changes in the preterite

CD4, Track 11 **LM 6-10 | Un día muy ocupado** Marina will tell you all about her day yesterday. Match what she says with the illustrations below.

1. ______________________

2. ______________________

3. ______________________

4. ______________________

5. ______________________

CD4, Track 12 **LM 6-11 | ¿Es cierto?** Marina's husband Gabriel thinks he knows what Marina did yesterday. For each statement he makes about Marina's day, select **cierto** *(true)* or **falso** *(false)*. Look at the pictures in the previous activity to help you select your answer.

1. cierto falso

2. cierto falso

3. cierto falso

4. cierto falso

5. cierto falso

6. cierto falso

Nombre ______________________ Fecha ______________________

CD4, Track 13 **LM 6-12 | ¿Y tú?** Marina wants to know if you did the same things she did. Select ***sí*** or ***no*** to answer her questions.

1. sí no

2. sí no

3. sí no

4. sí no

5. sí no

6. sí no

ESTRUCTURA Y USO 3 Giving detailed descriptions about past events: Verbs with stem changes in the preterite

CD4, Track 14 **LM 6-13 | Una romántica indigestión** Olga and Roberto went out to dinner. However, Roberto ate too much and got sick! Listen to what happened, and fill in the blanks with the verbs in the preterite that you hear.

Roberto **1.** ______________ muchos, pero muchos camarones y a Olga el camarero le **2.** ______________ carne de res asada. A Roberto le **3.** ______________ mucho los camarones y **4.** ______________ kilos. Los dos se **5.** ______________ mucho pero él **6.** ______________ una horrible indigestión.

CD4, Track 15 **LM 6-14 | ¿Cierto o falso?** Listen to each statement based on the story you just heard in the previous activity, and indicate if it's **cierto** *(true)* or **falso** *(false)*.

1. cierto falso

2. cierto falso

3. cierto falso

4. cierto falso

5. cierto falso

6. cierto falso

CD4, Track 16 **LM 6-15 | Tus amigos** Listen to the questions about your friends who went to a restaurant yesterday, and answer them conjugating the verbs provided in the preterite.

Modelo ¿Qué prefirieron beber tus amigos? (preferir beber vino tinto)
Prefirieron beber vino tinto.

1. (dormir)

____

2. (tomar cervezas)

____

3. (sonreír a las chicas guapas)

____

4. (vestirse muy elegantemente)

____

5. (reírse mucho)

____

6. (despedirse a las diez)

____

PRONUNCIACIÓN 1 *m, n,* and *ñ*

CD4, Track 17 The consonants **m** placed in all positions of a word and **n** before **b, v, f, m** are pronounced like the English *m* in *men*: **más, morir, amor,** and **invertido** [i-**m**-vertido], **anfiteatro** [a-**m**-fiteatro], **inmenso** [i-**m**-enso].

Before the letters **k** and **g,** the letter **n** is pronounced like the *in* sound in *sink* and/or *sing*: **angustia** [a**n**-gustia], **pongo** [po**n**-go], **canguro** [ca**n**-guro].

In all other instances, **n** is pronounced like the English *n* as in *no!:* **nube, nieto, Anita, honor.**

The letter **ñ** is similar to the sound *ni* in *onion:* **Muñoz, España, niño.**

To learn more about the letters **n** and **ñ,** go to Heinle iRadio at www.cengage.com/spanish/viajes.

CD4, Track 18 **LM 6-16 | ¡A escribir!** Listen and repeat the list of words that have the sounds that you just learned. Then, fill in the missing words.

Letter **m:**

1. mamá, comida, ______________
2. mucho, ______________, camarones
3. ______________, champiñón, mantequilla

Letter **n:**

4. nuevo, cena, ______________
5. un poco, ______________, una empanada
6. jamón, mineral, ______________

Letter **ñ:**

7. español, ______________, año
8. ______________, pequeña, niña

Nombre ______________________ Fecha ______________________

¡A VER!

LM 6-19 | ¿Comprendiste? After watching the first scene in the video segment for Chapter 6, **¿Quieres ir de compras conmigo?** read the following statements and indicate if they are **cierto** *(true)* or **falso** *(false)*.

	cierto	**falso**
1. Antonio y Javier se van de compras.	☐	☐
2. Valeria quiere cocinar comida venezolana.	☐	☐
3. Valeria va a preparar chiles rellenos.	☐	☐
4. Valeria llama a su mamá para pedirle ayuda con la receta.	☐	☐
5. Alejandra quiere que Valeria llame a su mamá.	☐	☐
6. Valeria no entiende bien la receta.	☐	☐

LM 6-20 | Vale como cocinera Watch the video segment for Chapter 6 again, as Valeria recalls her horrible cooking experience. Then read the following statements and complete them with the right answer.

1. La cena fue…

- **a.** un éxito.
- **b.** un desastre.
- **c.** una delicia.

2. El queso estaba…

- **a.** muy azucarado.
- **b.** muy bueno.
- **c.** muy salado.

3. Los chiles se me…

- **a.** quemaron.
- **b.** sirvieron.
- **c.** comieron.

4. Valeria le echó a la salsa…

- **a.** mucha pimienta.
- **b.** mucho picante.
- **c.** mucho vinagre.

5. Antonio se comió…

- **a.** una chuleta.
- **b.** un sopa.
- **c.** un chile relleno.

Nombre ______________________ Fecha ______________________

De compras: Argentina, Paraguay y Uruguay

VOCABULARIO 1 La ropa

CD4, Track 19 **LM 7-1 | La ropa** You will hear the name of an article of clothing twice. First repeat it, and then write its letter under the correct illustration.

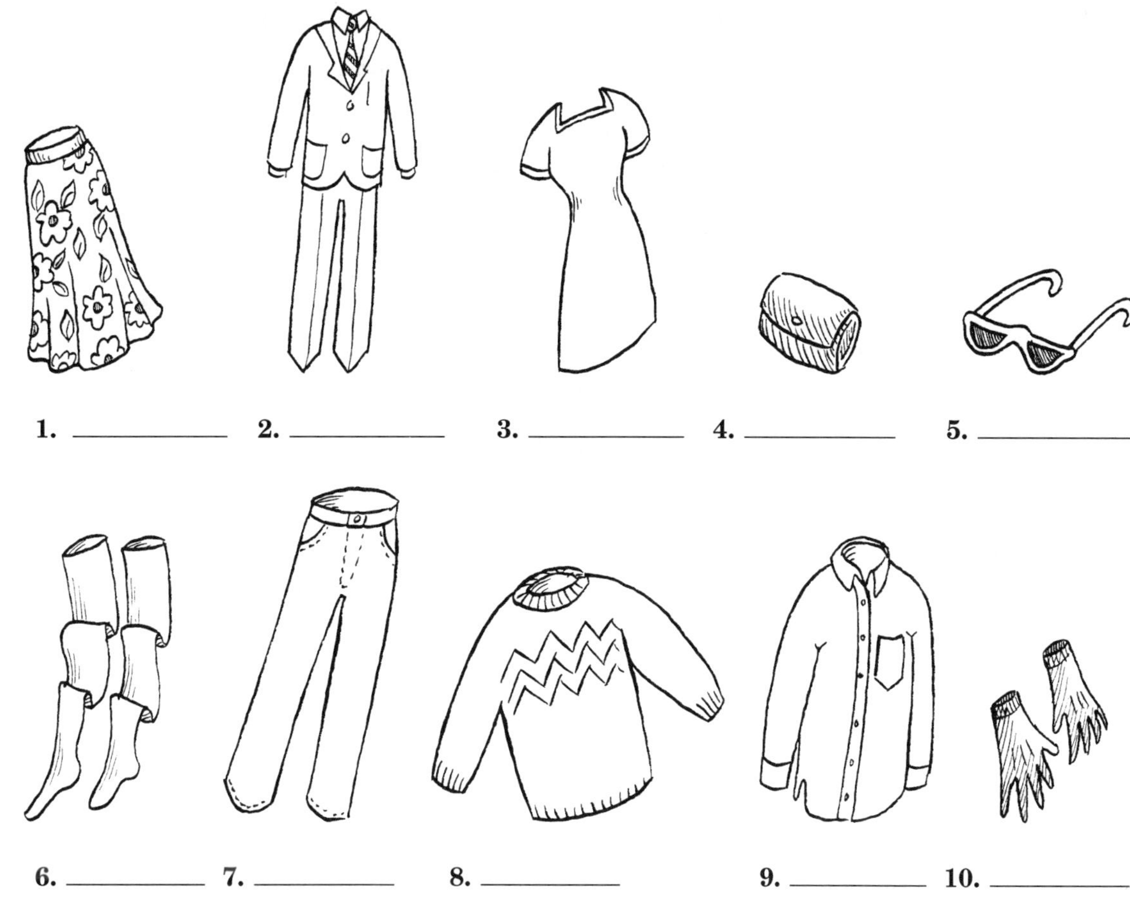

1. ________ 2. ________ 3. ________ 4. ________ 5. ________

6. ________ 7. ________ 8. ________ 9. ________ 10. ________

CD4, Track 20 **LM 7-2 | ¿Qué me pongo?** One of your friends is asking you what to wear for each situation. Listen to the questions and answer by writing the most appropriate clothing item. Follow the model.

Modelo ¿Qué me pongo para ir a la piscina?
el traje de baño

1. ______________________
2. ______________________
3. ______________________
4. ______________________
5. ______________________
6. ______________________

CD4, Track 21 **LM 7-3 | Los famosos y la ropa** You're listening to an online broadcast of interviews with the stars on the red carpet minutes before the Oscar ceremony. Pay attention to what they're wearing and indicate if it is **posible** or **imposible.**

1. posible	imposible	**4.** posible	imposible
2. posible	imposible	**5.** posible	imposible
3. posible	imposible	**6.** posible	imposible

ESTRUCTURA Y USO 1 Talking about singular and/or completed events in the past: Irregular verbs in the preterite

CD4, Track 22 **LM 7-4 | Un día de compras en Buenos Aires** Listen to the story about a husband and wife who go shopping. Complete the story by filling in the blanks with the irregular verbs in the preterite tense.

1. Ayer mi esposo y yo ________________ de compras.
2. ________________ ir a una de las boutiques de la calle Florida.
3. Mi esposo ________________ conmigo.
4. Me ________________ un vestido muy bonito en una tienda.
5. Pero no ________________ comprarlo.
6. ¡Mi esposo y yo no ________________ la cartera!

CD4, Track 23 **LM 7-5 | Más sobre las compras** The sentences that you just heard in the previous activity each had an irregular verb in the preterite. Identify the infinitive of the irregular preterite verbs. Choose the correct infinitive from the choices below.

1. ir	ser	estar
2. saber	poder	querer
3. decir	venir	tener
4. poder	poner	querer
5. poner	poder	saber
6. querer	tener	traer

CD4, Track 24 **LM 7-6 | ¡Yo también!** Listen to what the following people did last week. You did exactly the same things! For each statement, write the same activity in the first-person singular. Follow the model.

Modelo Ayer Amalia se puso el traje de baño para ir a la playa.
¡Yo también, *me puse* el traje de baño!

1. ¡Yo también ________________ de compras!
2. ¡Yo también ________________ de Rosarito!
3. ¡Yo también ________________ comer en un restaurante argentino!
4. ¡Yo también ________________ hacer la tarea!
5. ¡Yo también ________________ en el cine!
6. ¡Yo también ________________ un regalo!

Nombre ______________________ Fecha ______________________

VOCABULARIO 2 De compras

CD4, Track 25 **LM 7-7 | Definiciones** Listen to the items and choose the closest definitions from the choices.

1. es para pagar
   es para probarse
   es para llevar
2. es importante para rebajar
   es importante para probarse
   es importante para mostrar
3. cuando algo cuesta más
   cuando algo cuesta menos
   cuando algo no cuesta
4. cuando se paga con tarjeta
   cuando se paga con descuento
   cuando se paga con dinero en monedas y billetes
5. es la persona que depende
   es la persona que trabaja en una tienda
   es la persona que trabaja en las rebajas
6. es similar a ver
   es similar a cambiar
   es similar a gastar

CD4, Track 26 **LM 7-8 | Expresiones idiomáticas** For each idiomatic expression that you hear, match the equivalent expression and indicate its letter.

1. ____________ Es algo que no es nada caro. Es muy barato.
2. ____________ Ropa que está muy «in» y que todo el mundo lleva.
3. ____________ Es para preguntar si la ropa o los zapatos van bien o mal.
4. ____________ Es cuando la ropa o los zapatos no son de la talla o del número apropiados.
5. ____________ Es lo que se dice al dependiente antes de pagar.
6. ____________ Es para preguntar si uno se puede poner ropa o zapatos en una tienda.

CD4, Track 27 **LM 7-9 | En la tienda** Listen to the questions that clients ask in a store, and select the most logical answer from the choices listed below.

1. Le quedan divinamente.
   Te quedan divinamente.
   Te quedan baratas.
2. Me debe una talla 54.
   Me debe 10.000 bolívares.
   Me debe 54 por ciento.
3. Claro que sí, pruébeselo.
   Claro que sí, pruébeselos.
   Claro que sí, pruébeselas.
4. Sí, son muy grandes.
   Sí, tengo unos zapatos para Ud.
   Sí, tengo su número.
5. Sí, están en rebajas.
   Sí, están en efectivo.
   Sí, están de su talla.
6. Sí, puede llevarse otras gafas.
   Sí, puede ver con las gafas.
   Sí, hacen juego con sus ojos.

ESTRUCTURA Y USO 2 Simplifying expressions: Direct object pronouns

CD4, Track 28 **LM 7-10 | ¿Qué tal las compras?** Your friend is curious to know how your shopping day went. Listen to the questions and choose the correct answer. **¡OJO!** Pay attention to the pronouns!

Modelo ¿Te probaste un vestido?
Me lo probé.

1.	Me lo compré.	Me los compré.	Me las compré.
2.	Me la llevé.	Me las llevé.	Me los llevé.
3.	Me la probé.	Me las probé.	Me los probé.
4.	Lo cambié.	La cambié.	Los cambié.
5.	La compré.	Las compré.	Lo compré.
6.	Me la llevé.	Me las llevé.	Me los llevé.

CD4, Track 29 **LM 7-11 | ¡Especifica!** Now your friend tells you about her day at the mall. She does not specify what she bought, tried on, and exchanged. Depending on the pronoun that you hear, choose the correct item. Follow the model.

Modelo Me lo probé.
el impermeable

1.	el collar	los chalecos	la bufanda
2.	los vaqueros	la pulsera	el abrigo
3.	el traje	las sandalias	la camisa
4.	la gorra	el cinturón	los guantes
5.	los calcetines	la falda	las blusas
6.	los sombreros	el anillo	la chaqueta

CD4, Track 30 **LM 7-12 | ¿Quién?** Listen to the sentences, paying attention to the object pronouns. Then choose from the list below to indicate the person(s). Indicate to whom each pronoun refers. Follow the model.

Modelo No me queda bien.
yo

1.	vosotros	ellos	nosotros
2.	nosotros	ellas	vosotros
3.	ellas	él	ellos
4.	ella	usted	tú
5.	yo	ustedes	tú
6.	él	ella	ellas

Nombre ______________________ Fecha ______________________

ESTRUCTURA Y USO 3 Describing on-going and habitual actions in the past: The imperfect tense

CD4, Track 31 **LM 7-13 | Cuando Valeria Mazza era niña** Listen to the famous Argentine model, Valeria Mazza. Identify the verbs in the imperfect tense and write them in the spaces provided.

Cuando **1.** ______________ niña **2.** ______________ ser modelo. No **3.** ______________ que las modelos **4.** ______________ que hacer tantos sacrificios. Por ejemplo, no **5.** ______________ que las modelos duermen y comen poco y trabajan tanto. Pero **6.** ______________ decidida a afrontar las dificultades, y así empecé: con mucha fuerza de voluntad.

CD4, Track 32 **LM 7-14 | La niñez de Crystal** Listen to Crystal's childhood years in Argentina. Write the conjugated verbs that you hear and indicate whether they are in the imperfect or the preterite tense.

1. pretérito imperfecto
2. pretérito imperfecto
3. pretérito imperfecto
4. pretérito imperfecto
5. pretérito imperfecto
6. pretérito imperfecto

CD4, Track 33 **LM 7-15 | ¿Y tu niñez?** Answer the following questions by conjugating the verbs that you hear in the preterite or the imperfect tense. Then select the choice that best applies to you.

1. De pequeño, (yo) ______________________
   un ángel. un demonio.
2. Mis padres me ______________________
   "Eres muy malo(a)". "Eres muy bueno(a)".
3. (Yo) ______________________
   de vacaciones a la playa. de vacaciones a la montaña.
4. (Yo) ______________________
   a la pelota *(ball)*. a las muñecas *(dolls)*.
5. Mi pasatiempo favorito ______________________
   mirar la tele. practicar deportes.
6. (Yo) ______________________ en
   el continente americano. el continente europeo.

PRONUNCIACIÓN 1 *c* and *qu*

CD4, Track 34 The letter **c** can be pronounced with two different sounds: a hard sound and a soft sound. When the letter **c** is combined with the vowels **a (ca), o (co), u (cu),** the sound is hard (like the English *k*): **cor**bata, **ca**misa, **cu**ñado. When the letter **c** is combined with the vowels **e (ce)** and **i (ci)** the sound is soft: co**ci**na, **ci**ta, él di**ce**, abe**ce**dario. In Spain, the softer sound is pronounced like **z** and in Latin America like **s**.

If you wonder about the Spanish letter **k** (also pronounced like the **c** in **ca, co, cu),** it only appears in very few words in Spanish: **ki**lo.

The letters **qu** combined with **i** and **e** are pronounced like the sound **k: Qui**to, **qui**ero, ¿**qué** tal?

 For more information, visit Heinle iRadio at www.cengage.com/spanish/viajes.

CD4, Track 35 **LM 7-16 | ¡Así suena!** Listen to a list of words with the soft **c** sound and the hard **c** sound. For each word, indicate if the **c** sound that you hear is soft or hard.

1. soft hard
2. soft hard
3. soft hard
4. soft hard
5. soft hard
6. soft hard

PRONUNCIACIÓN 2 *l, ll,* and *y*

CD4, Track 36 The letter **l** in Spanish is pronounced like the English *l:* **Lol**a, ca**lor**, ca**l**cetines.

The sound **ll** is pronounced like the English *y* as in *yet:* Me **ll**amo, **ll**evo, **ll**ueve, ca**ll**e.

However, Argentinians and Uruguayans pronounce it like the English **z** as in *measure*.

The letter **y** is like the English *y* as in *yet*: Re**y**es, ma**y**or. However, when it is placed at the end of a word, it is pronounced like the English sound **ee** as in **Lee**: so**y** [so-**ee**], vo**y** [vo-**ee**], ho**y** [o-**ee**].

CD4, Track 37 **LM 7-17 | ¡Así suena!** Listen and repeat.

l:	sa**l**sa	chi**l**e	enchi**l**ada	guacamo**l**e	frijo**l**es
ll/y:	torti**ll**a	po**ll**o	pae**ll**a	Gui**ll**ermo	**Y**olanda

CD4, Track 38 **LM 7-18 | ¡A escuchar!** Identify the sounds of **l** and **ll/y** in the words that you hear.

1. l ll/y
2. l ll/y
3. l ll/y
4. l ll/y
5. l ll/y
6. l ll/y

Nombre ______________________ Fecha ______________________

¡A VER!

LM 7-19 | ¿Cierto o falso? Watch the **¡A ver!** video segment and indicate if the following statements are **cierto** or **falso.**

	cierto	falso
1. Los zapatos de Sofía están nuevos.	☐	☐
2. A Alejandra le gusta mucho comprar ropa.	☐	☐
3. Alejandra y Sofía van a la piscina.	☐	☐
4. Sofía se pone el traje de baño de Alejandra.	☐	☐
5. Antonio lleva una gorra roja.	☐	☐
6. Alejandra tiene tanta ropa como Sofía.	☐	☐

LM 7-20 | ¿Quién lo dice? Watch the **¡A ver!** video segment again and identify who says the following statements.

1. Tus vaqueros están pasados de moda.

Alejandra   Sofía

2. ¿Para qué quieres tantos zapatos?

Alejandra   Sofía

3. ¡Enséñame tus cosas!

Alejandra   Sofía

4. ¡Ya pasó de moda!

Alejandra   Sofía

5. ¡Te ves muy bonita!

Antonio   Javier

6. Yo llevo la camiseta de fútbol del mejor equipo del mundo.

Javier   Antonio

Nombre ________________ Fecha ________________

8 Fiestas y vacaciones: Guatemala y El Salvador

VOCABULARIO 1 Fiestas y celebraciones

CD5, Track 2 **LM 8-1 | ¿Qué haces ese día?** Listen to the descriptions of a celebration, a holiday, or an occurrence and indicate what you do that day. Write the correct letter in the spaces provided below.

_______ **1.** ¡Me asusto!

_______ **2.** Lo paso bien.

_______ **3.** Doy una fiesta.

_______ **4.** Les digo: «¡Felicitaciones!»

_______ **5.** Me pongo triste.

_______ **6.** Lo paso muy mal (me preocupo mucho).

CD5, Track 3 **LM 8-2 | Días festivos** Listen to the name of holidays and write their English translations.

1. ________________

2. ________________

3. ________________

4. ________________

5. ________________

6. ________________

CD5, Track 4 **LM 8-3 | ¿Quién hace qué?** Listen to the story. Then read the questions and write the name of the person from the list provided below to indicate who does the following things or reacts the following way.

Ana Patricia Victoria Juan

1. ¿Quién da una fiesta sorpresa? ________________

2. ¿Quién se reúne con su familia? ________________

3. ¿Quién se pone un disfraz? ________________

4. ¿Quién hace un pastel el 24 de diciembre? ________________

5. ¿Quién le desea muchas felicidades a su hermana? ________________

6. ¿Quién tiene una celebración de cumpleaños? ________________

ESTRUCTURA Y USO 1 Inquiring and providing information about people and events: Interrogative words

CD5, Track 5 **LM 8-4 | Identifica la palabra interrogativa** You will hear a series of questions. Listen to the questions and write the equivalent interrogative in English. Follow the model.

Modelo ¿Adónde vas esta tarde?
where

1. ______________________________
2. ______________________________
3. ______________________________
4. ______________________________
5. ______________________________
6. ______________________________

CD5, Track 6 **LM 8-5 | Respuesta correcta** Listen to the questions and choose the correct answer from the two choices provided below. Write the letter that corresponds to the correct answer.

1. ________ **a.** Son de Manuela. **b.** Es de Manuela.
2. ________ **a.** Está muy bueno. **b.** Es una tarta de chocolate.
3. ________ **a.** Porque me gusta tener dos. **b.** Pagué trescientos dólares por la televisión.
4. ________ **a.** Es de Ricardo. **b.** Es Ricardo.
5. ________ **a.** Es una profesora de Guatemala. **b.** Es la profesora Rodríguez.
6. ________ **a.** Hay treinta estudiantes. **b.** Hay un estudiante muy simpático.

CD5, Track 7 **LM 8-6 | ¿Cuál es la pregunta?** You will hear some answers. Based on the model, write logical questions for each answer.

Modelo Estudio español para trabajar en Guatemala.
¿Para qué estudias español?

1. ______________________________
2. ______________________________
3. ______________________________
4. ______________________________
5. ______________________________
6. ______________________________

Nombre ____________________ Fecha ____________________

ESTRUCTURA Y USO 2 Narrating in the past: The preterite and the imperfect

CD5, Track 8 **LM 8-7 | Preguntas personales** Listen to the following questions about your childhood. If the question is based on something that already happened, write **pretérito.** If the question is based on a repeated or a habitual event, write **imperfecto.** Follow the model.

Modelo ¿Ibas a la playa de vacaciones cuando tenías nueve años?
imperfecto

1. ____________________
2. ____________________
3. ____________________
4. ____________________
5. ____________________
6. ____________________

CD5, Track 9 **LM 8-8 | ¡Contéstame!** Listen once again to the questions in activity **LM 8-7** and answer them.

1. ____________________
2. ____________________
3. ____________________
4. ____________________
5. ____________________
6. ____________________

CD5, Track 10 **LM 8-9 | ¿Qué pasó con Patricia y Victoria?** Listen to the story of Victoria and Patricia. They are vacationing on the Guatemalan coast. For each sentence, choose the correctly conjugated verb from the two choices provided. Then write the verbs, conjugated as you hear them. Follow the model.

Modelo Victoria y Patricia celebraron Semana Santa en la costa.
celebraron

1. ____________ se ponía se puso
2. ____________ tenían tenía
3. ____________ fue fueron
4. ____________ había hubo
5. ____________ nadaban nadaron
6. ____________ estaba estaban

VOCABULARIO 2 La playa y el campo

CD5, Track 11 **LM 8-10 | ¡De vacaciones!** Listen to the following descriptions of places to go on vacation and write the letter that best describes each place.

______ **1.** la playa ______ **4.** el balneario

______ **2.** la montaña ______ **5.** la costa

______ **3.** el campo ______ **6.** el mar

CD5, Track 12 **LM 8-11 | ¿Posible o imposible?** Listen to the following statements and write in Spanish if they are possible **(posible)** or impossible **(imposible).**

1. ______________________ **4.** ______________________

2. ______________________ **5.** ______________________

3. ______________________ **6.** ______________________

CD5, Track 13 **LM 8-12 | ¿Dónde?** Listen to the following activities and write down the most logical places where they can be done. Choose from the list provided.

en el balneario en el campo en el lago en el mar en la montaña en la playa

1. ____

2. ____

3. ____

4. ____

5. ____

6. ____

ESTRUCTURA Y USO 3 Stating indefinite ideas and quantities: Affirmative and negative expressions

CD5, Track 14 **LM 8-13 | ¡No estoy de acuerdo!** Listen to the following statements and write the contrary using affirmative or negative expressions as appropriate.

1. ____

2. ____

3. ____

4. ____

5. ____

6. ____

Nombre ______________________ Fecha ______________________

CD5, Track 15 **LM 8-14 | ¿Qué ves?** Look at the drawing and answer the following questions with the most logical affirmative or negative expressions.

1. ______________________
2. ______________________
3. ______________________
4. ______________________
5. ______________________
6. ______________________

CD5, Track 16 **LM 8-15 | ¡Nunca y nadie!** Listen to the sentences and answer negatively using **nunca** or **nadie** accordingly. Choose from the two choices.

1. ________ **a.** Nunca voy al gimnasio. **b.** No voy con nadie al gimnasio.
2. ________ **a.** Nadie me ve fuera de las clases. **b.** No veo a nadie fuera de las clases.
3. ________ **a.** No hablo nunca cuando duermo. **b.** No hablo con nadie.
4. ________ **a.** Nunca tomo el sol. **b.** Nadie toma el sol.
5. ________ **a.** No voy a la playa con nadie. **b.** Nunca voy a la playa.
6. ________ **a.** No llamo a nadie por la mañana. **b.** Nadie llama a mi casa por las mañanas.

PRONUNCIACIÓN 1 *x*

CD5, Track 17 In Spanish, the letter called **equis** is not very common at the beginning of a word, and it is pronounced like an **s**, as in **xenófobo.** Between two vowels it is pronounced like the English *x,* as in *exam*. However, when it is before a consonant, **x** is pronounced almost like an **s,** as in **extranjero**. In Mexico**, x** sounds like a **j** even if the word is written with an **x.** For example, **México** is written with an **x** but pronounced like a **j: Méjico.** In Spain, numerous words, such as **Javier** and **Jiménez,** used to be spelled with an **x (Xavier, Ximénez),** but these words have changed their spelling, transforming **x** into a **j.** Only in Latin America have some words kept the **x** spelling (but **j** pronunciation): for example, **México.**

 To learn more about the letter **x,** visit Heinle iRadio at www.cengage.com/spanish/viajes.

CD5, Track 18 **LM 8-16 | ¡Así suena!** Listen, repeat, and write.

x: (between two vowels)

1. ______________________________

x: (before a consonant)

2. ______________________________

x: (initial position)

3. ______________________________

x: (in Mexico)

4. ______________________________

x: (in different positions)

5. ______________________________

x: (in a sentence in different positions)

6. ______________________________

PRONUNCIACIÓN 2 La entonación

CD5, Track 19 When we ask a question, the intonation changes—it rises or it falls—depending on the expected answer.

- In Spanish, the intonation rises if the expected answer to the question is affirmative or negative:
  ¿Tiene Victoria su traje de baño?
  ¿Se reúne Juan con su familia en Navidad?
  ¿Hay olas en el mar?
- The intonation also rises if the expected answer confirms something in the question:
  Toño es el novio de Patricia, ¿cierto?
  San Salvador es la capital de El Salvador, ¿no?
  Guatemala está al sur de México, ¿verdad?
- However, the intonation falls if the questions are requesting information:
  Por favor, ¿me puede decir qué hora es?
  Me gustaría alquilar un velero. ¿Cuánto cuesta una hora?

Nombre ______________________ Fecha ______________________

CD5, Track 20 **LM 8-17 | ¿Pregunta o respuesta?** Indicate whether what you hear is a question or an answer. Pay particular attention to the intonation. Then, select the arrow pointing up or the arrow pointing down to show if the intonation rises or falls.

1. pregunta respuesta ↑ ↓
2. pregunta respuesta ↑ ↓
3. pregunta respuesta ↑ ↓
4. pregunta respuesta ↑ ↓
5. pregunta respuesta ↑ ↓
6. pregunta respuesta ↑ ↓

DVD ¡A VER!

LM 8-18 | ¿Cierto o falso? Watch the **¡A ver!** video segment for Chapter 8, then read the following statements and mark whether they are **cierto** or **falso.**

	cierto	falso
1. Alejandra va a hacer ejercicio.	☐	☐
2. Es el cumpleaños de Valeria.	☐	☐
3. Valeria se pone muy contenta por su cumpleaños.	☐	☐
4. Valeria cumple veinticinco años.	☐	☐
5. Valeria tenía fiestas de cumpleaños muy, muy grandes cuando era niña.	☐	☐
6. Cuando era niña, Alejandra celebraba sus cumpleaños con sus compañeritos y la maestra.	☐	☐

LM 8-19 | El cumpleaños de Valeria Watch the **¡A ver!** video segment again and complete the following statements with the correct choices provided below.

1. Alejandra le pregunta a Valeria: "¿Te pasa algo?" Y Valeria le contesta...
   - **a.** "No, no es nada".
   - **b.** "No, no me pasó nada".
   - **c.** "No, no es de moda".
2. Valeria está triste porque...
   - **a.** ya no tiene amigos.
   - **b.** ninguno de sus amigos vino.
   - **c.** ninguno de sus amigos la felicitó.
3. Alejandra le dice a Valeria que sus amigos en Venezuela seguramente piensan que está muy ocupada en Puerto Rico porque...
   - **a.** casi nunca está ocupada.
   - **b.** casi nunca está en casa.
   - **c.** casi nunca está contenta.
4. El año pasado, en su fiesta de cumpleaños, Valeria tuvo...
   - **a.** cincuenta invitados.
   - **b.** cien invitados.
   - **c.** ciento cincuenta invitados.
5. La mamá y la hermana de Valeria siempre le preparaban su...
   - **a.** comida favorita.
   - **b.** postre favorito.
   - **c.** fiesta favorita.
6. Al final, Javier, Antonio, Sofi y Alejandra le dicen todos a Valeria...
   - **a.** "¡Felicitaciones!"
   - **b.** "¡Feliz día!"
   - **c.** "¡Felicidades!"

Nombre ______________________ Fecha ______________________

De viaje por el Caribe: Cuba, Puerto Rico y la República Dominicana

VOCABULARIO 1 Viajar en avión

CD5, Track 21 **LM 9-1 | Un viaje en avión** You will hear some statements about Patricia and her sister, two students from the University of Colorado who studied abroad at the University of Puerto Rico in San Juan last semester. Put the sentences in a logical order by entering the letter that corresponds to each one in the space provided.

1. ______ **4.** ______

2. ______ **5.** ______

3. ______ **6.** ______

CD5, Track 22 **LM 9-2 | ¡Esa no!** Listen to the words associated with flights and traveling. First, repeat each word or expression that you hear. Next, write the word or expression that does not belong in the group in the space provided.

1. ______________________________.

2. ______________________________.

3. ______________________________.

4. ______________________________.

5. ______________________________.

6. ______________________________.

CD5, Track 23 **LM 9-3 | Tus preferencias cuando viajas en avión** You are planning your next vacation. At the travel agency, the agent, in order to find the ideal place for you, asks that you fill out a form indicating your preferences. Select your preferences: **sí, no,** or **es posible.**

1. sí no es posible **4.** sí no es posible

2. sí no es posible **5.** sí no es posible

3. sí no es posible **6.** sí no es posible

ESTRUCTURA Y USO 1 Simplifying expressions (I): Indirect object pronouns

CD5, Track 24 **LM 9-4 | ¿A quién le sucede?** Ester Carranza is assisting her clients at the travel agency. Listen to what she does for each client, and select the option with the indirect object pronoun that best reflects Ester's actions. Write its letter in the space.

1. ______ **4.** ______

2. ______ **5.** ______

3. ______ **6.** ______

CD5, Track 25 **LM 9-5 | ¿Quién es responsable?** Identify the individual that carries out the action you hear by entering the correct letter in the space provided.

1. el agente de viajes ______
2. el piloto ______
3. mi amigo ______
4. el asistente de vuelo ______
5. la madre ______
6. el oficial de aduana ______

CD5, Track 26 **LM 9-6 | Un viaje especial** Julio and Gloria went to the Caribbean on a romantic getaway. Listen to what they did, and answer the questions following the model.

Modelo Julio y Gloria trajeron fotos para mí.
¿A quién le trajeron fotos Julio y Gloria?
Me trajeron fotos a mí.

1. ____.
2. ____.
3. ____.
4. ____.
5. ____.
6. ____.

ESTRUCTURA Y USO 2 Simplifying expressions (II): Double object pronouns

CD5, Track 27 **LM 9-7 | ¿Qué hicieron?** Answer each travel-related question by selecting a logical response from the list below. **¡OJO!** Pay special attention to the use of double pronouns in the answers.

1. Se los dimos a nuestros padres. ______
2. Se las mandaron a sus amigas desde la República Dominicana. ______
3. Se lo mandé a Visa para pagar nuestro viaje al Caribe. ______
4. Me lo abroché durante el vuelo. ______
5. Se lo enseñaste al oficial de aduana. ______
6. Se lo dio al asistente de vuelo. ______

Nombre ______________________ Fecha ______________________

CD5, Track 28 **LM 9-8 | ¡Qué bien se lo pasa uno en el Caribe!** Listen to each sentence carefully. Then, replace the direct and indirect objects in the sentences with direct and indirect object pronouns and write them down in the space provided. Follow the model.

Modelo Mi amigo compró el boleto para mí.
Me lo *compró.*

1. ________ ________ enseñaron.
2. ________ ________ recomendó.
3. ________ ________ prestaron.
4. ________ ________ regaló.
5. ________ ________ ofreció.
6. ________ ________ escribimos.

CD5, Track 29 **LM 9-9 | Abreviando** Abbreviate each statement you hear by replacing the subjects and the objects with their respective pronouns. Write the sentences in the blanks provided. Follow the model.

Modelo Julio y Gloria trajeron fotos para mí.
Me las trajeron.

1. ______________________________.
2. ______________________________.
3. ______________________________.
4. ______________________________.
5. ______________________________.
6. ______________________________.

VOCABULARO 2 El hotel

CD5, Track 30 **LM 9-10 | En el hotel** Manny and Teri are spending their honeymoon in a hotel in La Habana. Listen to their story and write the letters in the spaces to put their statements in logical order.

1. ______ 4. ______
2. ______ 5. ______
3. ______ 6. ______

CD5, Track 31 **LM 9-11 | ¿Qué recuerdas de los recién casados?** Listen to the following statements about the newlyweds Manny and Teri. Show how much you know about their honeymoon by indicating **cierto** or **falso** after hearing each statement.

1. ____________ 4. ____________
2. ____________ 5. ____________
3. ____________ 6. ____________

CD5, Track 32 **LM 9-12 | ¿Qué parte del hotel es?** Listen to the definitions and choose the correct vocabulary word by entering its corresponding letter in the space provided.

1. la llave ______
2. la recepción ______
3. un baño privado ______
4. la cama doble ______
5. un hotel lujoso ______
6. la reserva ______

ESTRUCTURA Y USO 3 Giving directions: Prepositions of location, adverbs, and relevant expressions

CD5, Track 33 **LM 9-13 | ¿Dónde están?** Study the map below. As you hear the locations described, indicate where things are located by selecting the correct direction.

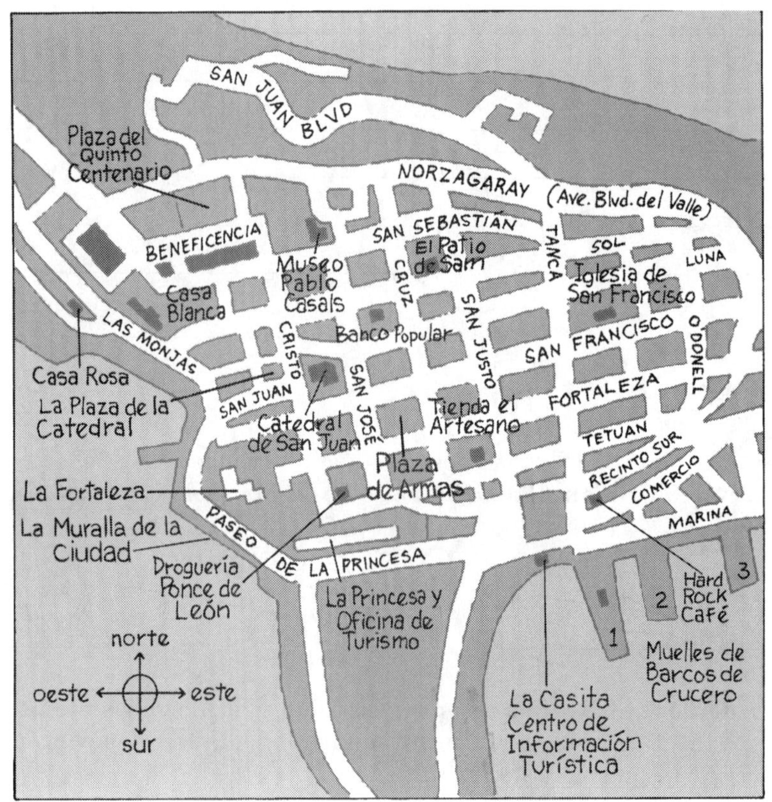

1.	norte	sur	este	oeste
2.	norte	sur	este	oeste
3.	norte	sur	sureste	suroeste
4.	norte	sur	sureste	suroeste
5.	norte	sur	sureste	suroeste
6.	norte	sur	este	oeste

Nombre ______________________ Fecha ______________________

CD5, Track 34 **LM 9-14 | ¿Cómo llego?** You are lost in San Juan and forgot your map at the hotel. You ask a local for directions. As reference, the local will show you a map identical to the one in activity **LM 9-13**. Listen to the directions and then select which route the directions are for. Enter the appropriate number in the space provided.

1. ____________ de la Droguería Ponce de León al Museo Pablo Casals
2. ____________ del Hard Rock Café a la Plaza del Quinto Centenario
3. ____________ de La Casita Centro de Información Turística a la Muralla de la Ciuda
4. ____________ de los Muelles de Barcos de Crucero a la Casa Blanca
5. ____________ de la Iglesia de San Francisco a la Catedral de San Juan
6. ____________ del Banco Popular a la Plaza de la Catedral

ESTRUCTURA Y USO 4 Telling someone to do something: Formal commands and negative *tú* commands

CD5, Track 35 **LM 9-15 | Durante un vuelo** Listen to the instructions that the flight attendant Silvia Vargas is giving to the passengers on the plane. Identify each command with the corresponding drawing.

1. ______________________ 2. ______________________ 3. ______________________

4. ______________________ 5. ______________________

CD5, Track 36 **LM 9-16 | Las promociones para viajes especiales** Tere is listening to the radio when she hears a commercial from the travel agency Caribetel. Listen to the commercial at least twice and then write down the commands in the spaces provided.

1. ______________ 7. ______________
2. ______________ 8. ______________
3. ______________ 9. ______________
4. ______________ 10. ______________
5. ______________ 11. ______________
6. ______________ 12. ______________

CD5, Track 37 **LM 9-17 | En el aeropuerto** Verónica and Juan are at the airport. They are both very excited about going to Aguadilla, Puerto Rico, but Verónica is so afraid of flying that she is giving orders to Juan, constantly telling him what not to do. **¡OJO!** She is so nervous that some of her commands make no sense! First listen to the affirmative commands and then write them in the negative form.

1. ____.
2. ____.
3. ____.
4. ____.
5. ____.
6. ____.

PRONUNCIACIÓN 1 *j*

CD5, Track 38 The Spanish **j** has a sound somewhat like the *h* in *hill,* but harder. It is never pronounced like the English *j* in *jet.*

CD5, Track 39 **LM 9-18 | ¡Así suena!** Repeat and write each sentence.

1. ____.
2. ____.
3. ____.
4. ____.

Nombre ______________________ Fecha ______________________

PRONUNCIACIÓN 2 *g*

CD5, Track 40 The Spanish **g** before an **e** or **i** is pronounced like the **j** in **Juan.** In all other cases, **g** is pronounced like the *g* in *go.*

To learn more about **g, gu,** and **ga,** visit Heinle iRadio at www.cengage.com/spanish/viajes.

CD5, Track 41 **LM 9-19 | ¡Así suena!** Repeat and write each sentence.

1. ______________________.
2. ______________________.
3. ______________________.
4. ______________________.
5. ______________________.
6. ______________________.

CD5, Track 42 **LM 9-20 | ¡Así suena!** Repeat and write each sentence.

1. ______________________.
2. ______________________.
3. ______________________.
4. ______________________.

¡A VER!

LM 9-21 | Comprensión After watching the video segment for Chapter 9, read the following statements and decide whether they are **cierto** or **falso.**

	cierto	**falso**
1. Valeria fue de compras por el Viejo San Juan.	☐	☐
2. Antonio gastó mucho dinero, se perdió y se siente celoso.	☐	☐
3. Ale desea establecer una agencia de ecoturismo y vivir en el extranjero.	☐	☐
4. Antonio y Ale fueron al Paseo de la Princesa y ahora están jugando a las cartas.	☐	☐
5. El sueño de Javier ya tiene un itinerario.	☐	☐
6. Aunque no le gusta hablar con extraños, Valeria le pidió a una señora direcciones para llegar a la Plaza de la Rogativa.	☐	☐

LM 9-22 | ¿Consejos para Javier o para Valeria? You will read a few statements from someone giving advice to Javier and Valeria. Read each sentence, and then decide if the advice is intended for Javier or for Valeria, based on what happened in the **¡A ver!** video segment.

1. No viajes por avión en Costa Rica. ¡Las carreteras son muy bonitas!

   Javier Valeria

2. Pregúntale a una señora cómo llegar a la Plaza de la Rogativa.

   Javier Valeria

3. Ve a una agenica de viajes para tener más información sobre Centroamérica.

   Javier Valeria

4. No les digas mentiras a tus amigos.

   Javier Valeria

5. No tengas celos de Alejandra.

   Javier Valeria

Nombre ______________________ Fecha ______________________

10 Las relaciones sentimentales: Honduras y Nicaragua

VOCABULARIO 1 Las relaciones sentimentales

CD6, Track 2 **LM 10-1 | ¿Qué definición es?** Listen to the definitions about relationships. In the spaces provided, write the letters that correspond to the definitions.

_______ **1.** los recién casados

_______ **2.** el ramo

_______ **3.** los invitados

_______ **4.** la luna de miel

_______ **5.** la boda

_______ **6.** el divorcio

CD6, Track 3 **LM 10-2 | Tú, ¿qué piensas?** Listen to the sentences and fill in the missing words in the following sentences. Then, give your opinion by writing one of the following expressions in the space provided.

Estoy de acuerdo. or **No estoy de acuerdo.**

1. No creo en el amor ______________________. ¡Es imposible!

____

2. ______________________ es una institución anticuada y muy tradicional.

____

3. Muchas veces ______________________ no es fácil.

____

4. El ______________________ a alguien y que sea recíproco es una sensación muy bonita.

____

5. Vivir en pareja y no ______________________ es la mejor situación.

____

6. Después de muchos años de matrimonio, solo hay ______________________ y no amor.

____

CD6, Track 4 **LM 10-3 | ¿Cúal no pertenece?** Listen to the following word sequences and write the word that does not belong to each group.

1. ____

2. ____

3. ____

4. ____

5. ____

6. ____

ESTRUCTURA Y USO 1 Describing recent actions, events, and conditions: The present perfect tense

CD6, Track 5 **LM 10-4 | Eva en una boda** Eva went to her cousin's wedding last week. Listen to her story and complete the sentences with verbs you hear in the present perfect.

1. Primero, los invitados ______________________ en la iglesia.
2. La solista ______________________ el «Ave María» de Schubert.
3. Después del «Ave María», la novia ______________________ con su padre a la iglesia.
4. Las madres se ______________________ a llorar al ver a la novia entrar en la iglesia.
5. Los novios ______________________ «Sí, quiero».
6. Los novios se ______________________ al terminar la ceremonia religiosa.

CD6, Track 6 **LM 10-5 | ¿Qué ha hecho Eva ayer?** Listen to what Eva did yesterday before her cousin's wedding. Then match each sentence with its English translation by writing the correct letter.

1. __________ In the morning, Eva and her mother have gone to try on their dresses.
2. __________ After that, they have bought flowers for their dresses.
3. __________ Eva has come back home in the afternoon.
4. __________ Eva has read her fashion magazine.
5. __________ Eva has eaten with her parents.
6. __________ After dinner, Eva has seen a movie.

CD6, Track 7 **LM 10-6 | ¿Y los demás?** Now listen to what the other members in the family have done before the wedding. Pay attention to the verbs, because you will have to conjugate the verbs that you hear to agree with different family members (subjects) that appear below. The verbs that you hear are all conjugated in the third-person singular, "Eva".

Modelo Eva ha descansado en el sofá.
Sus padres *han descansado* en el sofá.

1. Sus hermanos ______________________ a la abuela a casa.
2. Nosotros ______________________ a la peluquería.
3. Tú ______________________ una botella de champán.
4. Ustedes ______________________ por teléfono con el novio.
5. Yo ______________________ mucho con toda la familia.
6. Usted ______________________ que el día de la boda será muy divertido.

Nombre ______________________ Fecha ______________________

ESTRUCTURA Y USO 2 Qualifying actions: Adverbs and adverbial expressions of time and sequencing of events

CD6, Track 8 **LM 10-7 | ¿Cómo?** Qualify Victoria and Juan's actions with the most logical adverbs. Follow the model.

Modelo Victoria llama a Juan. / frecuente
frecuentemente

1. ______________ 4. ______________
2. ______________ 5. ______________
3. ______________ 6. ______________

CD6, Track 9 **LM 10-8 | ¡Radio Chismes Increíbles!** Listen to the program **Radio Chismes** *(Gossip)* **Increíbles** about the rich and famous, and write how the celebrities did what they did. Use the adverbs of frequency based on what you hear in the sentences. Follow the model.

Modelo Julia Roberts ha tenido a su tercer hijo con un parto difícil.
Julia Roberts ha tenido a su tercer hijo *difícilmente*.

1. Jennifer Aniston salió del aeropuerto de Los Ángeles ______________.
2. Angelina Jolie ha adoptado a su sexto niño ______________.
3. Paris Hilton ha estado en la cárcel ______________.
4. Britney Spears se ha afeitado la cabeza una tercera vez ______________.
5. Madonna ha bebido cocteles *(cocktails)* ______________.
6. Gwyneth Paltrow se ha vestido ______________.

CD6, Track 10 **LM 10-9 | ¡Para mí, no!** You have different opinions from your friend. Listen to your friend's opinions and write the contrary, using the opposite adverbs. Write only the adverbs instead of the whole sentence. The adverbs that you will hear are the equivalents of: *well, best, poorly, a little, late, always,* etc.

Modelo Nunca me duermo antes de las doce.
siempre

1. ______________
2. ______________
3. ______________
4. ______________
5. ______________
6. ______________

VOCABULARIO 2 La recepción

CD6, Track 11 **LM 10-10 | Sinónimos** Listen to the definitions and the synonyms of the vocabulary. Write down the appropriate letter of the definition or the synonym next to each word listed below.

__________ **1.** terminar

__________ **2.** asistir

__________ **3.** la pareja

__________ **4.** la orquesta

__________ **5.** el banquete

__________ **6.** acompañar

CD6, Track 12 **LM 10-11 | Más definiciones** You will hear five words related to banquets and receptions. For each word, select the definition that corresponds to it by writing the correct letter in the space provided. Follow the model.

Modelo a. felicitar
Decir: "¡Felicidades!" ____*a*____

1. hacer ruido *(noise)* con las manos __________
2. las personas que vienen a la fiesta __________
3. tomar, obtener un objeto; por ejemplo, el ramo de la novia __________
4. una persona que lleva ropa muy elegante __________
5. expresar buenos deseos antes de beber champán *(champagne)* o vino __________

CD6, Track 13 **LM 10-12 | ¿Pudo ocurrir así?** Listen to the following statements about a wedding reception. Decide if the statements describe something that could have happened or not; write **sí** if the event could have happened or **no** if it could not have happened. Be logical!

1. ________ **2.** ________ **3.** ________

4. ________ **5.** ________ **6.** ________

ESTRUCTURA Y USO 3 Talking about future events: Future tense

CD6, Track 14 **LM 10-13 | Predicciones sobre los recién casados** Pepita and Pepito just got married. The wedding guests talk about how they predict the future of the newlyweds. Listen to their predictions and write down the verbs that you hear in each sentence (they are in the infinitive form) in the future tense.

Modelo Pepita y Pepito (ser) muy felices
serán

1. ________ **2.** ________ **3.** ________

4. ________ **5.** ________ **6.** ________

CD6, Track 15 **LM 10-14 | ¡Tú no decides!** Your future mother-in-law wants to organize your wedding for you. (She is very excited about you marrying her son!) She tells you how she envisions your day. Negate the verbs that you hear. Follow the model. (Do not forget to switch to the **yo** form when necessary).

Modelo ¡Te casarás con un vestido de diamantes!
¡No me casaré con un vestido de diamantes!

1. ¡ ______________ un vestido muy, muy largo!
2. ¡ ______________ un ramo de rosas rojas!
3. ¡ ______________ a toda la familia!
4. ¡ ______________ caviar!
5. ¡ ______________ en el jardín de la casa!
6. La recepción ______________ lugar en la casa.

CD6, Track 16 **LM 10-15 | ¿Y tu futuro?** You will hear some questions pertaining to your future. Answer them in complete sentences making certain you use the correct form of the future tense in Spanish.

1. ______________________________
2. ______________________________
3. ______________________________
4. ______________________________
5. ______________________________
6. ______________________________

ESTRUCTURA Y USO 4 Expressing conjecture or probability: The conditional

CD6, Track 17 **LM 10-16 | En un mundo perfecto...** Listen to the sentences about how couples would be in a perfect world. Pay attention to the verbs—they are in the infinitive form and must be conjugated in the conditional. Follow the model.

Modelo En un mundo perfecto, las parejas (quererse) siempre.
En un mundo perfecto, las parejas *se querrían* siempre.

1. En un mundo perfecto, los esposos no ______________ nunca.
2. En un mundo perfecto, las parejas no ______________ sobre cosas sin importancia.
3. En un mundo perfecto, los esposos ______________.
4. En un mundo perfecto, el marido y la mujer siempre ______________ la verdad.
5. En un mundo perfecto, no ______________ hijos no deseados.
6. En un mundo perfecto, las parejas ______________ una vida muy feliz.

CD6, Track 18 **LM 10-17 | Especulaciones** The bride never made it to the wedding yesterday. The guests speculate about what could have happened to the bride. Listen to the verbs in the preterite and write them down in conditional.

Modelo La novia no se despertó a tiempo.
La novia no *se despertaría* a tiempo.

1. La novia ______________________ un accidente.
2. La novia ______________________ a otro hombre.
3. La novia ______________________ de opinión.
4. La novia ______________________ del día de la boda.
5. La novia ______________________ con otro.
6. La novia ______________________ con el otro.

CD6, Track 19 **LM 10-18 | ¡Con educación, por favor!** Álex is a small child who does not yet have proper manners. You will hear him make a statement; change his command into a more gentle request by using the conditional. Write each reworked request in the space provided, and then repeat each one. Follow the model.

Modelo ¡Camarero, quiero agua!
Camarero, *querría agua,* por favor.

1. Mamá, ¿ ______________________, por favor?
2. Papá, ¿ ______________________, por favor?
3. Mamá, ¿ ______________________, por favor?
4. Papis, ¿ ______________________, por favor?
5. Papá, ¿ ______________________, por favor?
6. Mamá, ¿ ______________________, por favor?

PRONUNCIACIÓN 1 Review of accents

CD6, Track 20 One easy rule to remember is that all words ending in –**ión** have a written accent on the **o;** for example, **atención** and **información.** The voice always rises with the accent, emphasizing its placement on the **ó.** Listen to the following words ending in –**ión** and repeat: **interrogación, acumulación, constitución, argumentación, legión.**

All interrogative words have a written accent mark as well. The voice rises with the accent.

Listen to the following interrogative words and repeat: **¿Cómo estás hoy? ¿Qué tal estás hoy? ¿Por qué fumas tanto? ¿Cuándo llegas a casa?**

Now, compare **¿Por qué fumas tanto?** (interrogative) with **Porque me gusta** (affirmative statement). Do you hear the difference? Listen and repeat: **¿Por qué no vienes a clase? Porque estoy cansado**.

Some words have a written accent mark and are pronounced accordingly to distinguish one word from another: for example, **sí** and **si**. Listen and repeat: **¡Sí, quiero! Si te casas conmigo, serás muy feliz.**

To learn more about **Accents,** visit Heinle iRadio at www.cengage.com/spanish/viajes.

Nombre ______________________ Fecha ______________________

CD6, Track 21 **LM 10-19 | ¿Puedes distinguir?** Of the two options presented, write the words that you hear.

1. si sí ________

2. por qué porque ________

3. que qué ________

4. se sé ________

5. cuándo cuando ________

6. como cómo ________

PRONUNCIACIÓN 2 Review of pronunciation of vowels

CD6, Track 22 The vowel **a:** The Spanish **a** sounds like the English *a* in the word *father.*

m**a**r p**a**l**a**br**a** c**a**j**a** puert**a** mes**a**

The vowel **e:** The Spanish **e** sounds like the English *e* found in the word *get*.

P**e**p**e** du**e**l**e** m**e**t**e**r l**ee**r p**e**s**e**

The vowel **i:** The Spanish **i** sounds like the English sound *ee* in the word *India*.

L**i**l**i** P**i**l**i** m**i**l**i** t**í**a m**í**a p**i**stola

The vowel **o:** The Spanish **o** sounds like the English *o* in *cope*.

p**o**r am**o**r **o**l**o**r ag**o**st**o** **o**íd**o**

The vowel **u:** The Spanish **u** sounds like the English *oo* found in *choose*.

m**u**la m**u**ela t**u**t**ú** l**u**z s**u**ena

CD6, Track 23 **LM 10-20 | ¡Así suena!** Repeat and write the words you hear.

1. ________ **4.** ________

2. ________ **5.** ________

3. ________ **6.** ________

¡A VER!

LM 10-21 | ¿Cierto o falso? Watch the **¡A ver!** video segment from Chapter 10 and tell if the following statements are **cierto** or **falso.**

	cierto	falso
1. Valeria está enojada con César.	☐	☐
2. César no está celoso.	☐	☐
3. César es el ex novio de Valeria.	☐	☐
4. Antonio piensa que Valeria es muy guapa.	☐	☐
5. Antonio nunca ha tenido una novia.	☐	☐
6. El amigo de Antonio se llama Rubio.	☐	☐

LM 10-22 | Palabras exactas Watch the video clip again, and circle the correct statements.

1. Al principio del segmento, Valeria habla con César por teléfono. Ella le dice:
   - **a.** Yo pensé que podíamos ser amigos pero veo que no.
   - **b.** Yo pensé que podíamos ser amigos pero veo que es imposible.
   - **c.** Yo pensé que podíamos ser amigos pero veo que no es posible.
2. Cuando Valeria termina de hablar por teléfono y ve a Antonio en la piscina, le pregunta lo siguiente:
   - **a.** ¿Estabas espiando mi conversación?
   - **b.** ¿Estabas escuchando mi conversación?
   - **c.** ¿Estabas oyendo mi conversación?
3. Cuando Antonio le pregunta a Valeria que por qué César es su ex novio, Valeria le dice que César es muy machista y celoso. Antonio le pregunta lo siguiente:
   - **a.** ¿A poco tú nunca le diste razones para ser celoso?
   - **b.** ¿A poco tú nunca le diste motivos para ser celoso?
   - **c.** ¿A poco tú nunca le diste ocasiones para ser celoso?
4. Antonio también tuvo una novia a la que quería mucho. ¿Qué le dice Antonio a Valeria que pasó?
   - **a.** Su novia se enamoró de su mejor amigo y Antonio no la perdonó.
   - **b.** Su novia se enamoró de su mejor amigo y ya no le habló a Antonio.
   - **c.** Su novia se enamoró de su mejor amigo y dejó a Antonio por él.
5. Después de escuchar esa historia tan triste sobre la novia de Antonio, Valeria le dice a Antonio lo siguiente:
   - **a.** Yo no se lo podría perdonar.
   - **b.** Yo no se lo podría aguantar.
   - **c.** Yo no se lo podría tolerar.
6. Al final del segmento, Antonio le pregunta a Valeria que si la puede acompañar y le hace otra pregunta. ¿Cuál es la pregunta?
   - **a.** ¿Qué te gustaría comer?
   - **b.** ¿Qué te gustaría ver?
   - **c.** ¿Qué te gustaría hacer?

Nombre ______________________ Fecha ______________________

11 El mundo del trabajo: Chile

VOCABULARIO 1 Profesiones y oficios

CD6, Track 24 **LM 11-1 | ¿Profesión u oficio?** Listen carefully to the following items and indicate whether they are professions or trades by selecting the correct choice.

1. profesión / oficio **4.** profesión / oficio **5.** profesión / oficio

2. profesión / oficio **3.** profesión / oficio **6.** profesión / oficio

CD6, Track 25 **LM 11-2 | Las profesiones** Listen to the descriptions. Match the descriptions that you hear with the appropriate professions below and write the corresponding letter.

______ **1.** el (la) fotógrafo(a) ______ **4.** el (la) periodista

______ **2.** el (la) contador(a) ______ **5.** el (la) programador(a)

______ **3.** el (la) jefe ______ **6.** el (la) traductor(a)

CD6, Track 26 **LM 11-3 | ¿A quién llamas?** Listen to each situation and decide which person you would call by selecting the appropriate illustration. Make certain you write the letter corresponding to the situation, as well as the professional in question.

1. ______________________

2. ______________________

3. ______________________

4. ______________________

5. ______________________

ESTRUCTURA Y USO 1 Making statements about motives, intentions, and periods of time: *Por* vs. *para*

CD6, Track 27 **LM 11-4 | ¿Cuál de las dos?** Listen to each pair of sentences containing the prepositions **por** and **para.** Decide which one is correct by selecting the appropriate letter.

1. a / b **2.** a / b **3.** a / b **4.** a / b **5.** a / b **6.** a / b

CD6, Track 28 **LM 11-5 | ¿Por o para?** Listen to the dialogue carefully and decide which prepositions you need to use. Select the correct preposition.

1. por / para
2. por / para
3. por / para
4. por / para
5. por / para
6. Por / Para

CD6, Track 29 **LM 11-6 | Más decisiones** Listen to the following incomplete statements. Complete each sentence by choosing the appropriate preposition and writing it in the space provided.

1. ________________
2. ________________
3. ________________
4. ________________
5. ________________
6. ________________

VOCABULARIO 2 La oficina, el trabajo y la búsqueda de un puesto

CD6, Track 30 **LM 11-7 | Buscando trabajo** You are at an employment agency looking for a job. For the agency to match your qualifications with the right position, you must fill out a form indicating your preferences. Give your opinion (**sí, no,** or **no es importante**) after hearing each statement.

1. sí no no es importante
2. sí no no es importante
3. sí no no es importante
4. sí no no es importante
5. sí no no es importante
6. sí no no es importante

CD6, Track 31 **LM 11-8 | Cosas de trabajo** Match the definition with its appropriate term. Write the letter of the definition in the space.

___________ **1.** pedir un aumento
___________ **2.** la impresora
___________ **3.** contratar
___________ **4.** solicitar un puesto
___________ **5.** de tiempo completo
___________ **6.** despedir

CD6, Track 32 **LM 11-9 | ¿Qué hacer primero?** Listen to the necessary steps one must take to prepare for that perfect job. Place the statements in chronological order by writing in their letters in the spaces provided.

1. ________________
2. ________________
3. ________________
4. ________________
5. ________________
6. ________________

Nombre ______________________ Fecha ______________________

ESTRUCTURA Y USO 2 Expressing subjectivity and uncertainty: The subjunctive mood

CD6, Track 33 **LM 11-10 | El jefe de mis pesadillas *(nightmares)*** Julián had a dream that his boss was great; however, that is not the case. When Julián woke up he remembered how awful his boss is. Listen to what Julián says about his boss. Then indicate whether you agree (**Estoy de acuerdo.**) or disagree (**No estoy de acuerdo.**) that these traits make his boss intolerable.

1. Estoy de acuerdo. No estoy de acuerdo.
2. Estoy de acuerdo. No estoy de acuerdo.
3. Estoy de acuerdo. No estoy de acuerdo.
4. Estoy de acuerdo. No estoy de acuerdo.
5. Estoy de acuerdo. No estoy de acuerdo.
6. Estoy de acuerdo. No estoy de acuerdo.

CD6, Track 34 **LM 11-11 | ¿Qué le recomiendas a Julián?** Poor Julián is so tired of his awful boss that he comes to you for advice. Listen to the options and choose the one that will improve Julián's situation. Select the appropriate letters.

1. a / b
2. a / b
3. a / b
4. a / b
5. a / b
6. a / b

CD6, Track 35 **LM 11-12 | ¿Qué te parece?** You will hear a series of situations pertaining to the workplace. Offer your perspective or opinion by using the subjunctive to complete the sentences below.

1. Recomiendo que ______________________.
2. Deseo que ______________________.
3. No dudo que ______________________.
4. Es necesario que ______________________.
5. Es probable que ______________________.
6. Es posible que ______________________.

CD6, Track 36 **LM 11-13 | El trabajo ideal** Listen to the ideal job description. Pay close attention to the use of the subjunctive and write the subjunctive phrase in the spaces provided.

1. ______________________
2. ______________________
3. ______________________
4. ______________________
5. ______________________
6. ______________________

CD6, Track 37 **LM 11-14 | ¡Ese es!** Choose the correct form in order to complete the sentence correctly.

1. que se divierta / que se divierte
2. que me da / que me dé
3. que te aumenta / que te aumente
4. que no les pide / que no les pida
5. que vayan / que van
6. que escribe / que escriba

CD6, Track 38 **LM 11-15 | El empleo de mis sueños** Listen to the prompts and respond according to your preferences with regard to the perfect job. Pay close attention in using the present subjunctive.

1. ______________________________
2. ______________________________
3. ______________________________
4. ______________________________
5. ______________________________
6. ______________________________

DVD ¡A VER!

LM 11-16 | Comprensión After watching the video for Chapter 11, decide if the following statements are **cierto** or **falso.**

	cierto	falso
1. Javier quiere escribir un libro sobre la cultura taína.	☐	☐
2. El padre de Sofía quiere que estudie medicina.	☐	☐
3. Javier necesita hacer un plan.	☐	☐
4. Sofía es una inspiración para Javier.	☐	☐
5. Sofía y Javier quieren vivir en el extranjero.	☐	☐
6. Sofía busca un apartamento porque quiere abrir una agencia de deportes de aventura y ecoturismo.	☐	☐

LM 11-17 | ¿Quién fue? Watch the video again and decide which of the five characters in the video is responsible for the following actions.

1. Quiere viajar al extranjero.

   Sofía Valeria Antonio Javier Alejandra

2. Lucha por su sueño y fue una inspiración.

   Sofía Valeria Antonio Javier Alejandra

3. Busca un apartamento.

   Sofía Valeria Antonio Javier Alejandra

4. Quiere vivir en otro país y establecer una agencia de ecoturismo.

   Sofía Valeria Antonio Javier Alejandra

5. Toma mate.

   Sofía Valeria Antonio Javier Alejandra

6. Necesita hacer un plan.

   Sofía Valeria Antonio Javier Alejandra

Nombre ______________________ Fecha ______________________

12 El medio ambiente y las políticas ambientales: Costa Rica y Panamá

VOCABULARIO 1 La geografía rural y urbana

CD7, Track 2 **LM 12-1 | ¿Rural o urbana?** Listen to the words from the vocabulary. Identify the words pertaining to urban or rural geography. Write **rural** or **urbana** according to the vocabulary term that you hear. Follow the model.

Modelo la fábrica
urbana

1. ______________
2. ______________
3. ______________
4. ______________
5. ______________
6. ______________

CD7, Track 3 **LM 12-2 | ¿Es posible o imposible?** Listen to the following statements and decide if each one is possible or impossible. Write **Es posible** or **No es posible** depending on the information given.

1. ______________________________
2. ______________________________
3. ______________________________
4. ______________________________
5. ______________________________
6. ______________________________

CD7, Track 4 **LM 12-3 | ¿Dónde están?** Listen to the following words pertaining to urban or rural geography. Next to the choices provided, write the most logical place where each may be found.

1. el bosque, la carretera, la metrópolis, la basura ______________
2. la fábrica, la selva, la colina, el tráfico ______________
3. el arroyo, el bosque, la finca, la metrópolis ______________
4. la basura, la tierra, la selva, el ruido ______________
5. la catarata, la colina, la basura, los rascacielos ______________
6. la basura, la selva, el bosque, la carretera ______________

ESTRUCTURA Y USO 1 — Expressing emotion and opinions: Subjunctive following verbs of emotion, impersonal expressions, and *ojalá*

CD7, Track 5 **LM 12-4 | Y tú, ¿qué opinas?** You will hear statements made by six people who lead very different lives. Listen carefully, and express your opinion or reaction to each of one. You should use verbs of emotion (**me alegro de que, me molesta que, me sorprende que**, etc.) or impersonal expressions (**es bueno que, es necesario que, es mejor que,** etc.) in your responses. Follow the model.

Modelo Siempre utilizo el transporte público.
Es bueno que tú utilices el transporte público.

1. ______________________________
2. ______________________________
3. ______________________________
4. ______________________________
5. ______________________________
6. ______________________________

CD7, Track 6 **LM 12-5 | Sugerencias** Listen to your friend's opinions regarding lifestyles. Respond to her opinions by commenting on the way she lives. Follow the model.

Modelo Es una lástima no vivir en una metrópolis.
Es una lástima que tú no vivas en una metrópolis.

1. ______________________________
2. ______________________________
3. ______________________________
4. ______________________________
5. ______________________________
6. ______________________________

CD7, Track 7 **LM 12-6 | ¡Ojalá!** Your best friend just found a job in a big metropolitan area. Listen to the statements in the present tense, and then wish your friend the very best in the big city. Begin each of your sentences with the expression **ojalá** + *subjunctive.* Follow the model.

Modelo La vida en una gran metrópolis te gusta.
¡Ojalá que la vida en una gran metrópolis te guste!

1. ______________________________
2. ______________________________
3. ______________________________
4. ______________________________
5. ______________________________
6. ______________________________

Nombre ______________________ Fecha ______________________

VOCABULARIO 2 La conservación y la explotación

CD7, Track 8 **LM 12-7 | ¿Qué palabra es?** You will listen to some definitions. Write the letter of the appropriate definition for each word.

_____ **1.** destruir _____ **3.** reforestar _____ **5.** recoger

_____ **2.** el petróleo _____ **4.** acabar _____ **6.** el aire

CD7, Track 9 **LM 12-8 | ¿Verdad o mentira?** The president of the country is speaking about conservation and exploitation. Listen carefully to the president's message and select either **verdad** or **mentira** depending on the statements. **¡OJO!** Be logical!

1. __________ **2.** __________ **3.** __________

4. __________ **5.** __________ **6.** __________

CD7, Track 10 **LM 12-9 | ¿Es posible o es imposible?** Listen to the following statements regarding the environment and select either **Es posible** or **Es imposible** depending on the statements.

1. __________ **2.** __________ **3.** __________

4. __________ **5.** __________ **6.** __________

CD7, Track 11 **LM 12-10 | ¡Adivina!** Listen to the descriptions of animals or insects. Based on the descriptions, guess which animal or insect is being described.

1. __________ **2.** __________ **3.** __________

4. __________ **5.** __________ **6.** __________

ESTRUCTURA Y USO 2 Expressing doubts or uncertainty; hypothesizing and anticipated actions: The subjunctive with verbs or expressions of doubt and uncertainty; adjective clauses and time clauses

CD7, Track 12 **LM 12-11 | ¿Indicativo o subjuntivo?** Listen to the sentences and write the verbal mode that you hear: **indicativo** or **subjuntivo.** Follow the model.

Modelo Creo que hay mucha contaminación en las grandes metrópolis.
indicativo

1. __________ **2.** __________ **3.** __________

4. __________ **5.** __________ **6.** __________

CD7, Track 13 **LM 12-12 | ¡Lo contrario!** You are going to listen again to the statements from activity **LM 12-11.** Following the model, write the opposite of what you hear.

Modelo Creo que hay mucha contaminación en las grandes metrópolis.
No creo que haya mucha contaminación en las grandes metrópolis.

1. ______
2. ______
3. ______
4. ______
5. ______
6. ______

CD7, Track 14 **LM 12-13 ¡Cada cosa en su momento!** There is a time for everything! You are telling your best friend when you intend to accomplish important events in your personal and professional life. Listen to the statements and complete them in a logical manner about how you would like to plan your future.

Modelo No me voy a comprar una casa hasta que no…
tenga un buen puesto

1. ______
2. ______
3. ______
4. ______
5. ______
6. ______

DVD ¡A VER!

LM 12-14 | ¿Cierto o falso? Watch the **¡A ver!** video segment for Chapter 12 and then read the following statements. For each statement write **cierto** or **falso.**

	cierto	falso
1. A Javier le encantan las actividades y deportes al aire libre.	☐	☐
2. A Valeria le da miedo hacer esnórquel.	☐	☐
3. Los amigos toman el sol en el barco.	☐	☐
4. Al final, Valeria también salta del barco al agua.	☐	☐
5. Sofi va al mar siempre porque vive cerca del mar.	☐	☐
6. Todos se divierten mucho.	☐	☐

Nombre ______________________ Fecha ______________________

LM 12-15 | ¿Qué dicen exactamente? Watch the video segment a second time and then choose the right answer for each statement below.

1. Antes de hacer esnórkeling el guía le dice a Valeria que…
   - **a.** rápidamente se vaya a hacer esnórkeling.
   - **b.** no tenga miedo de hacer esnórkeling.
   - **c.** es normal que no le guste el esnórkeling.
2. El guía da instrucciones de cómo saltar del barco al agua y da la siguiente recomendación:
   - **a.** que brinquen (o salten) al agua de cabeza.
   - **b.** que brinquen (o salten) con los pies primero.
   - **c.** que no brinquen (o salten) del barco hasta que él lo diga.
3. Cuando Valeria se queda sola, dice:
   - **a.** «No sé hacer esnórkeling».
   - **b.** «No sé nadar».
   - **c.** «No sé bucear».
4. Alejandra comenta su experiencia y dice:
   - **a.** «No pude ver peces porque no podía respirar con la máscara».
   - **b.** «Estaba triste porque ese día no había peces en el mar».
   - **c.** «La experiencia del esnórkeling fue estupenda ».
5. Antonio también comenta su experiencia y dice:
   - **a.** «La experiencia de ese día es algo que nunca voy a recordar».
   - **b.** «La experiencia de ese día es algo que nunca podré hacer otra vez».
   - **c.** «La experiencia de ese día es algo que nunca podré olvidar».
6. Después del esnórkeling, Sofía le pregunta a Valeria lo siguiente:
   - **a.** «¿No quieres saber lo que hay bajo el agua?»
   - **b.** «¿No quieres saber cómo nadar bajo el agua?»
   - **c.** «¿No quieres saber lo que se siente bajo el agua?»

Autopruebas Answer Key

CAPÍTULO PRELIMINAR

WB P-12 Una conversación típica

Hola, Qué / estás / gracias / gusto / es mío / dónde / Soy / Adiós / Adiós / Nos

WB P-13 Números

1. quince / catorce
2. uno / cero
3. treinta / veintinueve
4. diecisiete / dieciséis
5. veinticinco / veinticuatro

WB P-14 Presentaciones

eres / Soy, es / son / somos

WB P-15 ¿Sois de España?

vosotros / nosotros, Yo, él / Ud. / Yo / Ella / tú / Yo / Uds.

CAPÍTULO 1

WB 1-18 Los cursos

1. b **2.** c **3.** a **4.** c

WB 1-19 ¿Qué hora es?

1. Son las tres menos cuarto de la tarde.
2. Es la una y veintidós de la tarde.
3. Es la una menos veintinueve de la tarde.
4. Son las cinco y cuarto de la mañana.
5. Son las nueve y media de la mañana.

WB 1-20 Está muy ocupada.

1. Los martes Nancy estudia alemán a las cuatro menos cuarto de la tarde.
2. Los miércoles Nancy estudia chino a la una menos cuarto de la tarde.
3. Los jueves Nancy estudia ruso a la una y media de la tarde.
4. Los viernes Nancy estudia italiano a las cinco y cuarto de la tarde.
5. Los sábados Nancy estudia portugués a las siete y media de la noche.
6. Los domingos Nancy estudia japonés a las diez de la mañana.

WB 1-21 Los colores

1. amarillo **2.** negro/anaranjado **3.** rojo **4.** marrón **5.** blanco **6.** verde

WB 1-22 Lupe y Lalo

1. una **2.** la **3.** una **4.** la **5.** las **6.** la **7.** las **8.** los **9.** el **10.** una **11.** La **12.** las **13.** la **14.** los **15.** la **16.** los

WB 1-23 Las actividades del día

1. Ramón trabaja todos los días.
2. Teresa y Evelia estudian matemáticas por la tarde.
3. Yo practico deportes por la mañana.
4. Nosotros descansamos a las cuatro de la tarde.
5. Tú enseñas ejercicios aeróbicos por la noche.
6. Uds. regresan a la casa a las seis de la tarde.

CAPÍTULO 2

WB 2-27 Los miembros de la familia

1. esposa
2. primo
3. apellido
4. sobrina
5. nietos

WB 2-28 Descripciones

1. es; mexicana
2. somos; simpáticas
3. son; tontos
4. eres; atlética
5. es; paciente

WB 2-29 Probablemente son...

Possible answers:

1. trabajadores
2. inteligente
3. tacaño
4. irresponsable
5. perezosa
6. gordos

WB 2-30 Los números

1. treinta y dos
2. noventa y nueve
3. veinticuatro
4. doce
5. quince
6. diecisiete
7. cuarenta y seis
8. setenta y nueve

WB 2-31 Una conversación

1. Tienes **2.** Mi **3.** tengo **4.** tienes **5.** mis **6.** tienen **7.** tienen **8.** su **9.** Su **10.** Tienes **11.** tengo **12.** Tienes **13.** tengo

WB 2-32 En la universidad

1. vives **2.** vivo **3.** vive **4.** Escribes **5.** escribes **6.** recibo **7.** debo **8.** tienes **9.** creo

CAPÍTULO 3

WB 3-23 Los meses y las estaciones

1. diciembre, el invierno
2. febrero, el invierno
3. enero, el invierno
4. octubre, el otoño
5. mayo, la primavera
6. noviembre, el otoño

WB 3-24 En la ciudad

1. a **2.** g **3.** b **4.** d **5.** c **6.** f **7.** e

WB 3-25 Los pasatiempos

Possible answers:

1. Me gusta ver películas en video.
2. Me gusta sacar fotos.
3. Me gusta jugar al tenis.
4. Me gusta tocar la guitarra.
5. Me gusta bailar con la música rock.
6. Me gusta visitar a mis abuelos.

WB 3-26 Entre amigos

1. vas
2. Voy
3. vas
4. vamos
5. va
6. van

WB 3-27 Un joven contento

1. salgo
2. hago
3. voy
4. hago / doy
5. pongo
6. Conozco
7. sé
8. veo
9. estoy

WB 3-28 ¿Saber o conocer?

1. sabe **2.** conocen **3.** saben **4.** conozco

WB 3-29 ¿Qué vas a hacer?

1. Voy a practicar deportes.
2. Voy a jugar al tenis.
3. Voy a nadar en la piscina.
4. Voy a montar a caballo.
5. Voy a levantar pesas.

WB 3-30 ¿Qué tiempo hace?

Possible answers:

A. Hace sol. Hace calor. Hace buen tiempo.
B. Hace sol. Hace buen tiempo. Está despejado.
C. Hace mucho calor. Está despejado.
D. Hace fresco. Está nublado.
E. Hace viento.
F. Hace mucho frío.

CAPÍTULO 4

WB 4-26 Los muebles

1. un escritorio **2.** un armario **3.** mi cama **4.** el inodoro **5.** el jardín

WB 4-27 Los electrodomésticos

1. un despertador
2. un horno de microondas
3. una lavadora
4. una aspiradora
5. la nevera

WB 4-28 En la casa

1. la cocina **2.** la sala **3.** el jardín **4.** el comedor

WB 4-29 Carlos y Eva

Possible answers:

1. piensas
2. Tengo
3. quieres
4. quiero
5. Prefiero
6. comienza
7. Comienza
8. queremos
9. preferimos
10. pienso

WB 4-30 Con mi familia

1. almuerzo
2. sirve
3. dice
4. almorzar
5. duermo
6. vuelven
7. vuelvo
8. jugamos
9. juego

WB 4-31 ¿Qué hago?

1. Haz tu cama todos los días.
2. Quita la mesa después de comer.
3. Saca la basura todos los días.
4. Ve al supermercado todos los sábados.

WB 4-32 ¿Cuántos son?

1. mil setecientos treinta y ocho
2. mil ciento sesenta
3. mil cuatrocientos dieciséis

CAPÍTULO 5

WB 5-24 El cuerpo humano

1. el ojo
2. el pelo
3. la(s) oreja(s)
4. la nariz
5. la boca / los dientes
6. el estómago
7. la pierna
8. el pie
9. la mano
10. el brazo

WB 5-25 Los problemas médicos

1. alergia, estornudo
2. catarro
3. enfermedad
4. congestionado(a)
5. escalofríos, síntomas
6. sano(a), enfermo(a)
7. examina
8. fiebre, toma la temperatura
9. náuseas, guardar cama

WB 5-26 La rutina diaria

1. Se despierta a las seis.
2. Se levanta a las seis y media.
3. Se ducha y se lava.
4. Se seca.
5. Se viste.
6. Se pinta. / Se maquilla.
7. Despierta a su hijo a las siete.
8. Se acuesta a las once.

WB 5-27 ¡Cómo vuela el tiempo!

1. Acaba de despertarse.
2. Acaba de levantarse.
3. Acaba de ducharse y lavarse.
4. Acaba de secarse.
5. Acaba de vestirse.
6. Acaba de pintarse / maquillarse.
7. Acaba de despertar a su hijo.
8. Acaba de acostarse.

WB 5-28 Lorena Bobada

1. es **2.** Es **3.** está **4.** está **5.** está **6.** está **7.** Es **8.** es **9.** está **10.** ser **11.** es **12.** es

WB 5-29 Gemelos distintos

1. No quiero esta, prefiero esa medicina.
2. No quiero ver a este, prefiero ver a ese médico.
3. No quiero comprar esta, prefiero comprar es a pastilla.
4. No quiero pedir estos, prefiero pedir esos jarabes.
5. No prefiero esto, prefiero eso.

CAPÍTULO 6

WB 6-24 La comida

CARNES:	jamón, res, pollo, bistec, pavo, chuletas de cerdo
PESCADO/MARISCOS:	calamares, camarones
BEBIDAS:	café, vino, agua mineral, té helado leche, cerveza, jugo
POSTRES:	helado, flan, queso
FRUTAS:	naranja, manzana, banana
VERDURAS:	lechuga, papas
CONDIMENTOS:	mantequilla, sal, pimienta, vinagre, aceite

WB 6-25 En el restaurante

1. c **2.** c **3.** a **4.** a **5.** b **6.** a

WB 6-26 ¡Viva la igualdad!

1. Beti come tantas verduras como Martín.
2. Beti almuerza en tantos restaurantes como Martín.
3. Beti pide tantas aprepas como Martín.
4. Beti es tan amable como Martín.
5. Beti toma tanto café como Martín.

WB 6-27 El más...

1. Guillermo es el mayor.
2. Alejandro es el más paciente de los primos.
3. El jugo es la bebida más dulce.
4. Kobe Bryant es el mejor jugador.

WB 6-28 ¿Qué hicimos?

1. almorzó
2. almorcé
3. comimos
4. tomé
5. bebió
6. terminaste
7. terminé
8. comencé
9. leí
10. leyó
11. busqué
12. compré

WB 6-29 Padre e hijo

1. se divirtieron **2.** pidió **3.** sirvió **4.** se durmió

CAPÍTULO 7

WB 7-23 La ropa

1. el traje de baño
2. el sombrero
3. los zapatos, los calcetines, las sandalias, las botas
4. la blusa, la falda, las medias, el vestido, los pantalones
5. los pantalones, el traje, la corbata
6. el impermeable, las botas

WB 7-24 En la tienda

1. En qué puedo servirle
2. probarme
3. talla
4. queda bien
5. Hace juego
6. moda
7. le debo
8. ganga
9. tarjeta de crédito

WB 7-25 ¡Fin de semana!

1. fuiste
2. Fui
3. hicieron
4. Tuvimos
5. vinieron
6. trajeron
7. estuvo
8. hiciste
9. fue
10. hice
11. quiso
12. supe

WB 7-26 A La hora de la cena

1. La **2.** lo **3.** me, te **4.** las

WB 7-27 Mi niñez

1. vivía
2. Tenía
3. sacaba
4. limpiaba
5. íbamos
6. compraba
7. gustaba
8. comíamos

WB 7-28 ¡Y ahora baila!

1. trabajábamos
2. llamó
3. éramos
4. se burlaba
5. invitó
6. bailaba
7. aceptaste
8. acepté

CAPÍTULO 8

WB 8-18 Una celebración especial

1. cumplió
2. entremeses
3. invitados
4. disfrazarse
5. máscara
6. disfraz
7. se reunieron
8. celebrar
9. brindis
10. gritaron
11. Felicidades
12. pastel
13. velas
14. recordar
15. regalos
16. llorar
17. lo pasaron
18. anfitriona

WB 8-19 En la playa y en el campo

1. f **2.** a **3.** d **4.** h **5.** c **6.** g **7.** b **8.** e

WB 8-20 Preguntas

1. De dónde
2. Dónde
3. Cuál
4. Adónde
5. Qué
6. Cuántas
7. Qué

WB 8-21 Un viaje inolvidable

1. era
2. hice
3. Fui
4. tenía
5. tenía
6. decidieron
7. vivíamos
8. era
9. había
10. podía
11. sabía
12. fui
13. empezó
14. nadaba
15. mordió
16. sentí
17. grité
18. se metió
19. salvó
20. tuve
21. fue
22. asustó

WB 8-22 Significados especiales

1. tuvimos **2.** supo, sabía **3.** quise **4.** pudo **5.** tenía

WB 8-23 ¿Algo quiere?

1. algo
2. algunos
3. algunas
4. también
5. ninguna
6. algunos
7. tampoco
8. ni
9. ni
10. nada

CAPÍTULO 9

WB 9-22 Viajes

1. c **2.** b **3.** d **4.** a **5.** f **6.** g **7.** e

WB 9-23 En el hotel

1. cuatro estrellas
2. cuartos
3. limpios
4. sucios
5. dobles
6. sencillas
7. privado
8. aire acondicionado
9. ascensor
10. recepción
11. cómodo

WB 9-24 ¿Dónde está todo?

1. al lado
2. detrás
3. a la izquierda
4. entre
5. a la derecha
6. enfrente

WB 9-25 Indicaciones

1. cruce
2. siga
3. Doble
4. suba
5. Siga
6. hacia

WB 9-26 Una carta

1. les **2.** les **3.** le **4.** le **5.** les **6.** me **7.** te **8.** me **9.** me
10. (mandar)les

WB 9-27 Elena, la buena

1. Sí, te la presto.
2. Sí, se la preparo.
3. Sí, se lo escribo.
4. Sí, me la pueden pasar. (Sí, pueden pasármela.)
5. Sí, se lo puedo comprar. (Sí, puedo comprárselo.)

WB 9-28 ¿Dónde está el banco?

1. Perdone **2.** deme **3.** Tome **4.** Dígame **5.** Salga
6. vaya **7.** Tenga **8.** Vuelva

CAPÍTULO 10

WB 10-23 El amor y los novios

1. noviazgo
2. amor
3. nos enamoramos
4. cariño
5. nos llevamos
6. enamorados
7. matrimonio
8. casados

WB 10-24 La boda

1. novios
2. casarse
3. se besan
4. recién casados
5. aplauden
6. recepción
7. tienen lugar
8. banquete
9. brindis
10. felicitan
11. orquesta
12. ramo de flores
13. agarrar
14. luna de miel
15. se separan
16. se divorcian

WB 10-25 ¿Qué han hecho?

1. Pablo ha leído tres libros.
2. Teresa y Ángela han visto una película nueva.
3. Mamá y yo le hemos escrito cartas a la familia.
4. Yo me he divertido con mis amigos.
5. Tú has vuelto de un viaje largo.

WB 10-26 Miguel lo hace así

1. Miguel lee el periódico detenidamente.
2. Miguel habla con las chicas nerviosamente.
3. Miguel come rápidamente.
4. Miguel saca buenas notas fácilmente.
5. Miguel va a las fiestas frecuentemente.

WB 10-27 La rutina

1. Todos los días
2. Muchas veces
3. Solamente
4. A veces
5. Una vez
6. Nunca
7. siempre

WB 10-28 ¿Cómo lo hago?

1. Primero te sacas una cuenta electrónica de Internet.
2. Después/Luego/Entonces, te compras software para el e-mail.
3. Luego/Después/Entonces le pides a tu novia su dirección electrónica
4. Entonces/Luego/Después puedes escribir el mensaje que quieres mandar.
5. Finalmente, le envías el mensaje.

WB 10-29 El primer día

1. tendrás
2. comenzará
3. será
4. vendrán
5. sabrán
6. querrá
7. dirás
8. habrá
9. durará
10. veré
11. podremos
12. haré
13. serás
14. irá

WB 10-30 Puros sueños

1. harías
2. viajaría
3. gustaría
4. Podría
5. saldríamos
6. iríamos
7. tomaríamos
8. Pasaríamos
9. querríamos
10. volaríamos
11. tendríamos

CAPÍTULO 11

WB 11-19 ¿Qué debe hacer?

1. arquitecto
2. peluquero
3. contador
4. periodista
5. programador
6. maestro
7. traductor
8. policía
9. siquiatra
10. dentista

WB 11-20 Solicitando trabajo

1. solicitar
2. currículum
3. computadora
4. imprimir
5. impresora
6. fotocopias
7. solicitud
8. llamar
9. entrevista
10. proyectos
11. beneficios
12. empleados
13. sueldo
14. contratar
15. tiempo parcial / tiempo completo
16. tiempo completo / tiempo parcial
17. jubilarte
18. despedir

WB 11-21 De vacaciones

1. por
2. por
3. Por
4. para
5. para
6. Para
7. por
8. para
9. por
10. para

WB 11-22 El amor y los negocios

1. escribas **2.** llames **3.** tengas **4.** mire **5.** pienses **6.** te enamores **7.** pierdan **8.** mandes **9.** vayamos **10.** nos divirtamos

WB 11-23 Entre amigos

1. salir **2.** venir **3.** sigamos **4.** trabajemos **5.** ir **6.** vuelva **7.** acompañes

CAPÍTULO 12

WB 12-22 La geografía rural y urbana

A **1.** metrópolis **2.** acelerado **3.** sobrepoblación **4.** ruido / tráfico **5.** tráfico / ruido **6.** contaminación **7.** transporte público **8.** medio ambiente **9.** basura **10.** recogen **11.** bella
B **1.** tranquila **2.** campesinos **3.** cultivar **4.** regar **5.** colinas **6.** arroyos
C **1.** resolver **2.** recursos naturales **3.** petróleo **4.** reforestar **5.** capa de ozono **6.** desarrollar **7.** explotar **8.** energía solar **9.** desperdicio **10.** destrucción **11.** reciclar **12.** escasez

WB 12-23 Un secreto

1. estemos
2. poder
3. venir
4. estén
5. digas
6. acompañen
7. pienses
8. vayan
9. tengan
10. sea

WB 12-24 Hablando del viaje

1. Yo creo que estas vacaciones son excelentes.
Sí, pero dudo que David quiera venir este año.
2. Gabriela no está segura que el hotel sea bueno.
Yo estoy segura que todos los hoteles van a ser muy buenos.
3. En San José nosotros tenemos que buscar un restaurante que sirva gallo pinto.
Yo conozco un buen restaurante que sirve gallo pinto.
4. Yo quiero visitar una reserva biológica que tenga muchas especies exóticas.
Manuel Antonio es una reserva preciosa que tiene todo tipo de animales exóticos.

WB 12-25 Consejos para la cita

1. limpie
2. venga
3. se asuste
4. llegue
5. está
6. guste
7. vas
8. invitas
9. diga
10. guste
11. decida